PUNCHING OUT

■

ALSO BY PAUL CLEMENS

Made in Detroit

Paul Clemens

Doubleday

■

New York

London Toronto

Sydney Auckland

PUNCHING OUT

▪ ▪ ▪

One Year WITHDRAWN

in a Closing

Auto Plant

The author wishes to acknowledge the generous support
of the John Simon Guggenheim Memorial Foundation
in the writing of this book.

DD

DOUBLEDAY

www.doubleday.com

DOUBLEDAY and the DD colophon are registered
trademarks of Random House, Inc.

A portion of this work previously appeared
in different form in the *New York Times*.

All illustrations courtesy of the author

Book design by Maria Carella

Library of Congress Cataloging-in-Publication Data
Clemens, Paul, 1973–
Punching out: one year in a closing auto plant/Paul Clemens.—1st ed.
p. cm.
1. Automobile industry and trade—Michigan—Detroit. 2. Automobile
industry workers—Michigan—Detroit. 3. Plant shutdowns—
Michigan—Detroit. I. Title.
HD9710.U53D4725 2010
338.4'76292220977434—dc22   2010019970

ISBN 978-0-385-52115-4

PRINTED IN THE UNITED STATES OF AMERICA

1   3   5   7   9   10   8   6   4   2

First Edition

FOR EDDIE AND THE GUYS

This was a very terrible and melancholy thing
to see, and as it was a sight which I could not
but look on from morning to night (for indeed there was
nothing else of moment to be seen), it filled me with
very serious thoughts of the misery that was coming
upon the city, and the unhappy condition of those that
would be left in it.

Daniel Defoe, *A Journal of the Plague Year*

Welcome to
The Budd Company Detroit Plant

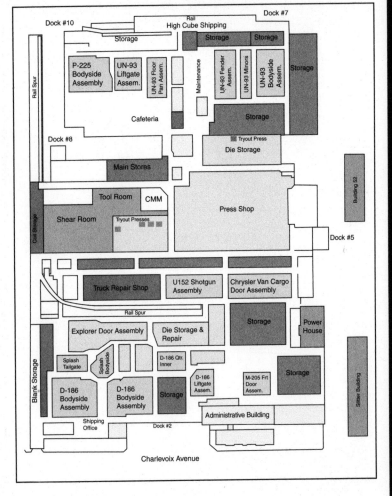

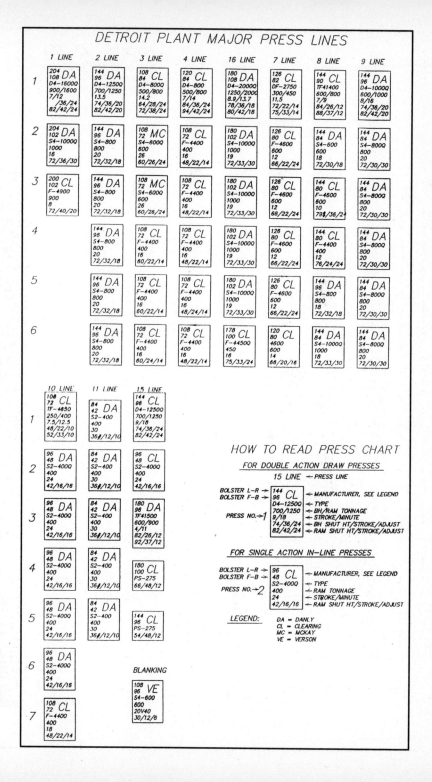

DETROIT PLANT MAJOR PRESS LINES

	1 LINE	2 LINE	3 LINE	4 LINE	16 LINE	7 LINE	8 LINE	9 LINE
1	204 108 DA D4-1600Q 900/1600 7/12 /36/24 82/42/24	144 96 DA D4-1250Q 700/1250 13.5 74/36/20 82/42/20	108 84 CL D4-800Q 500/800 14.2 64/28/24 72/38/24	120 84 CL D4-800 500/800 7/14 84/36/24 94/42/24	180 108 DA D4-2000Q 1250/2000 8.9/13.7 78/36/18 80/42/18	126 82 CL DF-2750 300/450 11.5 72/22/14 75/33/14	144 90 CL TF41400 600/800 7/9 84/26/12 88/37/12	144 96 DA D4-1000Q 600/1000 8/16 74/36/20 82/42/20
2	204 102 DA S4-1000Q 1000 16 72/36/30	144 96 DA S4-800 800 20 72/32/18	108 72 MC S4-600Q 600 26 60/26/24	108 72 CL F-4400 400 16 48/22/14	180 102 DA S4-1000Q 1000 19 72/33/30	126 80 CL F-4600 600 12 66/22/24	144 84 DA S4-600 600 18 72/30/18	144 84 DA S4-800Q 800 20 72/30/30
3	200 102 CL F-4900 900 8 72/40/20	144 96 DA S4-800 800 20 72/32/18	108 72 MC S4-600Q 600 26 60/26/24	108 72 CL F-4400 400 16 48/22/14	180 102 DA S4-1000Q 1000 19 72/33/30	126 80 CL F-4600 600 12 66/22/24	144 80 CL F-4600 600 10 79$/36/24	144 84 DA S4-800Q 800 20 72/30/30
4		144 96 DA S4-800 800 20 72/32/18	108 72 CL F-4400 400 16 60/22/14	108 72 CL F-4400 400 16 48/22/14	180 102 DA S4-1000Q 1000 19 72/33/30	126 80 CL F-4600 600 12 66/22/24	144 80 CL F-4400 400 12 76/24/24	144 84 DA S4-800Q 800 20 72/30/30
5		144 96 DA S4-800 800 20 72/32/18	108 72 CL F-4400 400 16 60/22/14	108 72 CL F-4400 400 16 48/24/14	180 102 DA S4-1000Q 1000 19 72/33/30	126 80 CL F-4600 600 12 66/22/24	144 96 DA S4-800 800 18 72/32/18	144 84 DA S4-800Q 800 20 72/30/30
6		144 96 DA S4-800 800 20 72/32/18	108 72 CL F-4400 400 16 60/24/14	108 72 CL F-4400 400 16 48/22/14	178 100 CL F-4450Q 450 16 75/33/24	120 80 CL 4600 600 14 66/20/16	144 84 DA S4-1000Q 1000 18 72/33/30	144 84 DA S4-800Q 800 20 72/30/30

	10 LINE	11 LINE	15 LINE
1	108 72 CL TF-4650 250/400 7.5/12.5 48/22/10 52/33/10	84 42 DA S2-400 400 30 36#/12/10	144 96 CL D4-1250Q 700/1250 9/18 74/36/24 82/42/24
2	96 48 DA S2-400Q 400 24 42/16/16	84 42 DA S2-400 400 30 36#/12/10	96 48 CL S2-400Q 400 24 42/16/16
3	96 48 DA S2-400Q 400 24 42/16/16	84 42 DA S2-400 400 30 36#/12/10	180 96 DA TF41500 600/900 4/11 82/26/12 92/37/12
4	96 48 DA S2-400Q 400 24 42/16/16	84 42 DA S2-400 400 30 36#/12/10	180 100 CL PS-275 66/48/12
5	96 48 DA S2-400Q 400 24 42/16/16	84 42 DA S2-400 400 30 36#/12/10	144 96 CL PS-275 54/48/12
6	96 48 DA S2-400Q 400 24 42/16/16		BLANKING 108 96 VE S4-600 600 20V40 30/12/6
7	108 72 CL F-4400 400 18 48/22/14		

HOW TO READ PRESS CHART

FOR DOUBLE ACTION DRAW PRESSES

15 LINE ← PRESS LINE

PRESS NO. → 1

- BOLSTER L-R → 144
- BOLSTER F-B → 96
- CL ← MANUFACTURER, SEE LEGEND
- D4-1250Q ← TYPE
- 700/1250 ← BH/RAM TONNAGE
- 9/18 ← STROKE/MINUTE
- 74/36/24 ← BH SHUT HT/STROKE/ADJUST
- 82/42/24 ← RAM SHUT HT/STROKE/ADJUST

FOR SINGLE ACTION IN-LINE PRESSES

PRESS NO. → 2

- BOLSTER L-R → 96
- BOLSTER F-B → 48
- CL ← MANUFACTURER, SEE LEGEND
- S2-400Q ← TYPE
- 400 ← RAM TONNAGE
- 24 ← STROKE/MINUTE
- 42/16/16 ← RAM SHUT HT/STROKE/ADJUST

LEGEND:

DA = DANLY
CL = CLEARING
MC = MCKAY
VE = VERSON

Contents

PROLOGUE

• • •

'Taint
Never Gonna
Come Back,
McGee

**Wherever you look...
you see Budd**

...because Budd makes body parts and
assemblies for Ford, General Motors,
American Motors, Chrysler, and others—
components used in 28 popular cars
and 14 leading trucks.

THE **Budd** COMPANY
AUTOMOTIVE DIVISION • DETROIT, MICH.

■ ■ ■

WHEN JON CLARK started his newsletter, *Plant Closing News,* in 2003, he promised subscribers that he'd report on the specifics of 25 plant closings a month—300 per year. In 2003, he reported on 983; the next year, 1,130; the next, 1,180. When I first talked to him, in October 2007, he'd reported who, what, when, where, and why on 980 plant closings in the calendar year—"that's so far," he stressed, "plus an additional 250 bankruptcies."

The newsletter comes out biweekly and is "targeted to surplus industry service providers," including "rebuilders, used equipment dealers, dismantlers, demolishers, remediation contractors, equipment riggers, craters, and equipment transport firms looking for current business opportunities, particularly those arising from the closing or relocating of North American industrial manufacturing plants." Each issue begins by noting the number of closings in the United States and Canada included in the issue. For instance, the January 15, 2007, issue is headlined: "44 Companies Closing 48 Plants + 18 Bankruptcies." These are then subdivided by industry— food processing, textile products, wood products, pulp, paper products, chemical products, rubber, plastics products, glass, cement products, metal products, electrical, electronics, other manufacturers—and again by state—"AL 2, FL 3, MI 6"— before the specifics of each closing are given. Clark recalled getting a phone call from a manager at a plant in Arkansas angry that his plant had appeared in the newsletter. Clark pointed out that the closing had already made the papers.

Clark has also written *Plant Closing Checklist,* which includes a couple hundred questions and comments covering areas pertinent to plant closure. "Know what one of the first things on the *Plant Closing Checklist* is?" Clark asked. "Tell your people what's going on!" His memory for individual plant closings is unusually good. When we first spoke on the phone, I told him I was working on a book about the closing of the Budd Detroit Automotive Plant, Stamping and Frame Division. "That was a two-million-square-foot facility," Clark said of the plant, whose closing had appeared in the July 15, 2006, issue of *Plant Closing News.* He has industrial facts and figures at his mental fingertips, and his knowledge of plant closings is sought after. The Democratic National Committee had contacted him in the buildup to the presidential election of 2004 in an attempt to determine "how many jobs had been exported under Mr. Bush." It was a question impossible to answer exactly but one that led Clark to a larger point. "I tell you what," he said he told the Democrats. "If you can get everybody to vote for you that's lost their job in this country, you can easily be elected." He added, "And that was four years ago. And that's five thousand plant closures ago. And I think that had a big impact on Obama being elected."

We met over breakfast in the Houston airport a week after the 2008 presidential election, when the depth of the country's financial crisis was becoming clear. The Great Recession had officially begun eleven months before, and later that month the leaders of Detroit's Big Three would arrive in Washington for a public flogging—a prelude, for General Motors and Chrysler, to the bankruptcies to come. Auto suppliers—Delphi, Lear, Tower Automotive, Dana, Dura—were ahead of the downward curve, beating GM and Chrysler into bankruptcy by years. Budd, a major Tier 1 supplier, avoided the possibility of a similar fate by simply closing.

I had flown from Detroit to Houston to talk to Clark while en route to central Mexico to see a press line. Once the largest press line in the Budd Detroit plant, stamping body sides for the Ford Explorer and Ford Expedition, it had been sold after the Budd plant's closure to Gestamp, a Spanish auto supplier. Gestamp had the disassembled presses moved, piece by piece, a couple of thousand miles to its newly expanded plant in Aguascalientes, Mexico, where it was now stamping body sides for the Dodge Journey, the Chrysler crossover assembled in Toluca, Mexico.

I'd observed the disassembly of that press line, along with much of the rest of the Budd Detroit plant's equipment, for the better part of a year. The trip to Mexico would cap a process that had begun two and a half years before, on May 15, 2006, when ThyssenKrupp Budd, citing the declining sales of the Ford SUVs for which it supplied components, announced that it would close its Detroit plant by year's end. The Budd plant had been built in 1919 by Liberty Motor—which, like most motor companies in Detroit's early days, would soon go bust—and bought by the Budd Company in 1925. The German steel giant Thyssen bought Budd in the late 1970s and merged with the German steel giant Krupp in the late 1990s. The Budd Company became the ThyssenKrupp Budd Company in 2002, though no one called it that. "Budd," "Budd's," and "Budd Wheel"—so-called after its former Wheel and Brake Division—were the plant's names around town. The new name with the German prefix lasted just four years anyway: the Detroit plant closed, officially, on December 4, 2006. A sign saying "ThyssenKrupp Budd Detroit Plant" still hangs on the exterior of the empty plant—a misleading headstone on an exhumed industrial grave. At its peak, plant employment approached ten thousand.

The papers took note of its announced closing. The headline in the *New York Times,* via Bloomberg, got what and where ("Detroit Parts Plant Closing"), the headline in the *Detroit News* got why ("Landmark Plant Shuts as Sales of SUVs Fall"), and the headline in the *Detroit Free Press* got who ("ThyssenKrupp to Shut Down Detroit Plant"). The story was small and faded fast. The next day brought bigger news, when the FBI began to dig, at a horse farm in suburban Detroit, for the remains of Jimmy Hoffa.

I read the articles, read the company press release, and then called the vice president for public affairs at Thyssen-Krupp Budd who'd penned the release. I explained over lunch weeks later that I wanted to observe, up close, the plant-closing process. The public affairs VP, a pleasant man, said he'd support the project. Some time after, his decision was reversed. Someone above him had said no, or *nein,* and so I looked for other avenues into the plant. In Detroit, as in any big city, there are always several ways to get somewhere.

The headline appears daily in some American city: "Plant to Close." I wondered—what then? I was born and raised in

Detroit, world capital of closed auto plants, and I hadn't a clue. I knew what such plant closings meant—more lost jobs, another abandoned building—but no clear sense of what they actually entailed.

The locations of auto plants and car shops were the latitude and longitude lines that oriented my upbringing. My father worked in shops all over town. I'd worked a couple summers for a small Detroit camshaft shop—now closed—in which my father had worked when I was a small boy. I'd begun life, according to Catholic belief, in a Detroit plant now so thoroughly closed it's nonexistent. The Uniroyal Tire plant, formerly the U.S. Rubber Company plant, where my mother worked as a secretary while pregnant with me, was on Jefferson Avenue, a couple miles south and west of the Budd plant. At the time, it employed five thousand. "There's Uniroyal," my mom would say, years later, as we drove down Jefferson, motioning to an empty parcel of land. The British writer Geoff Dyer, visiting the city early this century, noted that "in Detroit . . . everything is where something used to be." This is true, though Dyer shows himself an outsider by saying so. The "where something used to be" clause is, to Detroiters, a bit of implied conversation, like the "good" that country folk habitually omit from their "Mornin'!"

As a plant on the city's East Side, Budd was in my industrial backyard. An uncle of mine had grown up on Anderdon, a block east of the Budd plant. My grandmother had gone to Southeastern High School, a couple blocks west of the plant. My grandfather had lived on Springle, three blocks east of the plant. I had long harbored vague plans for a book on the decline of the American working class, and when I scanned the papers on the morning of May 16, 2006, I was looking, in the unseemly way of writers, for a symbol of that decline. That the Budd plant was within Detroit's city limits, as old as the hills, and four miles from my front door made me feel light-headed with dumb luck.

The American working class has not only declined; it has transformed. During the last presidential campaign, the *New York Times Magazine* noted that though factory workers may still represent the working class for purposes of political theater, the United States now has more choreographers than metal casters, more people dealing cards in casinos than running lathes, and almost three times as many security guards as machinists— a massive shift away from industrial work among the working class. Productivity increases had greatly reduced the need for industrial workers, and such workers as were needed were easily and cheaply found outside the United States. On the day of the Michigan presidential primaries, National Public Radio reported that the state had lost 200,000 manufacturing jobs since 2000. The country as a whole had lost 4 million since 1999. One stumbled across such statistics at every turn. Figures differed, depending on source and date, but went in one direction, demanding additional commas and zeros. Industrial work, for working-class folk, was hard to come by.

The working class is to Detroit what immigrants are to New York, prospectors to California, prisoners to Australia: the people who put the place on the map, and who continue to populate its psychic space. There are few in Detroit who would describe themselves as anything but. If someone has done particularly well, he'll cite, proudly, the working-class stock from which he springs. Typically, though, the poor round up, the middle classes round down, and everyone, in the American spirit of self-selection, meets in that broad stratum of society that, by the sweat of its brow, scrapes by. What I thought I had seen inside the closed Budd Detroit plant through a particularly bad summer, fall, winter, and spring was the American working class, mopping up after itself.

■

"We publish on the first and the fifteenth of the month," Clark said of *Plant Closing News* over a breakfast of sausage, bacon, and gravy. He explained that he'd be busy later in the week, when he wrapped up work on the November 15 issue. It would be a big one, though not as big as the November 1 issue, which covered 66 plant closures. For November's second issue he anticipated "in excess of 50. Both of 'em in October were over 50. We average about 100 plants a month, and sometimes it goes upward from there to 120, 130. And we don't report on everything, because we can't find everything. I'm always seeing auction brochures, on hundreds of plants per year, that I never heard of." The entries in the newsletter are little prose poems, compact of tragedy:

Broyhill Closing Lenoir, NC, Case Goods Plant
Broyhill Furniture Industries has announced the closing of its Pacemaker case goods manufacturing facility located in Lenoir, North Carolina. The Pacemaker plant is a 522,000 square foot facility employing nearly 700 people.

Delphi to Close Mississippi Auto Parts Plant

Mississippi's smallest Delphi plant—located in Laurel—will close or be sold under the company's latest bankruptcy reorganization plan. Delphi has indicated they will close 21 of their 29 manufacturing plants.

The above entries come from the July 15, 2006, issue of *Plant Closing News* ("42 Companies Closing 44 Plants + 15 Bankruptcies"), which included the Budd Detroit plant, one of ten metal-products plants to be listed in the issue:

Detroit-Area Auto Parts Plant Closing

ThyssenKrupp Budd Co., an automotive supplier, said it was closing Liberty Motors, its Detroit-area factory. The plant, where about 350 people work, makes metal stampings and assemblies such as roofs, doors, fenders, tailgates, liftgates and body side panels for cars, trucks and sport utility vehicles. The closure will be gradual and conclude around the end of the year.

I pointed to the September 1, 2008, copy of *Plant Closing News* ("General Motors has announced that they will close four truck and SUV plants") that I'd brought with me.

"I started doing that"—Clark nodded toward the newsletter—"five years ago, because nobody else would, or nobody else did. I buy and sell used machinery. Mainly utilities. Emergency generators, chillers, transformers, propane tanks, CO_2 tanks, storage tanks. Things that are common in a lot of plants. A new thirty-thousand-gallon propane tank is sixty-five thousand dollars, and a used one is forty thousand dollars. And they're worth eight thousand dollars scrap steel today. Those are generic numbers, but you can see relative value. So people that need propane tanks are going to buy used propane tanks if they can find 'em."

He stopped and stepped back. "All these plants are closing down," he said. "I want to buy some equipment out of each and every one of them. Sewing plants are closing. I don't want anything to do with a sewing machine, but if they got an emergency generator there, I'd like to buy the emergency generator. Semiconductor plants are closing. I don't know anything about semiconductors. But if they've got big transformers, or storage tanks . . ." His search among closed plants for used utility equipment had exposed him to the scope of what was occurring and to the opportunities it created, opportunities it seemed sensible to share, since he could never buy and sell all the equipment available to be bought and sold. "I started doing *that*"—the newsletter—"in order to tell people, 'Here's what's happening in the marketplace. Here are the people you need to be talking to.' " Of the birth of *Plant Closing News,* he said, "I kind of backed into the newsletter."

From the May 1, 2007, *Plant Closing News* ("46 Companies Closing 46 Plants"):

City Machine Closes Muncie, IN, Facility
Changes in the manufacturing industry have driven a Muncie, Indiana tool and die business to close its doors. City Machine Tool & Die, founded in 1935, closed in mid April. Much of

the company's work for farm equipment giant John Deere was lost to a plant in China.

Lear Closing Detroit Plant

Lear executives have informed employees at its Detroit arm-rest and headrest plant that it will be closed. About 300 hourly workers will be affected. Lear said closing the Detroit plant is part of a $300 million restructuring investment.

Chrysler to Close Newark, DE, Assembly Plant

About 13,000 Chrysler workers will lose their jobs under a plan designed to cut the struggling automaker's costs and return it to profitability by next year. In part the plan calls for closing the company's Newark, Delaware assembly plant and a parts distribution center near Cleveland will also be closed.

"I consider this to be consulting work," he said, pointing to the newsletter. "I do two things. I do consulting work, and then I buy and sell equipment. I can make a lot more money buying and selling equipment than I can doing consulting work. But you can't depend on it. Consulting work is a fairly steady income." I asked him where his work buying and selling used equipment was taking him these days. "Right now it's not taking me anywhere," he said. We had originally planned to meet in Columbus, Ohio, rather than Houston, but the Columbus deal got postponed. "There's just not much work going on. Here's the thing: There are a lot of plants closing. In order for the plant-closing business to be substantially meaningful, you have to have buyers. Not a lot of buyers right now." He added: "Don't feel sorry for me. I'm ain't gonna go hungry. It's just a truism: for there to be a vibrant used-equipment market, there needs to be both companies closing and companies opening.

"I've been called a vulture by more than one company," Clark said. "That's okay: vultures have to eat. I feel like I provide a service, just like all the people making the calls off of my newsletter are providing a service to the plant. You're closing— what are you going to do, just walk off and leave it?" The business never ceased to amaze him. Earlier in the year, he'd been at a closed plant in Massachusetts. "I'm on the fourth floor," he said, "inventorying some equipment. We're going to tear the end off of the building, move the equipment out, and then tear the building down—within the month." He was hired by the company that had closed the plant to "sell the equipment off their job site," he said. "So, I'm on the fourth floor, inventorying this equipment, and I hear this *errerrerr*—strange noise. So I walk to the stairwell and go down to the first floor, and, I swear to God, there, on the first floor, is a guy buffing the floor. Of a building that's going to be torn down the next month. The only two people in the building are him and me. And I stopped him and said, 'What are you doing? This building's going to be torn down in a month.' And he said, 'Really? I wondered.' "

It was, Clark said, force of habit. "That's why people sit in the shadow of a plant that has closed down and twiddle their thumbs waiting for it to come back," he said. " 'The biggest employer in town is closing'—that's one of *the* most common statements in that *Plant Closing News.* 'The biggest employer in town is closing.' Single-employer towns are losing their single employer. Waiting for it to come back. 'Taint never gonna come back, McGee.

"It's amazing that we use all these euphemisms," he went on. "Downsizing, outsourcing, rightsizing. When all it means is you just lost your job and you have no way to pay your house note. Don't know where your kids are going to get money for clothes or for food. We've lost the human pathos, the empathy, the drama.

"I hear all the time—'We've built many plants, but we've never closed one. We don't know what to do, don't know how to start, don't know where to go.' From people that are closing plants. It's because I sell that checklist. One company called me—'We're thinking of buying your checklist. What does it have in it?' And I said, 'Here's my question: Why don't you write *me* a checklist? Why doesn't your firm document and collect all of your closing experiences? Because you've closed well over a hundred manufacturing plants.' And the guy said, 'We have?' And I said, 'Yes, you have.' They didn't say, 'This is the wave of the future. This is what we need to go through.' It's a very unpleasant task. So, as a result, it's often done very poorly. Not that there's a nice way or an easy way or a good way to close a plant, because unfortunately plants involve people.

"I'm gonna preach a minute," Clark said. "There's something about the moral decline of this country that goes hand in glove with what we're seeing with the manufacturing base being moved offshore. It's true Rome still exists, but the Roman Empire fell a long, long time ago and went into utter decay. Because the people wanted to be entertained by the circuses, and see the Christians eaten by the lions. I'm not saying we're going to see the end in my lifetime, or maybe even yours. But we're on a progressively downward track, and it's really, really hard, if not impossible, for me to see how we can turn it around, unless people suddenly come to their senses, and the Bible specifically says, in 2 Chronicles 7:14, 'If my people, who are called by my name, will *humble* themselves and seek my face and call upon my name, then I will heal their land and they will hear from heaven.' You know what? It's that desperate. We've lost our horizon. We don't know whether we're flying right side up or upside down. Preaching over.

"There will continue to be a lot of plant closures," he said. "I will continue to write the newsletter, as long as anybody will read it and subscribe to it. There's a conservative estimate of 25 to 125,000 manufacturing plants in this country, depending on how you define them. Well, if we're closing 1,200 to 1,500 of 'em a year, we're gonna have twenty years, thirty years, fifty years—some finite period of time."

Clark and I talked for several hours in Houston, with breakfast extending into lunch. He seemed to enjoy hearing of the afterlife of a plant that had appeared in his newsletter. I pretended, as I did in such situations, that he was an editor—better, a producer—and that I was pitching him this story. Could I keep him turning the pages? My pitch, by this point, had developed grooves from repeated telling, and still it wasn't much good. I was worried. I'd long completed most of my research for the book; all that was left was the trip to Mexico, and I'd soon get on a plane to see to that. I'd collected more material than I could use in ten books, but hadn't yet put anything of value on paper. My story, discussed to death with anyone who'd listen, had no shape that I could discern. Worse, it had no stakes. Another plant closed—who cares?

I kept talking. I told Clark of the Budd plant's location, bookended by two Chrysler plants. I told him of the cast of characters in the closed plant. I talked about the Budd press lines—their makes, their ages, the parts they'd stamped. Clark knew that I was on my way to Mexico after we were done, and he summed up the process that I was about to complete. In so doing, he provided it with something that as yet I hadn't: a point. Here was someone who knew how to frame a nonfiction narrative.

"People pick that stuff up," he said of the Budd presses, "and take it halfway around the world and reinstall it and put their people to work. You know, it makes you wonder what went wrong, that a plant could sit between two manufacturing plants and could push parts out the door, and now they can pick up the equipment and take it two thousand, three thousand miles, and run the same equipment to make the same parts and ship 'em back cheaper." He spoke as a man pained by the very phenomenon he tracked—a crime reporter saddened by a spate of homicides.

"That oughta be a story," he said.

CHAPTER 1

• • •

Settle
Labor Issues

A. J. LIEBLING once noted that "the Manhattan waterfront is not hard to find. You start in any direction and walk." He was highlighting the nonexistent nautical sense of many Manhattanites, notwithstanding the fact that they live on an island. Finding an auto plant in Detroit is just as straightforward, even for residents lacking car consciousness. Such plants—the still functioning and the long-since shuttered—ring this region, just as the East River and the Hudson encircle Manhattan. Living and dead, they dot Detroit's interior, singly and in clusters. To find one, you start in any direction and drive.

Begin at the crest of the bridge on westbound I-94, the Ford Freeway. This is more or less midtown, and it is the highest driving height you'll hit for miles around. The view is good but brief—unless there's a backup. Just past this peak, the right lanes of the Ford descend and intersect with I-75, the Chrysler Freeway, and occasionally a clogged interchange (north to Flint, south to Toledo) can buy you a bit of time at elevation. Let's assume there's not just a backup but an accident ahead, the kind of pileup that causes people to settle in—to kill the engine, get out of the car, sit on the hood. You might want to stand, actually, the better to see over the retaining walls, and to take in the sights full circle.

The most striking structure on view is not a plant, though its past is pure auto. The old General Motors Building, a neoclassical lovely half a mile off in the city's New Center area, was completed in 1923, when the company moved its headquarters to Detroit. You've seen the inside. In its lobby, a film-maker once sought to learn from the company chairman what was happening to a GM plant in Flint, the company's first home. A decade before that, at its peak, GM had employed over 600,000. Weeks after my meeting with Clark, GM's chairman and CEO appeared before Congress and noted—by way of making a "too big to fail" case for government funds—that his company employed 96,000. Since 2000, GM has closed more than a dozen North American assembly plants.

A couple thousand of those still on the company payroll work at the General Motors Detroit-Hamtramck assembly plant, though no one calls it that. The plant is north and east of the interchange at I-94 and I-75 and referred to, in these parts, as Poletown. In the early 1980s, Detroit's mayor, Cole-man Young, orchestrated the acquisition of the closed Dodge Main plant that sat on the site, along with the subsequent acquisition, under eminent domain, of the surrounding resi-dential area, which was then cleared to make way for the larger GM plant. Historically Polish but by this point racially mixed, the area remained "Poletown" to those seeking to save it. Detroit's first black mayor, Young felt this was a "deliberate misnomer," one calculated to "elicit public sympathy—as if the little old ladies in black dresses and babushkas weren't enough." Unbowed by Babushka Power, Young proposed the more demographically accurate "Afro-Poletown." It found few takers.

I drove by Poletown on the first day of the last strike there, in the fall of 2007. I was on my way, along eastbound I-94, to the Budd plant a few miles down the road. When I got off the freeway, I saw a helicopter circling Poletown. News crews, some picketers, and a few Detroit cops stood in front of the plant entrance along the Ford service drive. Two hours later, on my way back by, there were no cops, no copters, no news crews, and just a few picketers. Two days later, the strike was over. One national observer said that "the latest installment of the UAW-GM battle has the makings of this fall's Army-Navy football game—a match between two ancient powers whose rivalry once dominated the headlines but who now play a largely symbolic role." The plant has been intermittently idled since the strike and was part of the blanket idling under the company's bankruptcy.

To the south and east of Poletown, just across the Ford Freeway, is the Packard plant. Closed since 1956, it is said to be one of the largest abandoned industrial sites on the planet. From the height of the I-94 bridge a mile away, where we are still stuck in traffic, the Packard plant can appear to be a minor mountain range massed in the distance. It forms such a large part of the landscape that there are people who can't see it. I've known residents of Macomb County who've passed the plant on their way to and from work for years on end who claim to have no idea where the Packard plant is located. At its peak, the plant employed twelve thousand. In its three and a half million square feet—described, in a *Detroit Free Press* article, as "a labyrinth of rusted steel, shattered glass, crumbling concrete, standing water, freshly dumped trash, vivid graffiti, junked cars and crud-encrusted artifacts"—it now employs no one.

To the north and west of Poletown is American Axle & Manufacturing. You'll see it as an immense field of blue steel stretching into the industrial distance. The last strike at American Axle, a GM supplier, was in 2008, running from the end of February until the middle of May and causing production problems at thirty-two GM plants. American Axle workers picketed daily at company headquarters, a mile up the Chrysler Freeway. Since the strike's end, the plant has been occasionally idled due to weak demand, and the company has moved portions of the production from the Detroit plant to a company plant in Mexico.

Beyond American Axle and a bit to its east you'll see, if you squint, the spire of St. Florian set against the sky. You'll also see the crosses atop St. Josaphat, across the Chrysler Freeway, and Sweetest Heart of Mary, tucked behind a trash incinerator. (Beyond both, on a clear day, you'll see in the downtown distance two white letters—GM—atop Detroit's tallest building.) Straight ahead is the golden Virgin Mother atop Our Lady of the Rosary, where my sister was married. And that's just among the churches metaphorically facing Rome. There are others on view, belonging to denominations not mine. The Detroit metropolitan area is home to nearly as many active, abandoned, and barely hanging-on churches as auto plants; the correspondence between church and plant in each category can sometimes seem one to one, and they can be linked in the "abandoned" category by comparing rusty, graffiti-covered water towers with crooked crosses.

Ahead is the abandoned Fisher Body Plant 21 (b. 1919), a

white, six-story rectangular immensity that occupies the corner and more of Piquette and St. Antoine. Down the street from Fisher Body, invisible from the bridge, is Henry Ford's Piquette Avenue plant, the Ford Motor Company's first. So, too, was an old Studebaker plant, destroyed by fire in 2005. Visible a bit over from Fisher Body is a small, active supplier, New Center Stamping, which—as New Detroit Stamping— served as the place of employment of Marshall Mathers in the movie.

With the accident now clear you can climb down from the hood, get back in the car, and begin to drive. There are all kinds of routes you could take. For starters, get in the right lane at the interchange of I-94 and I-75 and take the Chrysler Freeway north. In twenty minutes you'll see, to the right, Chrysler world headquarters. (Minutes before, you'll pass the headquarters of Delphi, GM's main parts supplier, bankrupt beginning in 2005.) When this book opens, the building head- quartered DaimlerChrysler. It then became headquarters of plain Chrysler, owned by the private equity firm Cerberus. Then it headquartered Chrysler bankrupt. At present it is the headquarters of Chrysler Group LLC, partnered with Fiat and kept afloat by the American taxpayer. Unless my eyes deceived me as I drove past, workers at Chrysler's 8 Mile and Mound plant had covered the "Daimler" on their plant's sign with duct tape after the German sell-off.

Rather than turning off, you could remain on I-94 and continue in the westward direction you're facing. Just past the Ford-Chrysler interchange is the exit for Woodward Avenue. Take it and head north. In five minutes you'll cross the Davison, the country's first urban, depressed freeway, a term that now succeeds—given the bleak city landscape the Davison traverses below terra firma—on more than one level. By this point you'll be in Highland Park, a small city within Detroit. On one of these side streets a film icon parked his Ford pickup, drank beer on his porch, and barked at the passing world. Ahead, to your right, will be Henry Ford's Model T plant, the company's main base of production after leaving the Piquette plant and before moving to the Rouge. The disconnect between the Model T plant's historic significance and its present lack of upkeep is considerable.

You could, of course, ignore the Woodward exit and continue west. In a few minutes, you'll reach the interchange for I-96. Take I-96 west, and half an hour down the road you'll see, to your right, the Ford Wixom plant, though nothing identifies it as such from the freeway. Ford, exhibiting the smarts that kept it out of bankruptcy, has removed the company name from prominent signage at the closed plant. Nearly five million square feet, Wixom opened in 1957, producing Thunderbirds, and closed—one of eight Ford North American assembly plants to close since 2000—weeks after hitting the half-century mark.

You could, finally, continue in the westward direction you're facing and ignore all exits and interchanges. In five minutes you'll see, to the left, the Ford Rouge, once the world's largest industrial complex, and once the employer of a hundred thousand. It is so large a complex, sitting on so much land—two thousand acres—that, as with Packard, there are people who can't see it, or can't seem to find it. The plant is located just outside the Detroit city limits in Dearborn, where the Ford Motor Company has its world headquarters. Begun in 1917, the Rouge, sitting along the river of the same name, was completed a decade later. Henry Ford's concept was automobile production done on-site and from soup to nuts, with the Rouge handling everything from steel processing to final assembly. In 1943, my great-uncle, Father Hector Saulino, founded St. Bernadette—now closed—blocks from the Ford Rouge, then at the peak of its war production and employing countless Catholics. The plant is still in operation, with a fraction of its former workforce. Guided tours are available; buses leave every twenty minutes, every day but Sunday, from the Henry Ford Museum.

Our brief tour concluded, beat a retreat back to the bridge where we began. Take a last, elevated look around the city, and recall that a Frenchman named Cadillac—Antoine de la Mothe Cadillac—settled this place in 1701. Recall as well that this city once *was* a Cadillac, before becoming a Buick, then an Oldsmobile and a Pontiac (both defunct), and, finally, a Chevy, a high-mileage hauler that has done honest work but can sometimes seem closer and closer to coming to a halt. To reflect current reality, perhaps the history books should be recast. A Frenchman settled Detroit, but his name wasn't Cadillac. It was Chevy—Antoine de la Rusty Chevrolet.

Turn completely around (impossible outside these pages), so that, having jumped the median, you now face eastbound on the I-94 bridge. The view is good but brief. Traffic flows at seventy per as you descend the bridge and drive past Poletown, past Packard, past the closed Gemmer plant, a personal favorite, where steering gears were made. A couple miles ahead will be the Conner Avenue exit—which, as the highway sign says, is the exit for Detroit City Airport. This fact means less than it once did, since City Airport has been without a major carrier for more than a decade.

Exit the Ford Freeway at Conner Avenue. The Budd Automotive plant, Stamping and Frame Division, will be a mile down the road, on your right.

■

At the time of its closing, Budd Detroit was solely a stamping plant. There are all kinds of auto plants, and there are auto plants of all kinds in Detroit, but the three predominant types, by size and conspicuousness, are stamping plants, engine plants, and assembly plants. Assembly plants are the final stage, where the auto body parts from stamping plants and the engines from engine plants and the countless other components, big and small, come together to make a car. Poletown, for instance, is an assembly plant. Fisher Body was a GM stamping plant. New Center Stamping—stamping. Ford Wixom was an assembly plant. The Ford Rouge, as originally conceived, was all-inclusive. Some of these plants, such as Budd and New Center Stamping, are, or were, suppliers. Others belong to the Big Three. But all belong to the same industrial ecosystem.

Assembly plants are distinguished by their assembly lines— Henry Ford's great innovation—which produced middle-class prosperity as surely as movable type made possible widespread literacy. Similarly, stamping plants like Budd are identifiable by their press lines—the linked presses, arranged in rows, that stamp out auto body parts, with each press performing a separate but sequential operation: blank, form, trim, pierce.

Should you ever find yourself near an active press line, you'll no doubt know it. Like the liftoff of an airliner, the stamping of auto body parts requires inhuman force, producing decibels registered by your internal organs. The presses sound, unmistakably, as if they could kill you, which they could, without much interrupting their normal functioning. You'd notice the collision more than they would. The force required to cut, bend, and form steel—a force mechanical stamping presses producing auto body parts exert many times per minute—is orders of magnitude more than what is required to separate you from life and limb. The first of the six stamping presses in 16-line, one of the Budd plant's primary press lines, had a two-thousand-ton rating—that is, it was capable of delivering a force of that tonnage. By comparison, your femur will snap under less than a single ton of pressure. It'd be difficult to find a stamping plant of long standing without a history of tragedy. In recent decades, OSHA and automation have helped to reduce the human loss—the latter, in large part, by reducing the need for humans altogether.

To be anywhere near an active press line is a total sensory experience. To have stood in a press shop such as Budd's would have been to see, spread across 140,000 square feet, several Stonehenges of steel. What you'd have felt, for a moment or two after a press struck, was a not-so-distant rumble, as if you were standing astride a fault line. What you'd have heard would depend on whether or not you wore earplugs—though you really should've. What you'd have smelled, and to some extent tasted, was the oily mist that, like industrial dew, hovers in the air and then settles atop surfaces in a press shop.

To stand in front of a stamping press and see it up close is to encounter a sight. (I speak here of an inactive press. The space between presses in an active line will be caged off, allowing the robots to do the repetitive work, once supplied by humans, of moving the stampings from press to press along the line.) A couple of stories or more, and a million pounds plus or minus, presses such as those in the Budd press shop seem stuck in another era, a bloated Gilded Age when brute force was the road to riches and when humanity, not yet overcome by its mania for miniaturization, hadn't figured out how to get what it needed by finesse.

Most of the behemoths in the Budd press shop were, by brand, either Danly or Clearing. Whatever their make, the main components of a stamping press are, beginning from the bottom, its base, its bolster, its die, its ram, its crown, and—running from base to crown—its side columns, on which the crown sits and between which the ram slides. (Some call the ram the slide for this reason.) The one impermanent piece of the structure is the die, which will be changed out depending on the part. Each stamped part has a specific die that produces it; though necessary, die changes create downtime along a press line. In a state-of-the-art stamping plant, die changes are quick—a matter of minutes—and completely automated.

Budd was not state-of-the-art. A spring 1987 plant newsletter, the *Budd Communicator,* ran an article on the Budd Detroit die transition team, which competed against the Budd plants in Philadelphia and Kitchener, Ontario, to see which plant could complete die changes most quickly. The photograph accompanying the piece pictured thirty or so men on the team—"truck drivers, crane operators, hook-up, die setters, maintenance, sanitation and supervisors." A caption beneath a photograph of a group of men guiding the die noted that "teamwork and muscle are required." Philadelphia won the inter-plant contest. Detroit, where "the elapsed time was 89 minutes," came second.

Depending on the part it's producing, a die can be an industrial cookie cutter, a waffle iron, a three-hole punch, or some combination thereof. It comes in a top and bottom half, with the bottom half attached to the press's bolster and the upper half attached to the press's ram. The ram, at the bottom of its stroke, drives the die's halves together, forming, trimming, and punching the steel that has been fed into the press by the robot. The press's crown, up top, contains the motor, the gearing, and the flywheel driving the ram.

When there is no die in a press, as is the case in a closed stamping plant, a straight-side stamping press forms an arch, and one can walk through it as if entering Washington Square Park. That first press in Budd 16-line with the two-thousand-ton rating was a Danly—specifically, a model QDC D4-2000-180-108, meaning that its bolster was 180 inches, or 15 feet, from left to right, and 108 inches, or 9 feet, from front to back.

One can walk under an industrial arch of such size arm in arm with several friends.

Beneath a running press line, down in its pit, will be a conveyor to collect and carry away the steel scraps that the dies trim from the stamping. In a big stamping plant such as Budd, the conveyors beneath each press line will carry their scraps to a baler. Down in the pit will likely be oil, though the amount will depend on the press, much as the amount of oil in your driveway depends on your car. (Some of this oil will be from the tooling, and is no sign of malfunction.) The oil will be carried, by a series of pumps, to a skimmer pit outside the plant. In Budd, much of the flooring around the presses was wood—squares of pecan and bricks of pine—into which Saudi Arabias of oil had soaked. You could walk around the press shop for centuries and not wear out your shoes.

Compared with a state-of-the-art assembly plant such as Ford's Dearborn Truck Plant, the scene in an old, closed stamping plant such as Budd is hellish, backlit by Goya. (There were in fact foam fingers in the Budd plant that said "GOYA." It stood for "Get Off Your Ass.") To see what I mean, visit Dearborn Truck during the Rouge tour. There's a better than even chance, if you have kids, that the plant is both cleaner and quieter than your house. It smells clean, too: the plant uses only pneumatic tools, and so lacks the telltale scent of oil and hydraulic fluid. The more modern the plant, the more the robot-to-people ratio tilts toward the robotic. If your pulse is quickened by efficiency and precision, a modern assembly plant is for you.

Its floors will absorb no oil. Computer message boards above the assembly lines will broadcast abbreviations and numbers, as if the plant were an industrial stock exchange. In essence, it is. Assembly plants look forward to the finished product (there's the windshield, here comes the dash). One can see, in the near distance, the car being driven onto the transport truck and then glistening in the dealer's showroom. A few days later, ideally, there will be the signing of the loan document, the handing over of the keys, and the smiling drive off the lot. Assembly plants provide closure: they finish what stamping plants and engine plants start.

In a stamping plant, the inclination is to look backward. A stamping plant's finished product—a floor pan, a roof—is of little or no use in and of itself. And it is difficult to envision the basic material of a stamping plant—coils of steel—as the door of a Ford Explorer, say, unless one is a poetic sort who looks at sand and sees a castle. The sight of all that steel calls to mind, instead, the foundry of its forging. And that's not to speak of all the steel—hundreds of thousands of tons of it—contained in all of the plant's presses, and the thought of all the equipment that it took to make *that* equipment, et cetera and so on, until one is left contemplating the seemingly infinite regress of parts that make the parts that make the parts that produce, at the end of the process, the car that the average American commuter spends an hour each day inside. The core message that the Big Three executives sought to express before Congress and bungled—that the automotive industry is immensely complicated; that a car requires thousands of parts; that these parts are provided by countless suppliers, who, in turn, are supplied by countless suppliers; and that all of these suppliers employ hundreds of thousands, the vast majority of the UAW's membership, with the whole industrial supply chain stretching back as far as the eye can see—this message, bungled however badly, remains absolutely sound.

■

That, more or less, is what a stamping plant does—when active.

After reading the May 16, 2006, articles about Budd's arrival on industrial death row, I returned several times to a *Detroit News* cyber-survey that asked for memories of the Budd plant. A week or so later I printed the comments—there were a couple dozen in all—and put them in a banker's box of material marked "Budd." Soon that box would have siblings, the brood taking over my basement.

By late summer, after the company had declined to cooperate with what I'd come to call "my book," not a word of which was written, I went back to those comments, searching them anew for a way into the plant. One comment stood out. "Signed" by a couple, Pat and Dom Capoccia, on May 19, 2006, it began: "Yesterday, May 18th my husband and I both attended our Retirement Ceremony from the Budd Detroit Plant. I retired with 30 years and my husband with 32.75. My dad retired from the plant with 36 years." I liked the tone, the timing of the retirements, the family history in the plant, and the Italian last name. I called up, spoke to Pat, and drove out to Oakland County to talk to them shortly thereafter.

Aside from the Capoccias' entry, there were a handful of

others on the *Detroit News* site that stood out amid the dross. "My father is Budd's most senior pipe fitter. My father has worked for Budd for 31 yrs and his father worked there for 44 yrs." "My father retired from the Budd Co. after 42 yrs . . . Budd is where I learned my tool & die trade . . . I currently work at a Toyota plant in Kentucky." "The Budd Co. was a godsend for our family who came from the south in the 1930's. My father and (4) Aunts and (4) Uncles all worked for Budd." "I started working there in early 1973 and retired in Feb. 2005. The day I hired in the old timers said they were closing!" If the Capoccias didn't work out, I had others to contact.

There'd be no need. When I sat down at the kitchen table of their home in a northern suburb, Pat handed me a list of people that she'd drawn up prior to my arrival. Done on yellow legal paper, it contained twenty or so names of folks Pat felt worth my talking to, along with their telephone numbers, home addresses, job titles, plant departments, and job statuses (active, retired).

For the time being, though, I talked to the Capoccias. Pat told me of her father, who started at Budd when "he was seventeen. He lied about his age." She told me of her uncle, whose "first job was as a plumber in the Budd plant." She had family who, like mine, had lived on Springle, blocks over from Budd. Dom, less talkative, had worked in the Budd plant as an electrician. I liked listening to him when he did talk. An Italian immigrant with an excellent accent, he'd left his home in "a small town against the mountain, sixty miles from Rome," and come to this country by way of Canada. He spoke often of the plant's "rowboats"—"robots," I eventually surmised. He complained of any worker who brought into the plant a "radio," which he rhymed with the beatnik endearment "Daddy-O." Though retired, Dom still drove down to Budd from time to time, to see friends. He said he'd pick me up some night on his way into the plant.

I was desperate to take Dom up on his offer. The same *Detroit News* cyber-survey that had asked for memories of the Budd plant had asked for predictions about its future. One poster employed the pseudonym Last One Out—short, no doubt, for the Last One Out of Detroit, that final resident of myth, away from which the city retains a cushion of some, 800,000 souls, or 1 million fewer than formerly. Mr. Out's crystal ball foresaw the plant's "complete gutting by scrap metal scavengers," "coats of spray-painted graffiti to mark precious gang territory," and an "arson [that] levels the 'historic' building to the ground. Its burned-out hull remains for years." Whatever his motivations, Mr. Out was making educated guesses. Such was the typical progression.

I needed to get inside Budd before this occurred. Detroit has active plants that you can tour with a ticket. It has closed plants, tons of them, whose emptiness you can tour for free, needing only nerve and a contempt of trespassing laws. Detroit has lots of plants, living and dead, but Budd, by this point betwixt and between, was something rarer: a plant, still active, soon to be—but not yet—a shell. I thought of this process as a sort of reverse life cycle. Rather than observe the coming into being of a butterfly, I told myself, I wanted to document the re-creation of a chrysalis, cracked and shorn of its caterpillar. I needed to see the plant's people, and its equipment, and the process of emptying the plant of both before it was too late. Otherwise, I'd just be taking pictures of and compiling musings about another of Detroit's abundant ruins, a genre already bursting at its seams.

The arty delectation of Detroit's destruction—"ruin porn," as it's called—it sometimes seems to take up half the Internet. I understand the fascination completely, and I don't get it at all. I find it numbing, and yet I find myself happy to stumble upon pictures, say, of Michigan Central, Detroit's abandoned eighteen-story train station, which, like "The Most Photographed Barn in America" in Don DeLillo's *White Noise*—a barn distinguished by nothing but the number of times it's been photographed by tourists—people continue to capture, in part, so that they can say they were there and took that picture. For my part, I will continue to stare at the pictures of Michigan Central that people post.

Still, this curatorial impulse is creepy, and I'm not convinced that it doesn't possess a moral component. In a *New Yorker* article on Governors Island—the uninhabited, time-stopped island just off the tip of Manhattan that would seem, in this respect, to resemble Detroit more than any other part of New York—Nick Paumgarten captures the moral calculus of arty enthusiasm for urban obsolescence well. Discussing a photographer who, years before, had toured the island's "ambered, purgatorial state," eventually showing her photographs at an exhibit that "helped the uninitiated endow [the island] with a kind of idiosyncratic charm," Paumgarten writes that the photographer herself "recognized that the aesthetic enjoyment of dereliction was a recondite and ultimately unsustainable pursuit. 'I like the idea of a ghost town,' she said. 'But what good is that going to do anybody.' "

Later in the piece, Paumgarten compares a plan for Governors Island's rehabilitation to certain hip, contemporary parks, "the kinds that involve the clever transformation of dilapidated postindustrial wastelands or garbage dumps into useful and conscience-easing space. These are often, above all, artistic statements, celebrated by right-thinking urbanists . . . It's a nexus of arty cosmopolitanism, environmentalism, and transportation geekery." He goes on to compare such a plan to "the High Line, the New York Central Railroad viaduct on the West Side of downtown Manhattan which Conrail abandoned in the nineteen-eighties." Paumgarten writes:

> In its decay, [the High Line] became a clandestine aerie; connoisseurs of dilapidation sneaked up there for a glimpse of a city gone to seed. When word came that it was going to be demolished in order to make way for real-estate development, two neighborhood residents started a campaign to turn it into a park. The park opened in June. It is a strange and beautiful place, an architectural marvel, simultaneously rugged and delicate. It was also a fashionable cause, financed in large part by the donations of rich people who had discovered the pleasure of urban ruin, and of altered perspective. There is something decadent about the formal curation of rust and the fetishizing of decay.

Just so. The key difference, in Detroit, is that no one is putting up money to turn these places into parks, which increases the hipster quotient of paying them a visit. One is not only a connoisseur but—by illegally touring ruins and returning with pictures to tell the tale—a kind of socially conscious outlaw to boot.

That said, I'd take the artists over the social scientists. Years before, to fulfill one of the duties of my day job, I'd had to chaperone candidates for chair of a social science department at Wayne State University. I picked one particular candidate up at Detroit Metropolitan Airport—he'd flown in from Canada—and we drove into Detroit along the Ford Freeway from Romulus.

A young man (a relative term in academia—he was forty or so) with a wife and kids and the accent of his Quebec upbringing, he seemed concerned by what he was seeing out my car window. Unlike the Europeans who toured the ruins of the South Bronx in the 1970s, he wasn't just paying an aesthetic visit to the place. He was applying to uproot his family from Nova Scotia and plant it in Detroit. Where would they live? How safe was it? I said that the city itself, and certainly its suburbs, had nice, safe sections, same as anyplace else. He asked if he would be able to walk to campus from downtown. He could, though I wouldn't recommend it for the wife and kids. It was a mile or more, depending, and certain stretches of the walk were spotty.

What I thought to myself was: Why on earth would anyone want to *walk*? This was Detroit. One's civic duty was to buy a car, several in fact, and drive them into the goddamned ground. To do less was a breaking of the social contract. Perambulate and sing the praises of public transportation some-place else.

In any case, my spoken answers didn't seem to make much of an impression on him. We drove on. He needed to put what he saw into a social scientific context.

"Creative destruction," he said.

It was one of those terms with a high-syllabic count—"longitudinal study" is another—that lowers my immune system.

"Destruction, anyway," I said.

He didn't get the job, which was for the best, and Dom Capoccia never did pick me up and take me into the Budd plant, which was just as well. I knew who'd get me into the plant as soon as I saw his name. It was at the bottom of the contact sheet that Pat Capoccia had drawn up for me on yel-low legal paper:

Ray Dishman (Benefit Rep)
LOCAL 306
12720 WARREN
Det. MI 48215
(313) 822-5113

■

I called United Auto Workers Local 306 on the Friday before Labor Day 2006 and got the following message. It was spoken by a man whose deep voice contained the timbre of trustworthiness. "You have reached UAW Local 306," he began.

> The office is now in the plan for those employees needing help in writing résumés, looking for jobs online, or making application for unemployment benefits, and many more. The center is open from 6:00 a.m. until 4:00 p.m. Monday through Friday. Other important phone numbers and in some cases jobs may be posted in the center. Also, letters have been sent out from the local about separation pay. No, the company *still* has not provided us with the amounts or times while on the separation. If you want to leave a message for Ray Dishman, the benefit rep, press twelve.

Like certain sports stars, politicians, and supreme beings, Ray Dishman had referred to himself in the third person: it was his voice on the machine.

As that fall wore on and the plant closing approached, Ray and I spoke every so often. He was busy, and I tried to calibrate the frequency of my calls to take me up to but not beyond the point of trying his patience. In October, a ThyssenKrupp Budd news release announced that the company would "sell its North American automotive body and chassis operations to Martinrea International, Inc.," a Canadian auto supplier. Company plants in Hopkinsville, Kentucky (opened 1998), Kitchener, Ontario (opened 1967), Shelbyville, Kentucky (opened 1987), and Hermosillo, Mexico (opened 2005), were included in the sale. The much older Detroit plant was not. It was the profits from the now-unwanted Detroit plant, Ray said, that had made possible the building of the later Budd plants in places outside the American Rust Belt, and outside America altogether.

Ray and I arranged to meet at the Local 306 offices at the end of November, six days before the plant's last day. The local was in a one-story brick building on East Warren Avenue and had bubble letters atop boasting "Over 60 Years of Solidarity." I'd once asked Ray, over the phone, how up-to-date that sign was. "Our first union meeting was March 21, 1937, at Southeastern High School," he said. "The union hall didn't exist, because we didn't have a union yet."

"So it's been almost seventy years?" I calculated.

"That's why it says *over* sixty years," Ray said.

When I walked in that Tuesday morning, Ray was on the phone. "Well, you never know when you'll need health insurance," he was saying. The layout of the local resembled that of the credit union it had been before the UAW took over the space in 1975, a year before Ray began at Budd. I felt, as I walked toward his desk, as if I were going back to where they locked up the dough, a feeling reinforced by the fact that Ray was talking dollars and cents into the receiver. "It's seventy-five K," he said, still on the line, "but they tax that as a bonus. One-third of that is gone."

On Ray's desk, along with a copy of *Knowing God*, were pictures of his parents. His father, Orbie Dishman, a former Budd union steward, had come up to Detroit six decades before from Livingston, Tennessee, his hometown bride in tow. His mother's brother, Luther England, also from Livingston, was the first to arrive in Detroit, starting at Budd in 1926. Through his father, Ray began to do union work a decade before his official start date. "I was doing my dad's grievances when I was fourteen years old," he said. "He just wrote it down for me, and I typed it up for him." Beneath Ray's desk were a pair of slippers. A die setter in Department 110, the Budd press shop, Ray had so far had two back and five knee operations. His Ford Crown Victoria, parked out front, carried handicapped plates.

Ray was in his mid-fifties, bearded, graying, and bespectacled, with a reassuring solidity about him. He made a fine anchor for those who felt themselves adrift. His phone calls in the days, weeks, and months leading up to the plant closing ran to form, and the questions he fielded could be read in his responses. "I just don't like the idea," he continued saying to the same caller. The idea Ray disliked concerned converting health-care coverage into cash. There were three ways, he later explained, that a Budd Detroit worker could retire from the closing plant—at age sixty with ten years of service, at age fifty-five with twenty-five years of service, or "thirty and out." Anyone meeting those criteria by December 1, 2006, such as this caller, would receive seventy-five thousand dollars, a full pension, and medical coverage for life. "That's what *our* feeling is—it should be the length of their life," he told me later. "The company, more than likely, eventually, down the road, a number of years from now—somebody'll say, 'No, no, that ain't what we meant.' "

This caller was considering selling his lifetime health coverage for an additional seventy-five thousand dollars that the company had offered. "We've been negotiating these last so many years to get insurance benefits," Ray said into the receiver. "I just don't like that idea. You figure, you've worked all these years to get that particular benefit. Seventy-five thousand is absolutely nothing for that benefit." Some of the already-retired guys, he told me, were too willing to sign away future health care for up-front cash. The willingness arose when "their spouse is working—say if she's working at Chrysler—and they don't need the health benefit because they're covered under their spouse's." The scenario scared him. "What happens if their spouse loses their job?" Ray listened patiently to the caller and didn't press the point. "Okay. Need anything, give me a yell," he said, hanging up.

How many calls was he getting a day? "I gave up counting," he said. "Today is a slow day, because we're in the last week, but when this was all coming down, we were probably getting forty, fifty calls, easy." The callers, he said, "wanted to be reassured, or they wanted somebody to tell them exactly where they stood."

Ray's contract with the company ran until October 1, 2007, an arrangement that allowed him to tend to the concerns of the retired and the laid off while getting to "thirty and out" himself. "I got five thousand retirees," Ray said. Included in those thousands were retirees from the Budd Gary plant (closed 1982) and the Budd Philadelphia plant (closed 2002). Though they had their own locals, the Gary and Philadelphia retirees were covered by the same UAW contract as the Detroit workers. Ray was unclear about Local 306's future. A merger with Local 212, out on 15 Mile Road in Macomb County, was possible. "We have nobody paying union dues," he said. "You got property taxes, utilities." He anticipated a spike in calls over the summer, when the unemployment benefits of laid-off Detroit employees would end. "It's going to be tough. We're going to get some calls: 'Are there any services available for me? I've not found a job. Is Catholic Services available? I've got three young kids. What can I do to try and provide for them?' "

■

At the time its closing was announced, six months earlier, Budd Detroit was making "roofs, doors, fenders, tailgates, liftgates and body side panels for cars, trucks and sport utility vehicles"—this, from the May 15, 2006, company news release that made public ThyssenKrupp Budd's "plans to phase out its Detroit manufacturing plant" by year's end. The Ford Explorer, the Ford Expedition, the Ford Excursion, and the Lincoln Navigator were among the SUVs that, before their sales fell, provided the Budd Detroit plant its last big stamping jobs. When those sales fell, so did the plant's prospects.

The plant's prospects had never been great. A 1937 *Fortune* magazine profile of the company founder begins: "In 1912, Mr. Edward Gowen Budd of Philadelphia went into the business of building all-steel automobile bodies. At that time steel was used *on* rather than *in* bodies—that is, steel plates covered and reinforced the wooden body but did not hold it together or give it any structural strength. Makers of automobile bodies, most of whom had graduated from the carriage business, ridiculed the notion of replacing wood with steel. Automobile manufacturers were stubbornly indifferent to Mr. Budd's idea. Yet Mr. Budd stuck to his heresy and eventually the motorcar industry caught up with him. Today nearly every automobile has an all-steel body."

The *Fortune* article is titled "Pioneer Without Profit." Its thesis, constantly recurring, is that the company Mr. Budd founded should have made a hell of a lot more dough than it did. "The Budd story has been far from a success story," *Fortune* laments. "Although the Briggs Manufacturing Co."—a competitor and next-door neighbor to the Budd Detroit plant—"was making wooden automobile bodies in 1912 it followed Budd into steel and is now estimated as having between two and three times the Budd volume with an incomparably better earning record. From 1926 through 1929 Briggs made $16,000,000; Budd lost $300,000. From 1930 through 1934 Briggs made $9,400,000; Budd lost $4,800,000." And so on. Mr. Budd was a visionary, and a very bad businessman.

The *Fortune* article gives him his visionary due. "None of which is to deny Mr. Budd's unusual talent in the development of new product," it grants after noting his losses. But what's the point of new product if there are no dollar signs attached? The article spends ample time on the Budd Company's other great innovation, the stainless steel train, and notes in passing that "the steel automobile wheel is another Budd development, but the wheelmaking activities have been segregated in the Budd Wheel Co. . . . and so [do] not have a large place in this story." The Budd Detroit plant was never part of the company's train business, centered as that was on Philadelphia. (By 1950, the Budd Company was "second only to Pullman as a railroad passenger car builder," according to *Time*.) But Budd Wheel was so much a part of the Detroit plant that it served, locally, as the synecdochic term for the whole place, the plant and its stamping operation included.

According to *Fortune,* the Budd Detroit plant's prospects had been bad well before SUV sales fell—since the plant's inception, in fact. Mr. Budd's worst business decision, according to *Fortune,* was to set up shop in Detroit in 1925 in the first place. "Mr. Budd got into Detroit," the article says, "and hardly had he arrived there when he heartily wished he had stayed home in Philadelphia. The Detroit operation was a failure almost from its beginning. Its hopes for immediate volume were based mainly on a large order that had been secured from Chrysler Corp. But soon Chrysler had some difference of opinion with Budd and its order was not renewed. This was a knock-down blow for the Detroit operation, especially since Mr. Budd's proximity to the automobile manufacturers did not result in any important new contracts after all. So, to all practical purposes, Mr. Budd went home. He still has the Detroit plant and it does some business, but on nothing like the scale that Mr. Budd expected."

He'd done much better automobile business a decade before. "In 1912," the article says, "Mr. Budd got his first order. The customer was Charles Nash ... Mr. Nash was President of General Motors and gave Mr. Budd's bodies a tryout on the Oakland touring cars. Next, and much bigger customers, were the Dodge brothers. John Dodge and Horace Dodge themselves had been metal workers and when they graduated from making parts for Henry Ford into making cars for themselves (1914) they bore no prejudice against steel. For many years they continued to be Mr. Budd's best customers."

A 1978 article by Stan Grayson in *Automobile Quarterly,* "The All-Steel World of Edward Budd," amplifies the point.

"In 1914," Grayson writes, "the Dodge brothers"—whom he describes earlier as "two hard-drinking, inseparable brothers"— "ordered 5000 all-steel touring car bodies even though neither Budd nor Ledwinka"—Budd's chief engineer, the Vienna-born Joseph Ledwinka—"could give them precise cost figures. 'At the end of the year, show us your books,' said the Dodges. 'If you have made too much out of us we'll yell; if you've lost your shirt, we'll lend you something on your cuff buttons.' " The next year, the Dodge order multiplied tenfold. "The Dodge's first order to Budd for 5000 bodies was followed by a second in 1915 for 50,000 and there were also orders for stampings—as opposed to all-steel assembled bodies—from Buick, Reo, Jeffrey, and Willys-Overland."

The same article's take on the flash of inspiration that led to Budd Wheel's creation is tidy and dramatic enough to have come from a Hollywood screenwriter. "One cold day in 1916," Grayson writes, "Edward Budd took a long look at one of his steel automobiles perched on its wooden wheels—which had broken in the cold—and decided the time had come for him to become involved in wheelmaking too."

Reading about the early days of the automobile business reminds one how little the excitement and chaos of bringing new creations to market has changed. "Looking back at the early days of the Budd Company," Grayson writes, "at the problems of welding and pressing, of bucking the established order of things, of getting business, Ledwinka once declared, 'We worked day and night and we all had nervous break-downs.' "

Mr. Budd, the *Fortune* piece implies, was just too goddamned nice to make much money from the ideas he'd hatched and from all the hard work he and his people had put in. "Mr. Budd held patents on all-steel construction but never achieved anything approaching a monopoly in building all-steel bodies. For Mr. Budd was desperately in need of customers. If he had held out for royalties, the automobile industry might have kept on making wood bodies or might have made steel bodies and fought Budd patents in the courts. So Mr. Budd waived patent rights in return for good will and orders on the books. He plugged along, saved his money, and grew up with, if not alongside, the automobile business." The *Automobile Quarterly* article begins with a discussion of Budd's consequent anonymity. "When it comes to naming automotive pioneers," Grayson writes, "the list is long and fairly predictable. Edward Budd is rarely mentioned. Perhaps this is because Budd never produced automobiles under his own name . . . yet Budd's automotive work and vision were as revolutionary as the moving assembling line or the mass production of standardized parts."

What knowledge there is of Budd owes more to the company's building of railcars. "Because Budd put its name upon them," an internally published company history—*Ideas That Move America . . . The Budd Company at 75*—says, "the public associated Budd more with trains than with automobiles or trucks," although "the automotive business would never account for less than eighty percent of Budd's total sales." The Detroit plant's production was always automotive, except during World War II, when it was military, and in the automotive arena Budd "operated as silent suppliers, and let their automaker customers take full credit for the revolutionary new automobile bodies that Budd helped produce."

Though Budd had made money for a time from his innovations, "since 1925"—the year he started in Detroit—"Budd has never made more than $2,300,000 in any year and his net losses have come to about $3,300,000." These numbers were through 1937, when the *Fortune* piece appeared. Of course, some of those losses came during the Depression. "It is estimated," *Fortune* notes, "that in 1929 Henry Ford spent $15,000,000 with Budd; in 1932 he spent $3,200,000. In 1929 Mr. Chrysler is said to have spent $12,700,000 with Budd; in 1932 only $3,000,000." Still, Mr. Budd and the men surrounding him seemed untouched by the profit motive to such an extent that *Fortune* was forced to vent. "To make a single general criticism of the Budd operations," the long article says near its conclusion, "it might be said that nobody in the organization seems to have much capacity for routine." When asked why Budd's profits were not commensurate with its technological achievements, a company executive replied, "Why be a Japanese?" It's the sort of statement, fair or not, heard in Detroit to this day: the Japanese imitate, often to great profit, but they don't innovate. "Mr. Budd strikes the same note," *Fortune* says, "when he says that it is not the pioneer who makes the profit, but the man who follows the trail that someone else has blazed."

The article in *Automobile Quarterly* contains several lovely touches. It notes various Budd campaigns to prove steel's fitness in automobiles and provides pictures of such stunts. One involved pushing a Chrysler Airflow with a Budd-supplied body down a cliff. Another involved "standing an elephant atop a 1930 Chrysler at Coney Island." An observer remarked afterward that the Chrysler "looked no more disreputable than one in which some woman had taken a driving lesson."

My favorite fact by far from the *Fortune* article concerns the company's early days in Philadelphia. The size of the company's stamping presses had been surprising from the very start, and to no less a person than Mr. Budd himself. "So poor was the Budd Co.," the article says, "that when it bought its first big stamping machine and found that the one-story plant was not big enough to house it, Mr. Budd had to buy a circus tent and operate for a whole year under canvas."

■

Seventy years after the appearance of the *Fortune* article, eighty years after the Detroit plant received its supposed knockdown blow, and not quite a century after the circus tent, Ray Dishman and I climbed into his Crown Vic and drove from the Local 306 offices to the Budd plant that would close in less than a week.

"I was brought up over there—the old Parkside projects," Ray said, pointing across the street from the local as we pulled away. "One-two-three-seven-nine East Warren—that was our address. I was brought up over here in the projects for years. They were considered low-income housing. A lot of them were for guys in the service, coming out of the war. Dad worked at Budd when we lived over here." I told Ray that my grandfather's family had lived on Springle, a few blocks down from the local. "I used to peddle papers on Springle," he said. "I used to peddle the *Detroit Times,* the *News.* I used to have pretty much all the apartments on Springle between Canfield and Mack."

Back then, the Parkside projects would have been mostly if not entirely white; now they are predominantly if not totally black. The neighborhood around the local has fewer businesses than are necessary both for the convenience of its residents and for the support of the city's tax base; such businesses as there are tend toward gas stations, fast-food restaurants, fast-food restaurants in gas stations, party stores, dollar stores, Rent-A-Centers, low-cost insurers, and seasonal tax services. Inside Local 306, the heroes on the walls—past UAW presidents— were white. On the mural that adorns the AAA Party Store ("Beer-Wine-Liquor-Lotto") just down the road, the heroes include Martin Luther King Jr., Marcus Garvey, Malcolm X, and a black Jesus. A nearby billboard, standing in the parking lot of another party store, pictures a white Jesus under the message "God Bless Detroit."

The first plant you'll pass as you drive south down Conner Avenue (to return to our plant tour) will be a pair of them, actually—Chrysler's Mack Avenue Engine Plants I and II, which collectively employ some 450 workers at present and build the engines for the Jeep Grand Cherokee, Jeep Commander, Dodge Dakota, and Dodge Ram. Budd, across Mack Avenue from the engine plants, sits between them and Chrysler's Jefferson North Assembly Plant—one of only ten remaining Chrysler assembly plants in North America—which currently employs 1,400 and assembles the Jeep Grand Cherokee and Jeep Commander. All three plant sites are bounded on their sides by Conner Avenue and St. Jean. Along Conner, you'll see UAW Local 51 and UAW Local 7, the locals representing Chrysler workers from the engine plants and assembly plant, respectively.

Though the Chrysler plants are impossible to miss, there are Detroiters who claim never to have noticed the Budd plant, in the same spot for ninety years. This is understandable. From Conner Avenue, the Budd plant's administrative building, a replica of Independence Hall, is turned sideways; it can be glimpsed only in profile. The rest of the plant's two million square feet looks a lot like a plant, neither more nor less, and noticing it as something distinct from the surrounding plants is a bit like picking out any cloud in particular on a particularly cloudy day. Detroit can be an overcast city.

This stretch of plants—Chrysler, Budd, Chrysler—was among the more impressive in modern Detroit. It was also nicely representative of the auto industry in that it included a Big Three engine plant, a stamping plant run by a supplier, and a Big Three assembly plant. (It remains representative, too, in these plants' evolving ownerships and partnerships—once German for all three, now Italian for the two remaining. What with Budd being owned at the end by Krupp, arms maker for the Third Reich, some might see in this an ironic encroachment by the Axis powers in the middle of the Arsenal of Democracy.) Yet this industrial stretch is hardly a patch on the plants that once populated the area, plants that, individually and collectively, provided exponentially more employment.

In 1975, the *Detroit News* marked the fiftieth anniversary of the Budd Detroit plant:

> In an era when big companies are moving manufacturing operations out of the big cities and into fancy suburban industrial parks, Budd bucks the trend with a solid commitment to remain in Detroit.
>
> "We're in the city to stay," insists Gilbert F. Richards, Budd chairman and chief executive officer. The plant is located on 86 acres on what was once the great east side manufacturing corridor with Chrysler, Hudson Motor, Continental, Briggs and a host of flourishing tool and die shops.

I once spent a couple afternoons in the Technology and Science wing of the Detroit Public Library, where I'd put in a request for copies of *The Directory of Michigan Manufacturers*, called the *Michigan Manufacturers Directory* in its later years. The library's holdings began in 1937 and were brought to me on a cart from down in storage. I flipped through volume after volume, decade after decade, to get a sense of the decline of the once-great East Side manufacturing corridor, and of the city of Detroit, and of the state of Michigan itself. Jotting down employment numbers and photocopying pages from the directories, hour after hour, was akin to reading a British novel about the collapse of a once-prosperous clan that had produced no heirs.

The Briggs Manufacturing Company, which so decisively outearned the Budd Company in the 1920s and 1930s, was located to the north and west of the Budd plant, in the spot where Chrysler's Mack Avenue Engine plants are now. In 1944, the first year employment numbers are given, Briggs, est. 1909 (according to the directory), employed 32,000 in total at its plants—M. 22,000, F. 10,000. It ran an ad in the directory boasting of its achievements:

For 30 Years America's Largest Independent
Automobile Body Builder . . . Now One of
America's Leading Producers of War Materiel
Briggs Manufacturing Company
Detroit, Michigan

The ad included drawings of what Briggs provided the war effort: bombers (gun turrets, bomb bay doors), fighters and observation planes (wingtips, tail cones), tanks (complete hulls, turret machining), ammunition (Howitzer steel shell casings), searchlights, airplane engine parts. The whole thing is headlined "Briggs War Production—1944."

The Budd Detroit plant, employer of 4,000, was entered twice at the same address, 12141 Charlevoix—once as "Budd, Edward G. Mfg Co.," employer of 2,500, and again "Budd Wheel Co.," employer of 1,500. Established in 1909, the Hudson Motor Car Company, to the south and east of Budd, employed 12,308 in total at its plants. Continental Motors, east of Hudson, employed 23,000 in total at its.

I kept flipping through the directories, my fingers getting dusty. In the 1950–51 directory, the Budd Detroit plant is listed as the employer of over 8,000—M. 7,895, F. 564. The state of Michigan as a whole now had some twelve thousand manufacturing plants. By 1955, the state had fifteen thousand manufacturing plants, with Budd Detroit employing over 6,000—M. 5,814, F. 538. The foreword to the 1957 directory was headed "Michigan Moves Forward—2,300 Added Manufacturing Plants—New Total Is 16,000" and ran:

> During the past two years, Michigan's manufacturing growth has been tremendous. Now, well over 16,000 manufacturing plants are required to accommodate the State's productions. Surely such growth and expansion attest highly to this State's favoring manufacturing facilities. Climate; rail, boat, air, and highway transportation; skilled labor in numbers; employers and men of management of the highest caliber . . . ample manufacturing finance and some of the strongest banks in the Nation: good homes and fertile acres; excellent and various recreational facilities; all combine to make Michigan the mighty manufacturing Mecca.

This text ran essentially unaltered for a number of years. The 1961 directory was headed "Michigan Moves Forward— 3,000 Added Manufacturing Plants—New Total Is 18,000," additions that made Michigan even mightier.

By 1963, Budd's numbers were back up to over 7,000— M. 6,602, F. 445. Briggs, by this point, had been out of business for a decade, its stamping plants, including the one neighboring Budd, bought by Chrysler. Hudson, nine years before, had been subsumed into the American Motors Corporation. The Continental plant now employed 733.

By 1965, the Budd plant was down to just over 4,000—

M. 3,985, F. 372. By 1967, the year of the riots in Detroit, the state of Michigan was back down to about sixteen thousand plants. In 1969, the state was still described as a "manufacturing Mecca," though this bit of boilerplate wouldn't last much longer. It wasn't just that the number of plants was slightly down or standing pat; it was that the numbers employed in each of the plants were tending to drop, a trend that would prove inexorable. GM, Ford, Chrysler: even the numbers in plants belonging to the big concerns were diminishing, and would for decades, up to the present day.

By 1976, Continental had closed, leaving just Budd and Chrysler in the East Side manufacturing corridor. The Budd plant's employment numbers would decline steadily over its final three decades. The first entry for the Budd Detroit plant, as renamed by its German owners—the ThyssenKrupp Budd Company—appeared in 2003, with plant employment listed at 1,100. The last entry for the Budd Detroit plant was in the 2006 *Michigan Manufacturers Directory:* "ThyssenKrupp Budd Co. Employs—500." By that summer, Budd's obituary would appear in *Plant Closing News.*

■

I'd asked Ray, before we left the local, if I should duck down as we entered Budd property. Not necessary, he said— the guard was a neighbor of his. Ray drove onto plant property without slowing, honking twice as we passed the guard shack and main gate. He parked farther on, in front of the steps of Independence Hall, and nodded to Jefferson North across the fence from us. Opened in 1992 across from the site of Chrysler's old Jefferson Avenue plant, Jefferson North is an anomaly: an active big-city auto plant built in an era when automakers—foreign automakers in particular—have proven fond of plant sites far away from the upper Midwest's unions, its infrastructure, and its demographics. "Never got a drop of work out of that plant," he said, with no trace of distaste. Though he had reason to, Ray harbored few resentments. Even the Germans who bought the Budd Company failed to infuriate him as they did other Budd workers I'd talked to.

As we entered the plant, a billboard had greeted us:

THYSSENKRUPP BUDD
DETROIT PLANT

The Thyssen folks, Ray said, were fine. They let the Budd Company name be when they bought it in the late 1970s, and were hands-off overall. It was only after Thyssen and Krupp merged twenty years later that things, including the company name, started to change. Ray, absent any malign intent, invariably pronounced "Krupp" "Krump." "When Thyssen bought us, we were okay," he said. "Then Krump got involved."

We walked up the front steps, passing beneath the word "Liberty," put there by the plant's first owners and still clearly visible in the scrollwork above the door. The plant's lobby was empty except for some boxes scattered about. Straight ahead was a wide wooden staircase that could have classed up a country inn. The front office building had undergone extensive renovation beginning in 1987; two decades later, amid the mess, the improvements were still evident. The work on

the front lobby, finished in 1989, was done by four men in the
Budd carpentry shop. One of them, Jim Russo, was "almost
single-handedly responsible for the refinishing of the staircase
banister," which "over the years had been covered with eight
coats of paint," according to the winter 1989 *Budd Communicator.* "To bring it back to its natural hardwood finish he had to
first strip, then sand and stain approximately 200 spindles,
before applying eight coats of varnish. The task took eight
months to complete." I'd have guessed eight years. A wall
alcove in the lobby, by this point empty, had once held a bust
of Edward G. Budd.

Beyond the bust of Mr. Budd and down the building's
western corridor was the plant manager's conference room.
Ray and I didn't visit it, but I'd enter the room over a year
later, on a cold day in February 2008, during a walk around
the closed plant with the Budd guard who was a neighbor of
Ray's. "We gathered here on May 15, 2006, and they told us
the plant was closing," the guard, Eddie Stanford, told me.
"The union was in shock." Tacked to the walls in the darkened
room—the plant's power was out at this point—were spreadsheets for the "Detroit Consolidation Project," which detailed
the transfer of in-progress Budd Detroit stamping jobs to the
ThyssenKrupp Budd plant in Shelbyville, Kentucky. The
entire plant consolidation was scheduled to take thirty-four
weeks, from May 15, 2006, to January 5, 2007. The transfer of
individual stamping jobs was staggered; the transfer of the
"Ranger Standard Roof" job for Ford, for instance, was to
take from June 30, 2006, through August 17, 2006. "Settle

Labor Issues" was scheduled to take six weeks, from May 15, 2006, to June 23, 2006.

I took the spreadsheets down off the wall and thought back to my day with Ray, when the laborers he spoke to still seemed deeply unsettled.

"Here's the old human resources office," Ray said that day, turning to the right of the staircase. A sign on the door said: "Human Resources Has Moved Upstairs." Two days after our tour, Ray would post the following notice for "Detroit UAW Represented Employees" upstairs:

> Please be advised all eligible employees must obtain, fill out, sign and return an Election Form (with a yes or no election) if you are eligible for either the retiree healthcare buyout or the mutual consent pension benefit buyout. Election forms are available in the Detroit Plant Human Resources Office. You must have this Election Form filled out, signed and returned to the Detroit Human Resource Office no later than DECEMBER 4, 2006. This posting serves as final notice.

Signed: "11/30/06 5:50 am Ray." I'd take this notice off the wall as well, half a year later, on another tour of the closed plant.

Ray took earplugs and a pair of goggles from a safety cabinet and handed them to me before we stepped onto the plant floor. As our tour started, Ray waved to a group of black workers who had huddled together. The oldest among them asserted mock control of the scene. "Trying to get these guys to work, Ray!" he yelled. Ray laughed. Amid the noise, this qualified as a lengthy give-and-take. The blunt talk of blue-collar workers is both virtue and necessity. It's hard to holler compound sentences.

We walked past stacks and rows of stampings, all of it under contract and waiting to be shipped. I asked Ray about each part we walked past. "To tell you the truth, some of this I'm ignorant on," he said. Each part had a destination. Ford Ohio Truck Assembly. GMC Flint Assembly. Wayne Assembly. Ontario Truck Assembly. We walked past Ford F-150 tailgates on a conveyor. Ray guessed they were going to Ontario and flipped through a binder to confirm. "No, this one here's going to Louisville," he said. He shut the binder. What difference did it make where they were going? The important thing was that they go.

In some sections of the plant, stampings were stacked to the height of a decent-sized tree. What if the shipping of parts under contract hadn't been completed by December 4? Ray chatted with an older black man in a gray skullcap who was driving a hi-lo and holding an application. "Get everything in? Sign everything?" Ray asked him. The man nodded. Ray told me that the man was applying to work where he already worked, doing more or less what he was currently doing. But since he would be doing it after December 4, 2006, he wasn't applying to ThyssenKrupp Budd. Anyone who wanted to stay on and work would be applying to "a job agency of some type," Ray said. The agency had a representative in the plant, processing applications. The men and women who signed on for further work would go from being unionized employees on Monday, December 4, to being independent contractors on Tuesday, December 5. Did Ray think a lot of people would apply? "Oh, sure," he said. "Especially the guys that are going to get laid off." At the end of their talk, the hi-lo driver pointed my way. "Don't worry about him," Ray said. "New guy." They both laughed.

We walked and talked, and I took notes and mental pictures, fearing that this was perhaps the last time I'd see the place. I felt like a student whose teacher, rushed for time, had flown through an important lesson before a pop quiz. Any questions? The problem, then as now, was that I didn't know enough to ask anything of intelligence. I had nothing but questions, and so couldn't come up with any specific reason to raise my hand.

Though only one floor was now in use, the plant was four floors in one spot, Ray said, five in another. Some of the upper floors were condemned. "These presses here are some of the biggest presses in the whole state," he said as we walked past the plant's first press line. We talked over booms that seemed to come from the other end of a cave. Watch your step, Ray said. Look out here. He talked to an unhappy woman on a hi-lo who had twenty-nine years and eleven months in. "She missed her insurance by thirty days," Ray said. Around the shop, flyers were posted for the plant-closing party on Friday, December 1, 2006, at Club Med on East Warren Avenue.

Outside the plant, Ray and I surveyed a field of storage racks, which from the road were the most noticeable feature of the Budd property. Most were stenciled "Return to Budd Det." What would happen to them all? "They're down there burning racks right now," he said, pointing to the smoke and fire coming from the plant's scrap yard. I wondered at the temperature necessary to burn solid steel racks. "These racks are hollow," he said. "A lot of them are not solid." He took a coin from his pocket and tapped a nearby rack. It sounded solid to both our ears. "See, that ain't hollow. So what they'll do is, they'll just start cutting." Up ahead, a giant magnet was lifting racks and dropping them into the flames. I said that it seemed as if it'd take a while to get rid of the racks. "No, no, they'll get this cleared out," he said, the can-do tone continuing, even with little left to do.

When we began our walk through the plant, Ray said he wanted to steer clear of supervisors. Now, on our way back, he said he didn't want to take me up to the second floor. "I don't want them to question you being in here," Ray said. We walked across the plant floor and through the causeway connecting the plant to the front offices. At the top of the stairs at the end of the causeway two white workers, an inspector and a tool-and-die guy, stopped Ray. Everyone who saw Ray stopped Ray. These guys had questions regarding their paperwork. Were they eligible for this? Did that apply? Could they skip this here? Ray was patient, paternal. They had the air of students cramming for a test they'd hoped would never come and so hadn't studied very hard for.

When Ray and I walked out of the Budd plant—it was November 28, 2006—we stopped on the porch of Independence Hall. It was a bit before noon, nearly sixty degrees.

The next Monday, closing day, would be more typical of the season—blustery, snowing. As we walked down the plant's front steps, I asked Ray about the two workers who'd just stopped him. They were too young to retire, their separation packages wouldn't float them for long, and their health insurance would expire in eighteen months. As we climbed into Ray's Crown Vic, I asked him what the younger of the two would do.

"Find him another job," Ray said.

"What?"

"Oh, I don't know. What would you do?"

I hadn't the slightest and said so.

Ray answered in a tone poised somewhere between God-will-provide and devil-may-care. "You figure—I was looking for a job when I got this one," he said.

Ray was pointing out that those still inside the plant had needed a job once before and had found Budd. And if it had happened once, what was to keep it from happening again?

CHAPTER 2

■ ■ ■

They Just
Closed the
Door

IF THE THEME of the *Automobile Quarterly* article is Mr. Budd's technological innovations, and that of the *Fortune* article his questionable business sense, then the theme of *Ideas That Move America . . . The Budd Company at 75,* the internally published company history from 1987, is the benevolence of Mr. Budd and the company bearing his name.

The history's author, Vincent R. Courtenay, embeds the company's story in that of the country. He employs the high style while painting his narrative background. Of 1912, the year of the Budd Company's founding, Courtenay writes: "The world's largest luxury passenger liner struck an iceberg in the North Atlantic and sank with a loss of 1,500 lives. She was called the Titanic." He's as fond of ellipses as Louis-Ferdinand Céline. He situates Mr. Budd among his era's "many men and women of sterling character and diamond hard conviction about right and wrong who were vitally interested in raising the condition of their nation and the lot of their fellow men and women." Courtenay writes: "Edward Budd and his colleagues were men of sterling character. The company they would develop would reflect this." And: "These were not men simply making a living, but men on a crusade."

A kindly crusade, concerned with the condition of its worker-soldiers. By 1916, Budd had "a company sponsored thrift savings club at a Philadelphia bank, where accounts could be opened with a single penny if need be, and all depositors earned interest at a rate of 3 percent per annum [. . .]

Budd Manufacturing had its own medical department, too, and fulltime doctor. He was the first fulltime industrial physician in America."

Courtenay states that "Edward Budd suggested his own altruistic leanings in an article he wrote in the December 1916 issues of the Buddgette," the company newsletter. "He stressed to all employees that, 'You are not working *for* someone, but *with* the Edward G. Budd Manufacturing Company' [. . .] A man who would not tolerate managers or foremen talking down to shop floor workers or flaunting authority, Budd wrote that he wanted every worker to speak out on all issues, to present his or her view on the best way to get the job done. He had started on the shop floor himself."

Defending Budd from "business historians and financial writers" for not enforcing patent rights on the all-steel auto body, Courtenay (who doesn't cite *Fortune* by name) claims of Budd and his colleagues, "These were the kind of men who knew that no matter how much money one could make, its impact upon the spirit would have a very hollow ring, if the intrinsic reward of self-accomplishment and meaningful social contribution were not also experienced."

As the Depression began, Budd did his best to keep workers, even though, in 1930, "automakers laid off more than half their workforce on a permanent basis. Suppliers like Budd Manufacturing and Budd Wheel were forced to follow suit." Still, Budd "formulated a strategy to try to hold as many members of the Budd team in place as possible. Cynics of the present day may well scoff and suggest that whatever new strategy Budd managers embarked upon was one of self interest, aimed at keeping profits flowing . . . And recorded history can refute that in a moment. Company correspondence makes repeated reference to Edward Budd's concern for preserving jobs, and this was the basis of his strategy."

Courtenay is careful on Budd's view of organized labor. "In his eyes, workers, managers, executives, were all players of the same team. He never changed that view, not even when his work force elected to become unionized in 1933. He personally thought his own benevolent policies could serve them better than those inspired by an organized union, but he respected their intelligence and choice, and allowed that they were in a much better position to make judgments about their own working conditions and futures than he himself was." This conflicts somewhat with the account in *Fortune*, which said that Budd broke "one of the first of the strikes that grew out of NRA"—the National Recovery Administration, a New Deal agency—"and its stimulus toward union organization." *Fortune* admits, though, that "he now has a company union."

Courtenay notes that by 1926—the year after Budd Detroit began production—"Budd Manufacturing was the largest sheet metal using company in America," and his story gains considerable steam when Budd's corporate output climbs during World War II and in the boom years to come. "Budd turned its full production to defense work as soon as America was in it," Courtenay writes of the war, "and was producing war material just eight days after the invasion of Pearl Harbor! Out went the sleek automobile bodies, fenders, doors, trunk lids, chassis frames . . . in came a tremendous lineup of nonautomotive products. In came munitions . . . eight inch and 340 millimeter shells . . . Bazooka rocket bombs . . . The company also produced many varieties of wheels for military use, as well as army truck body components, chassis and other vehicular parts."

A 1941 issue of *Time* noted patriotically, "Last week, Budd Wheel Co. (Detroit) celebrated the production of its 1,000,000th shell on a U.S. defense contract." Such production would increase geometrically. A photograph taken a year later at the Detroit plant, and now part of the *Detroit News* collection at the Walter P. Reuther Library, shows a dapper Mr. Budd holding a sizable shell with a uniformed military officer. Behind them both is a table with more shells of various sizes, a roped-off platform with empty chairs awaiting ceremonial VIPs, and, behind the platform, draping that resembles the flag. The notation on the negative, made by the *Detroit News* photographer covering the occasion, reads: "Edward G. Budd presents Col. A. Quinton, Jr. with the 10,000,000th shell produced by the Budd Wheel Co., 10/12/1942."

"Even before the war ended," Courtenay writes, "the Budd companies were planning for the return of their war veteran workers." This included the wounded. Mr. Budd "made it clear that this policy"—welcoming veterans back to their old jobs—"would not apply only to the able bodied, but to all former Budd employees. 'The wounded and distressed veterans . . . They are still our men!' he avowed. Budd would find work for all of them, whether badly wounded physically, or distressed psychologically. The Budd Manufacturing dispensary was expanded by 30 percent to provide special facilities for wounded or psychologically afflicted veterans."

The 1940s and 1950s would mark a high point for the company, though it was also the end of an era. "Employment had never been higher, nor production volumes so full in November, 1946," Courtenay writes, "when Edward Gowen Budd died at age 75."

■

Those sleek Budd automobile bodies came back after the war. One in particular would give the Budd Detroit plant its claim on posterity. Courtenay can hardly contain himself when, writing of the late 1940s, he foreshadows events of the early 1950s:

> In the wings, in the sanctum of sanctums of advanced vehi-cle research, Budd and Ford designers and engineers were already well into yet another futuristic car . . . a two seater sports car . . . but a sports car of the new jet age . . . one which would be an instant classic . . . which would look as modern and dashing thirty years later as the day of its first showroom appearance. It wouldn't emerge for several years because national and international events would intervene. Its distinct, aircraft inspired styling would make it the model for virtually all other cars on the road, regardless of their size or class. It would touch off a designing war which would gradually focus on rear fender tail fins, which would rise to almost outlandish proportions [. . .] The new two-seater sports car would be called the Ford Thunderbird.

But first things first. In 1949, "Budd did so very well that it outstripped its own capacity and actually had to defer new business orders." Not wanting to turn down business ever again, the company "allocated another $8.4 million for plant expansion. Seven million dollars would be used to construct a new, high output stamping plant at Gary, Indiana."

In 1950, *Time* called the Budd Company "the world's biggest independent producer of auto body parts." A Budd advertisement of the era—"Budd: Pioneers in Better Transportation"—features a Studebaker with a Budd body driving past a lighthouse in a coastal setting. At the bottom is the new company tagline: "The Budd Company, Philadelphia, Detroit, Gary." From Philadelphia, to Philadelphia and Detroit, to Philadelphia, Detroit, and Gary: hard to imagine, with mid-century plants in those three cities, a corporate history more interwoven with Rust Belt decline.

There is no decline without ascent, however, and just past mid-century Budd Detroit was above the clouds, where the sky is always clear. "The two-seater sports car Budd had been working [on] with Ford debuted in 1953 as the 1954 model Ford Thunderbird," Courtenay writes. "This sleek, graceful, aerodynamic car would attest to Budd's automotive capability and the craftsmanship of Budd workers. Budd would not only produce the components for the Thunderbird body, but would actually assemble the entire body, and deliver it ready for painting to the Ford assembly plant." For the first few years, the Thunderbird remained a two-seater—the Baby Bird, as it was called. By 1957, Budd was sending the bodies for the Thunderbird, now a four-seater, out to Ford's new Wixom plant.

"Budd built and assembled the T-Bird body through to September 2, 1960, producing 251,453 total units," the caption reads beneath a picture of a fully assembled 1955 Thunderbird sitting in the lobby of the Detroit plant. One female employee, from the sales department, sits in the driver's seat; another, from purchasing, stands by the driver's side door.

By 1955, "the Company was in the most efficient state in its history [. . .] In addition to producing steel bodies or body components for Ford, General Motors, Chrysler, Studebaker-Packard and American Motors (in that order of sales volume importance), Budd had greatly increased its sales of wheels, hubs, drums, [and] chassis frames." And: "A new three-year labor contract had been signed with the United Automobile Workers, which represented most of Budd's employees, and there was considerable labor and management harmony."

In 1960, the Budd Company "completed a foundry modernization program in Detroit, and expanded the Gary stamping facility." The Detroit plant needed modernizing, for "while Budd led the industry in the sale of steel disc wheels, it unfortunately did not do so at a profit. The Detroit plant was not efficient from a capital equipment standpoint. It was hoped that a heavy modernization program would correct this, and 'Project Progress' was launched." The process in Detroit took years; it "involved replacing or moving 1,600 major machine tools, and installing the latest state of the art material handling systems. This essential program interrupted operations at Detroit severely, so that the entire plant complex operated at a substantial loss."

Another problem for the Detroit plant: "Federal industrial emission regulations were now in full effect, with standards which varied from location to location. As it worked out, those in the Detroit area were the most stringent particulant regulations in the country. To comply, Budd spent a full million to install an air particulant control system at its Detroit gray iron foundry."

Despite the Detroit plant's mid-1960s troubles, the Budd Company as a whole was cooking. "Of the 31 American car lines," Courtenay writes, "Budd was supplying body components, wheels, brakes, hubs, drums for 28 of them, and wheels, hubs and drums for 14 out of 15 leading heavy duty truck and trailer manufacturers." A Budd ad of the era features a woman in reflective sunglasses, a car coming in one lens, a car going in the other. The tagline: "Wherever you look . . . you see Budd."

But in the background, massive social and economic forces were working to the detriment of Budd's urban plants. "With costs rising drastically," Courtenay writes, "many companies in the high cost centers of the Northeast and Midwest began looking toward the nation's sunbelt states. This was especially true in Detroit. Automotive suppliers, faced with the necessity of paying wages and fringe benefits equal to those of their automaker customers, bending under the burden of mounting local and federal taxes, of rising costs in insurance of all kinds, of new costs to meet federally mandated environmental and plant safety rules . . . had been heading South." The Rust Belt plants had another problem: "Rioting in the major urban centers where many large plants were located, tended to accelerate this process. It also started a new one: flight to suburbia [. . .] Nobody could question the business sense in leaving dangerous, unstable surrounds. The Budd Company, incidentally, vowed that, despite the ferocity of civil unrest in both Detroit and Philadelphia, they would keep their urban operations intact, to the extent that it was at all economically possible. The Company surely stood by its word."

By 1970, Budd's stamping division "was by far the world's largest independent supplier of car and truck stamping. Ford was the major customer, followed by Chrysler, General Motors, and American Motors." But, that same year, the Detroit plant's foundry closed. The headline in the Saturday, July 25, 1970, *Detroit News* said: "Budd Blames Foundry Closing on Disc Brakes." The article begins: "The Budd Co. says the trend to disc brakes on cars is a major reason it is going to close its Detroit foundry and stop producing passenger car brake drums and hubs. About 800 of the 4,200 employees in the Budd facility on the east side are going to lose their jobs by next year." The closing "would not affect other manufacturing areas at the Detroit plant. They include a press shop with 10 major press lines and related assembly facilities for making sheet metal body components for cars and trucks. There are also large facilities for building truck hubs, wheels and brake drums."

In 1972, forty-seven years after Mr. Budd opened the Detroit plant, "corporate headquarters were moved from Philadelphia to the Detroit suburb of Troy, so that senior management could be close to and maintain ongoing contact and rapport with their customer counterparts." Apparently, no one in the company remembered the *Fortune* piece and its claim, concerning the Detroit plant, that "Mr. Budd's proximity to the automobile manufacturers did not result in any important new contracts after all."

The 1975 *Detroit News* article that marked the fiftieth anniversary of the Budd Detroit plant, recalling its place in the once-great and now-vanished East Side manufacturing corridor, observed, "It's a plant that has been declared obsolete, near death but has risen time and again." The article noted that "the venerable plant processes nearly a thousand tons of steel a day" and that it "[hums] with two production shifts going full tilt and a third shift running on maintenance and die setups. Corporate sales in 1974 approached a record $863 million."

In 1976, according to Courtenay, "the Budd Company's sales now topped $1 billion for the first time in history." This success attracted the interest of "Thyssen AG, of Duisburg, West Germany, one of Europe's largest, most respected producers of steel, specialty steel, capital goods and manufactured products." Officially, "Thyssen AG and The Budd Company would join forces in April of 1978."

In 1980, though, Budd "recorded dramatic losses" and "would have to consolidate production facilities, consolidate its workforce and adopt new state-of-the-art production equipment. All of these measures required huge investments, yet the Company was recording losses on such a scale that it had quickly used up all its credit." The needed cuts were drastic. "Before Budd was restored to profitability," Courtenay writes, "employment would fall from some 21,500 workers to just 12,000. The effect of reduced volumes and of increased production efficiencies necessitated closing the huge body stamping plant in Gary, Indiana. Gary production was consolidated in Detroit and Philadelphia."

By 1984, the "leaner" Budd was "beginning to operate with a small profit [. . .] The United Auto Workers played a role in that improvement through concessions granted in labor contract negotiations in 1982 [. . .] With a new UAW contract pending in 1985, Budd officials took an unprecedented step, and opened up their financial records to representatives of the United Auto Workers. This showed them that Budd still was not 'out of the woods.' "

From the second-to-last page of the company history: "As The Budd Company celebrates its 75th birthday, employee morale is notably high at all facilities." And: "As a veteran worker at Budd's Detroit Stamping Plant said at the end of 1986, 'Budd employees understand what the Company's been through, and we understand the new kind of worldwide competition we're facing.' "

Last page: "Indeed, in 1987, The Budd Company surely has 'hit its stride!' The next 75 years in Budd's future will no doubt be as filled with achievement and adventure as the first."

■

There were nineteen years left, not seventy-five.

After the last 350 employees had been cleared out of Budd Detroit by December 2006, one employee—"I guess you'd call him the last plant manager," a friend of his told me—

remained to lead the mop-up operation. That friend, Tim Hogan, himself a third-generation Budd worker, put me in touch with Paul Pronze, the sort-of-last plant manager. I asked Pronze why he'd been chosen for the job.

"I could do anything," he said. "And I don't know why. They asked, and I said okay."

Pronze, a precise man in his mid-fifties, had experience in the role. A mechanical engineer from Purdue, Pronze grew up in East Gary, Indiana, and began his career at Budd's Gary plant in 1972. A decade later, he would be the last man standing when Gary shut down.

"When the plant closed, I was assistant superintendent in the maintenance department," he said. "December 22, 1982. When I say it 'closed,' that's when I walked out the door. I walked out with three other workers. There was nobody else left. We were in there the last two months by ourselves, shipping out equipment."

Despite his decades in Detroit, Pronze still considered Gary his home plant, referring to it with "our" and "we." "We mothballed the plant," Pronze said of those post-closing months in Gary. "All the oil was drained, preservative was put in all the equipment, all the equipment was washed. We coated all of the machine surface on the presses. It was thorough. All the basements were scrubbed. You walked through, it was clean concrete, everywhere. Our basements were absolutely clean."

There was a lot to clean. Gary was Budd's "largest stamping plant. Ours was the modern one. It had nineteen major lines. There were 210 pit line presses. We made the whole body of the T-Bird—the floor pans, the fenders, the doors, the roofs, the quarter panels. We were doing Chrysler. We made Ford Torino, Ford Galaxy, Cougar.

"There were seventeen rail sidings inside the building," Pronze said. "It was 120 acres that it sat on. We had two loco-motives of our own, to move railcars. We could have incorpo-rated, at the time of closing, both Detroit and Philadelphia's work into our plant." Gary, he said, was "putting out fifty thousand strokes"—parts—"a shift."

And yet it was Gary that closed first. Twenty-five years after Gary's closing, Pronze repeated his last-man-standing experience in Detroit. At different points, Pronze had been the Detroit plant's quality manager, maintenance manager, and industrial engineering manager. His last role came with no official title. "They didn't want to call me plant manager," Pronze said. "I was the only one there." He oversaw the shut-tered Detroit plant until its sale, for thirteen million dollars, to Crown Enterprises Inc.—owned by the billionaire Matty Moroun—on April 27, 2007, at which point Budd became a small part of the expansive real-estate portfolio of Michigan's richest man.

Portrayed in the press as a cross between C. Montgomery Burns and Charles Foster Kane, Moroun owns the Ambas-sador Bridge, connecting Detroit and Windsor, Canada—one of the world's busiest border crossings—and many of Detroit's ruins, Michigan Central train depot preeminent among them. Often called reclusive, he spoke publicly a couple years back, talking to a reporter after a homeless man had been found frozen in ice in one of his abandoned buildings.

Pronze stayed on for seven months after Crown's purchase

of the Budd plant, helping to keep an eye on things. But Pronze's expertise was less plants—the structures themselves—than the presses that went in them. "I've taken many presses apart, in different countries, and put them together," he said. Though he presided at two plant wakes, Pronze had assisted in a Budd birth as well. "I was the product engineer over all the equipment for Shelbyville," he said, referring to the plant Budd built in northern Kentucky in 1987. "I was the one that bought up all the presses for Shelbyville. That plant was built for the Explorer. It was originally three press lines. When we were finished, it had one of the fastest fender lines. We were making six hundred fenders an hour" for the Ford Explorer, he said.

As part of his Budd training back in the early 1970s, Pronze had traveled from Gary to the company plants in Philadelphia, Detroit, and Kitchener (in Ontario, Canada), seeing the company's scope and interconnectedness. When Gary closed, some of the presses ended up in Detroit. For my benefit, Pronze named them all. It was as if he were a baseball fan tracking players traded from one team to another and citing their new positions.

He always cited a press's make as well, a fact one is tempted to attribute to geography, since Pronze grew up within the orbit of the city—Chicago—that was home to Danly, Clearing, and Verson, the major American press makers of the last half century. He talked of presses as if they were life-forms. The shelf life of a press, Pronze said, "is indefinite. It depends on how much you abuse it." Speaking of some of the presses that had followed the trail of company plant closings, moving from

Gary to Philadelphia and finally to Detroit, Pronze said that they "were all built in '67, '68. When you take them apart, the bearings look brand-new. If you use them the way they're designed, thirty years to go without a rebuild is not unusual."

In the Detroit plant, Pronze said, the presses weren't always used as they ought to have been. "Detroit is a disaster," he said. "We would break parts on presses that I'd never seen broken before. They would just bust them."

This lack of preparation and precision extended to the plant closing itself. "They just closed the door," Pronze said. "They" had also shifted. Whereas Gary was closed by the Budd Company, Detroit was closed by ThyssenKrupp. "They left the water on; they left everything running. They left the equipment like it was. There was none of the prep. I was the last employee in the plant. I drove the hi-lo, took care of shipping. Do whatever they want. What's the difference?"

Pronze said that other ThyssenKrupp Automotive Group plants—"plants from England, plants from Germany"—came to Detroit and picked what equipment they wanted. "There was quite a few robots that were shipped," he said. "Then there was miscellaneous parts through the plant that were picked up, boxed up. And then another outfit that I'd hired came and sea-packed it, to preserve it."

After that was done, used-equipment dealers came in to assess the value of the rest of the plant's equipment and gauge their ability to sell it off. These two considerations were connected, and the scene Pronze described sounded like a Rust Belt stock exchange: men on cell phones, screaming, trying to line up financial backing, along with buyers for the equipment that they needed the backing to buy. "Machinery dealers out of Canada, machinery dealers out of New York, other ones in town came to look at the equipment," he said. Though he'd been a Budd man for thirty-five years, he didn't describe them as "vultures." A "seagull" was his diplomatic term for the local used-equipment dealer who succeeded in acquiring the Budd plant's remaining contents.

■

It's worth trying to describe the isolation one would have experienced during the months between the plant's closing and its purchase by Crown Enterprises.

Let's start with the isolation surrounding the plant. More than most, Detroit is a city of numbers. There are all sorts of numbers, and any civic-minded sort can cite them. Founded: 1701. Size: 139 square miles. Population: down one million or more from its peak of six decades previous. Here are some more stats: the city of Detroit, in land size, equals Boston, Seattle, and Manhattan combined. (You can pick other cities, and mix and match to taste.) Mark Twain's observation "Buy land—they're not making it anymore" could only have been made by someone who never observed modern Detroit, which makes land by the lot, by the block, by the square acre, by the square mile, and—in aggregate—by the city within the city. Detroit's empty spaces, if contiguous, would make a city the size of Boston.

Despite this abandonment, Detroit is vastly overpopulated. Though Detroit remains, in spirit, a working-class city, there is nowhere near enough work for the declining number of citizens it has. If there aren't enough jobs, why don't more people leave? Edward Glaeser, an economist at Harvard, once subtitled a 2005 paper, "Urban Decline and Durable Housing," something "along the lines of 'Why Does Anyone Still Live in Detroit?' " The question is a neat reversal of the usual lament—not "Why has Detroit lost so many people?" but "How does it still have as many people as it does?" According to a *New York Times Magazine* profile of Glaeser, the subtitle was dropped out of sensitivity, although the paper, in fact, seeks to answer that very question. "These places still exist," Glaeser said of Detroit and such cities, "because the housing is permanent. And if you want to understand why they're poor, it's actually also in part because the housing is permanent. Thousands of poor come to Detroit each year and live in places that are cheaper than any other place to live in part because they've got durable housing around."

Some of that housing is nearly free and there's still plenty of it, though there's a lot less than there once was. A February 2010 *Free Press* piece detailed the city's residential decline, tracking vacant lots and vacant homes via color-coded maps and pie charts. The citywide snapshot at the time: "91,000 vacant residential lots and about 31,000 empty residential structures."

The worst of it is on the East Side. Two of the three neighborhoods with the highest proportion of vacant houses— 54 percent and 50 percent, respectively—are Conner and Mount Olivet, both to the north of the Budd plant, across the Ford Freeway. These neighborhoods are next to each other. The house that I was born in sits (or sat: it's gone) on the far eastern edge of Mount Olivet, where vacant houses outnumber occupied houses, and where vacant lots outnumber both by a considerable margin. What the maps and charts don't tally, but what I'll call the combined vacancies—vacant lots plus vacant houses—exceed two-thirds of the total lots in Mount Olivet, and exceed three-quarters of the total lots in Conner.

The paper's citywide color-coded map of vacant lots—with lighter green indicating lower levels of vacant lots and dark green indicating neighborhoods where vacant lots exceed 50 percent—calls to mind an Ireland gone to seed. All of the neighborhoods to the Budd plant's east, neighborhoods I drove through again and again on my way to the plant, are dark green on the map (that is, more than half vacant land), as are the neighborhoods to its immediate west. To the plant's south is more dark green, and to its north and west is a huge expanse of still more dark green. Budd Detroit, in North America's most abandoned city, was smack in the middle of one of that city's most abandoned stretches.

The exterior of the Budd plant puts one in mind of a mansion that has passed through countless hands, with each owner having made additions in different aesthetic directions. The plant's footprint has shifted so many times—buildings added, buildings leveled—that it now resembles no shape known to ordinary geometry.

Part of this is due to the disparate roles the plant played. "That's what makes that an interesting facility," Tim Hogan said to me of Budd Detroit and the span of its production. If Budd's Detroit plant was a failure from its beginning, then the family of Tim Hogan witnessed its full, failed span. Hogan's grandfather "started with the first large wave of hiring. Nineteen twenty-six was the very beginning. My grandfather held a few jobs, but largely he was a screw machine setup man. The screw machines had to do with making the lug nuts and the lug studs—that's the Budd Wheel part of it." Hogan's father started at the plant in 1938 "as a tooling apprentice, but he spent the vast majority of his time in the Wheel and Brake Division as an engineer." His father was eighteen when he began. "He went off to Germany for a while, then came back," Hogan said.

Hogan himself started in Budd Detroit in 1974. His first job was as "a plant layout apprentice in the plant engineering department." He rose, for a time, to "the position of plant engineering manager, the top position." Concerning Budd Detroit's disparate roles, he went on: "Compared to a plant that is more single purpose—an assembly plant is an assembly plant, period—that plant was very clearly two plants. Not only was it the two plants, wheel and brake and the body stamping—completely different disciplines—then you had something that was part of wheel and brake, which was the foundry. Which is a whole different process. The foundry provided the castings for those products in wheel and brake that needed castings, which would be hubs, drums, and discs. That's *another* completely different discipline. And then, of course, you had the tooling departments that provided tooling for those manufacturing processes—and, again, the tooling for machining and wheel and brake is completely different than the tooling for stamping." The range of the Budd plant's production led to its being labeled "the mini-Rouge."

The Detroit plant, by the end, was approximately two million square feet. To walk its perimeter was to cover a mile, more or less. To walk its interior and see all there was to see could require a walk of five or ten times that distance, depending on the time of day, the quality of light, the level of one's curiosity, and the steel of one's nerves.

Even those trained to be realists, such as engineers, could find the isolation and the interior emptiness of a closed plant of such size and vintage spooky. "After the plant closed," Paul Pronze told me, "Mr. Budd's office began to fall apart. That's a true fact. It's got a new roof on top. I went and looked. And the plaster started to fall. And the fireplace itself—part of it fell apart. After the plant closed. There was nothing wrong with the room until after it closed."

■

Around the time Pronze finished his portion of the mopping up in the plant, I drove by the old Local 306 building on East Warren Avenue and noticed that the sign atop it—

LOCAL 306 UAW
OVER 60 YEARS OF SOLIDARITY

—had come down. Its two halves were wedged between a parking lot guardrail and the wall of the EEOC center next door. I called Local 306 and got a recorded message from a female employee of the phone company: "The number you have reached has been changed. The new number is area code (586) 795-0121. Please make a note of it." I noted it and called out to Macomb County, where I got the machine: "You have reached UAW Local 212. If you want to leave a message for Ray, please leave your message at the beep." As before, Ray had referred to himself in the third person. "Wind took half the sign down," he said when I got hold of him. "I took down the other so no one would get hit on top of the head."

At my request, Ray had given my number to his neighbor, Eddie Stanford, an old Budd guard who had just begun to work for the rigging company now taking the plant's presses down. Eddie and I spoke several times on the phone, with me saying I wanted to get inside and see what there was to see and Eddie saying he'd see what he could do.

"This is a new book for me," Eddie said, expressing my thoughts exactly, the first time we spoke.

I got into the plant with Eddie's help; I remained in it under his protection. As time went on, I came to carry Eddie's old business card with me, not because the information was still relevant, but because Eddie was:

The Budd Company

Stamping & Frame Division

Detroit Plant

E. R. Stanford

Human Resources Supervisor

Security

12141 Charlevoix Avenue, Detroit, MI 48215

823-9329

"If people saw my résumé, they wouldn't believe all the different jobs I done around here," Eddie Ray Stanford said, handing me the card from a stack that still sat in his desk drawer in the old security office. It was a day deep into the next winter, and we were in the closed plant's front office building, the replica of Independence Hall. Building #3, as Eddie referred to it, had housed the Budd administrative offices, and from time to time we toured it.

Over the course of nearly eleven months, from the beginning of June 2007 through the end of April 2008, Eddie and I toured just about every nook and cranny of the closed plant, visiting some crannies countless times. From Eddie's tour narration, and from the plant maps I took, and from old plant photographs and old company and union newsletters, I came to acquire a sense of my location within the plant and, with it, a sense of that location's age and import. There were Buildings A and C, the plant's tallest sections, both four- and five-stories and original to the plant that Liberty Motor had built; Building 30, north of Building C, added in the early 1950s, providing 135,670 square feet of floor space and "the first step in a long-range construction and plant rearrangement program," according to an old company newsletter; the press shop, due east of Building C; the train shed, along the building's western edge; Docks #10, #5, and #2; the shipping office, west of Dock #2; the powerhouse, which Eddie referred to as Building #5; and over a million square feet more of this and that, not all of which I knew what to call, but whose cracks and crevices I'd come to know.

With the power out in the closed plant, Building #3's internal offices were dark during daytime. It was necessary to carry a flashlight at noon, and I found it helpful to remind myself that I didn't believe in ghosts. Eddie did. "This place talks to me," he said as we tramped odd corners of the plant in the twilight, looking for tracks that "critters"—copper thieves—had made in the snow. To bolster his claim, Eddie would let loose a rebel yell. The Budd plant, its echo increasing by the day, always answered back.

Eddie had begun work at the plant in the late 1970s. It was his good luck to get in his thirty—a figure as full of meaning for factory workers as 3.14 is for calculators of circumference—before the plant shut down. Melville's line in *Moby-Dick*, that "a whale-ship was my Yale College and my Harvard," can be retrofitted for Eddie, who was educated at Budd, as others in Detroit were educated at Packard, Hudson, and Dodge Main. The Stanford family's matriculation in Motown extended back to the middle of the previous century, when Eddie's father took the Hillbilly Highway up from Tennessee to work at Budd Detroit. As with the Ivies, family connections helped get one in. As one former Budd worker put it, speaking of a co-worker whose father and grandfather had also worked at the plant, "He's a legacy, like me."

Eddie, a storyteller in the southern tradition, was born in La Follette, Tennessee. "I was eleven days old when I made the trip up here," he said. "I was wore out. I was so glad to get here." Like many in Detroit whose families came north, Eddie retained traces of the South. His nickname was Cornbread. A country singer, he owned a collection of guitars, "electric and a-cue-stick." With a friend accompanying, he performed at area nursing homes on Thursday nights, playing gospel songs and singing carols at Christmas. When contrite, Eddie would sing the old ballad "Three Men on a Mountain" for me:

Three men on a mountain
Up on Calvary
And the man in the middle was Jesus
He died for you and me.

Country music colored his perceptions. One fall day—it was the day I'd passed the strike at Poletown—Eddie told me that there was a Chinese fellow in the plant looking to purchase presses. I'd been told that the man was Korean. Eddie shrugged. "He didn't look like Waylon Jennings," he said. He was occasionally indifferent to distinctions between the Mexicans and the Brazilians who would spend months in the plant overseeing the dismantling of the press lines they'd purchased. Did the Brazilians ever talk? "Not American." I said I'd speak to them anyway. "Good luck," Eddie said. "Learn sign language." He loved the lady in his life, whom he called Mama. After three decades of marriage he still spoke of Mama with feeling, and from time to time he'd break into a few bars of "Does My Ring Hurt Your Finger" by Charley Pride.

Eddie bore a passing resemblance to our forty-second president. He was in his early fifties, a bit above six feet, a bit above his target weight, armed with slow southern charm and acute emotional intelligence and an encompassing curiosity about all things living. He had the same first-term head of salt-and-pepper hair, coupled in Eddie's case with the sort of mustache that in working-class circles marks one as a leader of men. As with many big fellows of a certain age, Eddie's toughness was a form of tenure, and he took it none too kindly when a twenty-year-old on the crew clocked a man two decades his senior, giving him a black eye. "That was disrespectful," Eddie said. "I tell you, any of these young kids grab me, they'll be grabbing a tiger. I'm fifty-three, but I don't drink, don't smoke, and I'm still strong." He possessed Gleason-like grace. "I got pretty good balance," he said as we descended a small but treacherous snowbank one winter day while on a tour of the plant's perimeter. "It takes a lot for me to go down."

For the eleven months I was within hearing of him, Eddie's talk was one of life's reliable pleasures, a healing compound equal parts fear of God, love of country, and reverence for the Good Book, King James Version. Stock phrases were freshened when he spoke. "The fruit don't fall from the branches too far," he said, in near-perfect iambic pentameter, of a father and son who mystified him. "It hurts," he once said, rolling his left wrist. "Musta sprung it." To convince the crew that the worst of a rigging job was behind them: "You've already done a lot of the brunt work." After delivering a diatribe: "Well, that's my spill." His neighborhood in an old, working-class suburb just north of the city was declining—"riff-rat" had started to move in. As a result, he'd built a home in a subdivision in the sticks; his new house sat at the end of a "cuddle sack." Verbs ending in *st* got an extra syllable in the third-person singular: "He trustes me." "It costes money."

"Eat slow. It digestes better." He often chided me about my eating habits, which struck him as deficient in red meat. "The Bible says, 'All things is good to eat.' It's in Romans, somewhere. Man has dominion."

Even on high holy days he wouldn't relent. "I'm gonna get a burger at Joseph's," he said at lunchtime, referring to the Coney Island at the corner of Conner and Jefferson avenues. "They got good burgers."

"It's noon on Good Friday," I said.

"So?"

"So, I'm not eating meat."

"The Bible says, 'All things is good.' That's in the King James Bible."

"The pope says otherwise."

"The pope don't take preference over the King James Bible. That's your road map. You yourself said that, writingly, it's one of the beautiful books."

Eddie ordered a cheeseburger and fries for himself. For me, he ordered a breakfast anytime of hash browns and eggs. He made much of the fact to the person taking the order that I'd be forgoing the sausage and bacon. "That's right," Eddie said, repeating my request. "We got a priest here."

The Budd security office, where Eddie's business cards still sat, was on the east side of Independence Hall. To get to Mr. Budd's old office, we had to walk through the building's lobby and climb the staircase to the second floor. Except for some trash, the lobby was empty; no factory-stock 1955 Ford Thunderbird, like the one the ladies posed with in the picture, was anywhere to be seen. There was no longer anything of value in the plant except for its presses, which couldn't be carried out beneath one's coat, and copper, which Eddie knew I lacked the capability and equipment to cut. I posed no security threat and provided good company.

On the second floor of the building's west side was the old office of Edward G. Budd. Fallen ceiling tiles and bits of plaster were piled in a corner. Over the months, Eddie often observed that "the old man would be mad to see the place like this." Such statements came from him whether we were in the plant's press shop, or its train shed, or its shear room, or its powerhouse, or its scrap yard. Through most of the fall, all of the winter, and on into the spring, there were fires in oil barrels in the press shop, to keep workers warm. The plant looked like a Hooverville. But the sight of Mr. Budd's old office, sad and silent as a ransacked museum, lent Eddie's observation an apocalyptic cast.

"If the world ends and he's on one of them horses," Eddie said, "we're in trouble."

CHAPTER 3

∎ ∎ ∎

Assets
Formerly of
Budd Company
Detroit

Left to right: Eddie Stanford and Guy Betts

IT WAS early June 2007 when, through Eddie's efforts, I first got into the closed plant. Though the rigging crew had been in Budd for a little more than a month by this point, I hadn't missed much. The crew was spending most of its time prepping for the upcoming auction, to be run by the Ashman Company of Walnut Creek, California. Along with the Ashman workers, the Detroit crew was sorting the plant's contents into auction lots. The auction preview would be on June 18, with the auction itself on June 19 and 20:

PUBLIC AUCTION
Assets Formerly of
Budd Company Detroit
Stamping Facility
1241 Charlevoix
Detroit, Michigan 48215

There were 1,242 lots included in the Ashman Company catalog. Among what was excluded were three large press lines, tagged "Not in Sale," that had already been sold overseas. These were 2-line, sold to Delga, a Brazilian auto supplier, and 9-line and 16-line, sold to Gestamp, a Spanish auto supplier that had, in turn, contracted Müller Weingarten, a German press maker, to help oversee 16-line's dismantling in Detroit and its installation in Mexico in the fall. There would be stretches during some days when Budd was no longer a primarily English-speaking plant.

"I see they got the plant address wrong," Ray Dishman said, scanning the Ashman Company catalog days before the auction. He was in his new Macomb County office, on 15 Mile Road. "It's not 1241 Charlevoix Avenue," Ray said. "It's one-two-ONE-four-one Charlevoix Avenue, Detroit." It was as if a substitute teacher had slightly misspelled his child's name: a small slip, but because of it you barely recognize your baby. On the auction's first day a suite of lockers, Lot 541, caught my eye. Covered in stickers—"Buy Union. Buy American," "I'll Fight for the Freedom to Have Unions"—it bore the names of dozens of ex-Budd workers, Ray Dishman's included.

Eddie Stanford had given my number to the rigging company's first crew leader, Jeff Jinerson, who left me a message on a sunny Saturday afternoon. We met for lunch two days later at a nearby bar—where, aptly, Jeff drank Bud. After we'd talked and he'd taken my measure, we drove down Charlevoix Avenue to the Budd plant, the cupola of Independence Hall visible in the distance. I trailed Jeff's truck, a Dodge Ram 1500 V-8 Magnum with Texas plates, and noted the sign—

DETROIT

FOUNDED 1701

—that I'd see time and again on my approach to the plant over the next eleven months.

The security gate of the closed Budd plant was staffed by Securitas, a national firm. The Securitas guards were responsible for the plant and the eighty-six-acre site, both owned by Crown Enterprises. Eddie, who handled security for the rigging company, was responsible for the plant's contents.

After thirty years in the plant Eddie knew it cold, and he resented rent-a-cops with no real knowledge of the plant and a poor grasp of security work in general pretending to take responsibility for the plant that his father had started working in fifty-seven years before. Some days, Eddie's feelings toward the Securitas guards were what impelled him out of bed and into Budd. Eddie referred to them as "Pinkertons" and did nothing to make their lives more pleasant. Guarding the same plant, Eddie and the Pinkertons were at cross-purposes.

I had no such problems with Securitas. Early on, I had to stop and sign in with the folks at the gate. Once the guards came to know me and to recognize my car, the gate would go up as I approached the plant. Like Ray Dishman, I'd drive on in without stopping, giving a wave and a honk.

I went to the Budd plant as often as I could—weekends, mornings, evenings, vacation days, holidays, lunch hours. At first, with the rest of the crew, I parked in the plant parking lot, beneath the "ThyssenKrupp Budd Detroit Plant" sign. At the end of the day, some guys would strip down to their underwear in the lot, removing their work clothes so as to not get their car's interior dirty or dirtier. Almost everyone switched from shoes to boots and back again before leaving, and many were sure to scrape the goop from the bottoms of their boots with metal rods, like little boys with sticks scraping dog shit from their shoes.

Though it entailed a walk into the plant proper, parking in the lot meant that I got to pass through the plant's turnstiles— an act not without emotional pull. This was working-class kitsch, but kitsch can be affecting. I listened for the factory whistle and regretted my lack of a toolbox or lunch bucket to lug.

On me, instead, were a notebook and pencil (come winter, ink could freeze in the plant's cold), a tape recorder and batteries, and occasionally a camera, for what Eddie called my "captures." The notebooks that I filled from early June 2007 through late April 2008 constituted my journal of the plague year. I told those who wondered at my presence that I wanted to see what happened to an auto plant right after it closed—to its equipment, its people, and to the old plant itself, the product of an industrial era, America's last, that would leave behind ruins to rival the Romans. Most found this fair enough, including those in a position to prevent my presence. At some point, I became part of the scenery.

That first day, Jeff Jinerson took me around, the two of us touring the closed plant on a golf cart. Jeff was forty, lean and rugged despite some hard living. He often wore a Jägermeister bandanna. He smoked continuously. A concerned crew member had left a brochure, "When Smokers Quit," on the steering wheel of the golf cart for him. "Fuck off, fuckers," Jeff said, chucking it. "I'll quit when you do your job."

Jeff's smoke-cured voice didn't just make sounds; it produced decibels. A terrifically talented rigger ("rigger" being the general term for the men, mostly, whose job it is to move immensely heavy stuff), he could function at near-optimal levels no matter what. "I was born and raised in a pile of grease," Jeff told me at the bar, by way of introduction. He was the grandson of a boilermaker and the son of a press repairman who owned the grease pile, American Welding and Press Repair, in which he had been reared. "I spent seventeen years putting shit in," Jeff said of the presses he'd installed, "and I've spent the last ten taking it out." Budd was the largest such taking-out job he'd done. "I'm running a 1.8-million-square-foot facility—water, power, elevators—everything, minus production," he said at the bar.

That very morning, he said, his crew had begun to take apart 16-line, bought by Gestamp for installation in its Aguascalientes, Mexico, plant. There was so much work to do that Jeff was looking to bring on four more skilled riggers. Starting pay, he said, was twenty-two dollars per hour. The Budd plant's old presses were "world-class," Jeff said—meaning, by American standards, not much, but first-rate to much of the rest of the world, including what used to be called the Third World. "We're clear-cutting the forest," Jeff said to me sometimes. Budd, in this metaphor, was just one of the trees being felled in a great industrial forest, one centered geographically and symbolically on the city of Detroit but spreading through parts of Wisconsin, Illinois, Indiana, Ohio, Pennsylvania, and New York state, and known as the American Rust Belt. Later that summer, splinter crews would leave Detroit to dismantle presses at the bankrupt auto supplier Tower Automotive's plants in Upper Sandusky, Ohio, and Kendallville, Indiana. By winter, crew members from Detroit would be in Newton, Iowa, to cut up presses in the closed, politically iconic Maytag plant.

Standing in the center of the press shop, 16-line had been the Budd plant's biggest line, with several of its presses having been shipped to Detroit from Budd Philadelphia in the 1990s. It had produced body sides for Ford's large SUVs: the Ford Expedition, the Lincoln Navigator, and the Ford Excursion. Gestamp had bought the line's first five presses—16-1, 16-2, 16-3, 16-4, and 16-5, in plant shorthand—for the new section of its expanded plant in Aguascalientes. The sixth press in the Mexican line would be 1-4, which had come to Detroit from the Budd Gary plant. Like the 16-line presses, it was a Danly. Gestamp also purchased 15-02 as its "tryout," or practice, press, for a total of seven presses to be dismantled and trucked the two thousand miles from Detroit to central Mexico. It was early June; the line's disassembly would take until mid-November 2007.

"The heart of the plant is the press shop," Eddie had said to me one day on the phone. "That's where the money is." As such, the press shop was where I would spend most of my time, since I wanted to observe the crew, and the crew followed the cash. The press shop was as pleasingly symmetric as a field of wheat, with presses planted in perfect rows. Moving west from the press shop's bay door, the lines were numbered 1, 2, 3, 4, 16, 7, 8 9, and 10. Now merely a pit, 10-line had been removed while the plant was still active. Outside the main press shop, in the plant's western half, were 11-line and 15-line. There were dozens of smaller, non-pit presses scattered about the plant.

Each line in the press shop contained six presses except for the 1-line, which contained four. The lines would come down not sequentially but according to the logic of sale date, scrap value, shipping schedules, and assorted considerations. To an outsider, even one who visited often, it seemed simply chaotic. The presses themselves gave the appearance of permanence until they were trucked away—as, by the end of April 2008, they all would be.

The rigging company's first makeshift headquarters in the plant were on the second floor of the central maintenance building, in the old Budd Employee Involvement Center ("No One Knows Your Job Better Than You. Only You Know How to Make Your Job Better"). Amid such slogans of corporate self-improvement were a TV and VCR, along with videos such as *Mechanical Maintenance Training: Rigging and Lifting.* These were shown to new guys on the crew. "I got cherries to pop," Jeff said. "I give them the video so that, when they die, I can sleep at night." He pointed to a skeleton. "That's our safety mascot, up there in the corner."

Beneath the skeleton, leaning against the wall, was a poster-sized aerial picture of the plant as it appeared on March 18, 1940. To the plant's east, the blocks that are visible—Anderdon, Algonquin, Springle—are dense with housing, though the postwar building peak is still a few years off, with some lots yet to fill in. Each Saturday at noon, Jeff said, he had a barbecue for the crew on the plant roof. Seen from above, the surrounding neighborhood looked a bit different now. "It looks like a crackhead's mouth," Jeff said, meaning lots of empty lots, resembling missing teeth. On a table in the

Employee Involvement Center, Jeff had a timeline of the weeks and months ahead—what he called "a conservative estimate" of the removals of 16-line and 2-line, extending seven months out, through Christmas 2007.

After our tour inside, Jeff and I took the cart outside the plant, where I met Eddie for the first time. Jeff introduced us, and Eddie and I talked about how often we'd talked on the phone, but how we hadn't yet met face-to-face, and how nice it was to, finally.

"Boss, I'm going to go at three," Eddie said to Jeff. "I'll be in early tomorrow."

Eddie stood outside his shack, which sat alongside the plant's scale, where the trucks that flowed in and out of the plant weighed in empty and weighed out heavy. A busted window air conditioner and an upside-down milk crate sat beside the scale, as steps, and a five-step ladder stood below the scale's readout, which was at about the height of a basketball rim. Once he had his numbers, Eddie would climb back down the ladder, walk back to the shack, and record the weight of the truck—along with some combination of who, what, when, and where—on the bill of lading. Trucks occasionally drove onto the scale for weighing one right after the other. "Two trucks!" he said, early in the summer, after weighing out one at 116,720 pounds. "I can't keep up with production like this."

A ten-by-ten dump, the shack was Eddie's castle. It was uglier than it was small, with just enough space inside for a desk, three chairs, a space heater, a fire extinguisher, and a table piled high with paper towels and boxes of breakfast cereal. A CD player occasionally played Waylon, Willie,

George Jones. When the shack was occupied, the door was typically roped or bungeed shut internally; when it was unoccupied, the door was padlocked externally. In winter, the keyhole would be stuffed with newspaper to keep out the cold. The shack's roof often leaked. Reroofing it meant putting down another layer of plastic weighted with bricks.

On the shack's walls were several maps of the plant, a couple more of the Detroit metropolitan region, a credit union calendar, a broken rotary phone, and a floor-to-ceiling American flag that covered the shack's east wall. The flag had flown at the corner of Mack and Conner avenues before Eddie brought it inside. He took it down because he said the boss didn't like it flying without a light on it. "This is going with me," Eddie said. "It's the last flag standing from the Budd plant. It belongs in the Henry Ford Museum."

On the desk in the shack were Eddie's Bushnell binoculars, so he could better see who was driving in and out of the plant. He spied not just possible thieves but—as part of the crew's management team—the trucks of crew members who'd left for lunch a little early or returned a little late. The window that served as his porthole was plastic, cracked, and half-covered by cardboard. The half not so covered was crisscrossed with packing and electrical tape. Eddie washed the window from time to time. In winter, when water was hard to come by, he used dew from the melting Faygo bottles that he had thawing in the shack.

But my view of the inside of the shack would come later, when it was the castle of a man I had come to consider a close friend. That first day, Eddie and I had just met, and he excused himself, saying, "I gotta work now." He nodded to the ladder and the contraption around it. "In the old days, I coulda grieved that. I'm calling OSHA."

■

Though the rigging crew comprised a rotating cast, the characters ran to form. Mostly, the crew was made up of men who had banged around a bit and who had landed, however briefly, at Budd—ex-UAW guys, roofers, plumbers, electricians, a vending machine deliveryman, a repo man, an Iraq war veteran, a Bosnian immigrant, a strip club bouncer, assorted jacks-of-all-trades. The collection called to mind a critic's description of the crew of the *Pequod*—men who had "come sulking away, address unknown, from howling creditors, accusing wives, alert policemen, beggary on shore." They almost all drove trucks; after a time, I'd identify guys by their Dodge Ram, Ford Ranger XLT, Chevy 1500, or Ford Custom F-150. These trucks tended to be dilapidated but basically dependable. Bumper stickers memorialized Dale Earnhardt. Some guys greeted me the same way, day after day. Switching their cigarettes to their left hand, they'd extend their right, then quickly retract it, inspect it for grease and grime, and—after succeeding in wiping away none of it on their work pants or plaid flannel—re-extend the hand with a shrug, to say: your call. Beards, mustaches, and stubble of various stages were near universal. A clean shave would have clashed with the surroundings.

For a short time, the crew had two black workers, one of whom was also the crew's only female worker, a young black woman whom everyone liked and called Z. Such exceptions aside, an entirely male and predominantly white crew took apart a plant in an almost entirely black city. The relative lack of blacks in the plant had less impact, behaviorally, than did the almost complete absence of female observation and oversight. You didn't need to shave, shower, brush your teeth, or wash your clothes before work; you didn't need to worry about your beer breath, your BO, your black eye, your smoking, your burping, your farting, your constant fucking cursing. Pretty much anything your body could do, you could do with impunity in the plant, which made its own sounds and smells, masking yours. The plant felt like a frat house, but of a peculiar, contradictory kind—one for men who had never set foot on a college campus.

Still, the fact that a predominantly white crew was taking apart the equipment in a closed plant in a predominantly black city gave the proceedings a peculiar feel. Several blocks over from the Budd plant, on Garland Street, is the onetime home of Dr. Ossian Sweet, the black physician whose move into the house in the then-all-white neighborhood resulted in a white mob, a death, and an acquittal, for Sweet, on the murder charge. The mob had gathered in 1925, the year that the plant became the property of the Budd Company. More than eight decades later, Sweet's old neighborhood was completely segregated a second time. With few exceptions, Detroit's neighborhoods have followed this pattern: longstanding segregation followed by a more rapid integration, with the neighborhood becoming so integrated that, soon enough, it is segregated again, this time in the other direction.

After this second segregation, the neighborhood starts, slowly, to disappear.

In Detroit, race is never not an issue, always at least subtext when it isn't quite text. Come January, Eddie would ask the boss about a day off for the Martin Luther King holiday. "You're not in the UAW anymore," Eddie quoted the boss as saying. Eddie complained, half-kidding, to a co-worker. "We're in the city of Detroit," he said. "We might get shot for working. It should be a double-time day."

A concern of blacks that one hears occasionally is that white people want to take the city of Detroit back over. This is demonstrably untrue: no city that loses 150,000 residents a decade for six consecutive decades can realistically claim that anyone wants to maintain it, let alone recapture it. And yet, in the closed Budd plant, this fantastic claim had, in some small way, come true: the white neighborhood that had become a black neighborhood that had become a vanishing neighborhood was filling up with white people again, at least in the Budd plant, which was itself vanishing.

By a considerable margin, the crew's most dependable member was Nedzad, a Bosnian immigrant who'd been with the rigging company since more or less the day he arrived in this country and who was nearly alone among crew members in working the Budd job end to end. His English was good enough, though Nedzad's proficiency and comprehension seemed conditional, dependent on how much he felt like saying, or hearing, in a given instance. His speaking role was somewhere between Harpo and Zeppo. Nedzad kept his own counsel, avoided the bars, and brought his lunch pail. He endured some good-natured ribbing. A crew member trying to remove a stubborn bolt covered in grease applied heavy-duty barbecue grill cleaner to a wire brush, in order to scrape the grease away. The foam bubbled on the wire bristles. "Hey, Nedzad," he said, holding it up. "Bosnian toothbrush!"

One noon, I said I was hungry—I didn't bring a lunch pail—and regretted saying so straightaway, as Nedzad immediately offered me a hunk of his chicken. "Wife," he said. "Cook every day. Bosnian food. Meat, mixed vegetable." Declining such an offer from a well-meaning immigrant is a delicate matter.

One of five children, two of whom still lived in Bosnia and two of whom were now in Austria, Nedzad arrived in the United States in January 2001. He started work with the rigging company weeks later. He was forty-eight and had two kids—"big boy, little girl."

I said that was nice.

"No, two is not nice," he said. "Five is nice." The cost of living in the United States, he said, made this impossible.

Gray chest hairs peeked out of Nedzad's work shirt, which in winter would be a heavy plaid flannel caked with crud. He was one of the few crew members to always wear a hard hat. His was white and unadorned. He had a bit of a belly, a European pot carried low, suggestive of small consolations after a day's hard work. He greeted most of what was said to him with a smile, a shrug, or both. To my winking admonitions that he get to work, he smiled. To many of my questions, he shrugged, as if to say, "What's the difference?" When, in late winter, Kosovo achieved its independence, I asked his opinion. "I'm here," he said.

That he was, day after day. On any given morning, my inquiring after this or that torch man, rigger, electrician, millwright, or wrench turner could draw a range of responses: he's late, he's drunk, he's dead, he's hungover, he's in the hospital, he's in custody, he's in court, he lost his license, he lost a fight, he got a flat, he couldn't find a ride, he's fucking fired. Amid such confusion, Nedzad was the crew's universal constant. He drove a gold Chevy Caprice Classic, not a truck, and where the trucks tended to be dirty and rusted, his Caprice reflected and gleamed. He said he had it washed every other day. This I didn't believe. No car could stay as clean as his—particularly not on heavily salted Detroit roads over the course of an exceptionally snowy Michigan winter—without a daily cleansing. Its wintertime sparkle suggested Southern California. On its back bumper was a "BIH" sticker for Bosnia and Herzegovina, his homeland.

Whereas Nedzad, near silent, would spend a year in the plant, the talkers tended to fall off the crew fast, forcing me to get them on the page before they departed. One such extrovert was Duane Krukowski. On a slow Saturday afternoon a few days before the auction I asked Duane, the job's first electrical foreman, what he and his men were up to. Two young "tunnel rats" under his direction, using cables, hooks, and safety harnesses, shimmied down beneath the presses of 16-line, from which oil still oozed. From there, it was a further twenty-foot drop into the deep pit beneath the press line and the pool of standing oil that a series of pumps carried out to the skimmer pit alongside Eddie's guard shack.

Duane pointed out that the floor of the plant, where we stood watching the tunnel rats work, wasn't really the floor. The floor was down there, where all the oil was. Those of us on the shop floor were, in a sense, standing above the plant's sea level. "Some greasy I-beams is what he's holding on to," Duane said as we watched a tunnel rat descend. "He's actually not holding on to anything but luck."

The tunnel rats, Jason and Paul, liked their work, which was easy compared with work they'd done before. Jason, who answered questions with a crisp "Yes, sir," had already dodged his share of death. "I got wounded, my last time, in Pakistan in 2004," he told me when he'd come up for air. In addition to Pakistan and Afghanistan and the border territory between the two, he listed "Iraq and Bosnia and Philippines and Colombia" as countries he'd fought in. He listed his injuries in said places. "Got my right knee shot off in Bosnia," he said. "I was incapacitated for six months." All together, he calculated, "I stayed in for five years, eight months. Got shot six times and did my time like I was supposed to. Iraq, I took three bullets, one in the right kidney, and two in the lung. I lost my right kidney. They couldn't save it. Said it had sepsis. In my right lung I lost 60 percent capability because it collapsed. And then in Pakistan, I took a .762 round. In April, I took a bullet right here"—entering near his temple and exiting by the bridge of his nose. That bullet hit him when he was "right on the border of Pakistan and Afghanistan."

"Hunting for bin Laden?" I asked.

"You could say that. We were hunting for the wanted list." His stint in Iraq included time in An-Nasiriyah, which he helped me to spell by pulling up his shirtsleeve and pointing to the tattoo on his shoulder. He was twenty-six years old and looked younger.

The other tunnel rat, Paul, was the youngest on the crew at twenty. The previous line on his résumé, a job he'd enjoyed, was that of repo man. "You get to steal cars, only it's legal," he said. He said that most of the cars he repossessed were in the city, that many had belonged to drug dealers, and that—since such tradesmen tend to exercise their Second Amendment rights—he'd heard his share of shots. Paul's grandmother, one of the area's few remaining white residents, lived two blocks from the Budd plant, in what Paul said was a company-built home that had belonged to his grandfather, who began working at Budd after World War II. Paul's early years were spent at the house. Since his grandfather's death, Paul had taken ownership of the home, next door to which were two former crack houses that he'd considered buying. On the day we visited, I saw notices in their windows stating that the homes were at present in possession of the Thirty-sixth District Court.

As Jason and Paul tunneled, Duane talked. He began his explanation of press electrical systems at the beginning. "This is the nervous system," Duane said. "Electrical is the nervous system. Nothing happens—nothing doesn't happen—without an electrical signal. There's actually an electrical signal that says 'Nothing's happening.' And there's an electrical signal that says 'Something's happening.' The computer knows the difference between something and nothing." It was the job of the tunnel rats, Jason and Paul, to remove the tangled wiring cables that dangled beneath the presses. It was the job of Duane to guide them. Some cables weighed as much as a hundred pounds. "They're full of wires," he said. "These aren't empty hoses. There's probably seventy-five to a hundred little tiny wires." As the cables were covered in oil, they were not just heavy but slippery besides. "We gotta break through the grease to get to the wire," Duane said.

I asked Duane how long the electrical disassembly on 16-line would take, making mention of the timeline Jeff had shown me. "That is a guideline," Duane said, angry at a floor grate that was preventing them from disconnecting a cable, "and that guideline has no way of knowing that it took us over an hour to get this grate off here. That timeline has no idea of the problems you run into. The guys that were putting this shit together, once upon a time, were laughing to themselves, saying, 'I'd hate to be the MF that has to take this shit apart.' And we're the MFs. So there you are." If he could get the wiring cable around the grate, he said, "I have a good afternoon. If that thing gets caught on something, I have misery."

That said, he was happy to be where he was—inside an auto plant on Detroit's East Side, like those before him. "The history of the place," he said. "I want to be here to take this apart. I told the guy that hired me in here, 'I want food, beer, and gas. You don't even have to pay me.' I've had grandparents who worked at Packard and Chrysler for forever. They retired from those places. And on and on. I come from a long line of this. I had to cut my teeth on it. I had no choice. It's like, if your dad's a doctor, you're gonna go to medical school." He looked around the press shop, then the plant itself, contemplating. "It's hard to believe that all of this stuff has to go into something making just a couple of parts for a car," he said. "And you can go into machine shops all over town, and there's so much more going on—just to make one car. That's why you cannot make one car. You have to make a million of 'em in order to make it pay off."

There was reverence in his voice. "The front of this building kind of looks like a church," he said. "I've known people, through the years, they thought that was a church out there."

I noted that it was a replica of Independence Hall.

"They wouldn't know Independence Hall," Duane said. "They went to public school." Duane was a product of Detroit's once-extensive system of Catholic schools, and he liked the idea—an error that wasn't mistaken—that the Budd plant was a sacred site.

"My dead relatives would be honored that I'm here taking this place apart," he said. "It's a crowning jewel. We're not the king of England, but it's something they passed on, and it's something"—the disassembly work—"that needs to be done. You can't leave this here, to rot in history. There's still life left in these machines. It's *real* important that they keep doing what they do, because a lot of people gave a lot of sweat and equity that has gone into these machines. You can't measure it. You can't measure the lives, you can't measure the lunches, the allowances, that people were able to give their kids." It's "what these kinds of machines do," he said. Duane hoped that Mexican families might now benefit as much as his own had. "It's why we're taking such care getting this thing out of here."

He learned these lessons early, getting inside the plants where family members had worked—Dodge Main, the old Cadillac Fleetwood plant. Later, his regard for machines increased out of necessity. "I used to work at Ford's," he said, applying the possessive, as working-class Detroiters do, "and I got laid off from Ford's. What they did was, they built a new assembly line. One day, we went over for a tour of the new line, and they showed me a machine that was doing my job. The line that I was working on was built in 1942, and this was in 1979. They turned the lights out, and the machine was still doing the job. So I said to myself, 'Now I gotta learn how to build machines.' It wasn't cry me a river or whine to the government. I said, 'Okay. Now I learn how to build machines.' Which is why I'm here taking 'em apart. Because I know how to put 'em together. Now I'm fifty years old, and I wouldn't give up being here for nothing.

"America's view of this world *works*," he went on. "We have no problem with Germans coming in, helping the Mexicans get this equipment out of here that helped to win the war. I think it's good. I'd rather have them try to make cars than make bombs and kamikaze pilots." Duane admired those who wanted to work, and had a deep respect for the Mexican ethic. "Mexico's come a long way," he said. "Those people have come a long way, if they've got time to deal with this"—that is, the hassle of getting 16-line across the border. "They're not sitting there, talking about revolution and saving the planet. They want to get down to *business* and support their kids and give their kids a better life. And I can appreciate that. That's why we're taking such pains and great care to take this thing apart."

Duane preferred to take pains without being told that he had to. He'd take care based on his own calculations. He found governmental interference infantilizing. "They gotta justify their jobs by stopping other people from doing theirs," he said of OSHA. " 'Oh, some idiot died.' Well, idiots die driving home from work. They die driving to work. They die going to the doctor's office."

"Sometimes they get home and their old ladies kill 'em," a nearby worker said.

"There's no guarantee stamped on your ass when you're born," Duane said. "And we come from a long line of people that make damn sure you know that."

Detroit is a union town, but anti-union feeling of this kind (unions organize precisely to get stamped guarantees, after all) is not uncommon. Pro-union and anti-union members of the working class can be as difficult to distinguish, for those who haven't made a study of the schism, as Shia and Sunni. Unless there's an obvious giveaway—a UAW jacket or bumper sticker or, as in Duane's case, a T-shirt that said "Proud to Be Union Free"—there's typically no outward tell. They live in the same neighborhoods, go to the same churches, share similar conceptions of the good life. Many people unconvinced that unions are an unqualified plus still drive American cars, since love of country trumps any competing dislike. Such folks are often called Reagan Democrats, a term that would make more descriptive sense if they hadn't also been Bush Democrats, Dole Democrats, Bush II Democrats, and, later, McCain Democrats, by which point it's both easier and more accurate to call them what they are, which is Republicans.

Though I vote with the unions, I find Duane's philosophy attractive. As approaches to life go, "Now I gotta learn how to build machines" has much to recommend it. It neatly distills working-class self-reliance, a virtue that unions, by their collective nature, can't, or don't, particularly encourage. Self-reliant should not be confused with stoic, by the way. You don't have to be stoic to be working-class; you can complain without ceasing so long as you do so without whining.

■

Duane would have had a hard time enduring the union meeting I'd sat through a couple days before our talk. At Ray Dishman's invitation, I'd attended a monthly meeting of the Budd Local 306 retirees in the UAW's Dave Miller Building, across Jefferson Avenue and down the road from Solidarity House, UAW world headquarters. I pulled up to the building and was about to park in its lot when I remembered my car—union made but German—and its inappropriateness on such property. I turned back around and parked next door at a McDonald's, my Volkswagen hidden behind a brick wall that I then had to hop to cross over to the UAW building.

Inside, a Maxwell House can sat next to the snacks at the meeting room's entrance. "Help Pay for Coffee and Donuts," the sign taped to it said. Copies of the *Voice of Local 306,* a twice-yearly newsletter, were stacked on a back table. Under "In Memoriam," seventeen deaths were listed. An article about the Employee Free Choice Act—more commonly called card check—began, "America's workers want to form unions." On the back page, a word-search puzzle contained the names of all sixteen presidents of Local 306.

The average age of the retirees was somewhere between elderly and ancient. About two-thirds of the crowd was black. After the meeting was called to order, everyone prayed "in Jesus's name" and then recited the Pledge of Allegiance, the words of which were printed on the meeting agenda.

"Play ball!" Ray said, dropping his hand from his heart.

Introduced as "Big Brother Dishman" to deliver his benefits-rep report, Ray got the best reception of the day.

"Morning, everybody!" Ray boomed.

Everybody had questions for Ray; Ray answered everybody. You sensed that if you listened closely enough to what Ray said, life was a problem with a solution. You just needed to call the right number and ask for the right person, information that Ray just so happened to have on hand. As he nodded to the retirees' questions about benefits and tried to alleviate their concerns, I flipped through the local's old newsletter, catching snippets of this back-and-forth.

"It's not under Blue Cross anymore," Ray said. "It's under UniCare."

"Speak up now, can't hear ya."

"The mike's broke."

"My doc is changing over to LensCrafters."

"If you're out of state," Ray said, "you're having a heckuva time getting someone to take UniCare."

"Stand closer to the mike!"

As Ray's presentation continued, with reports of death

and illness and insurance delays, an old black man began to spin the raffle box for the drawing to follow. I read Ray's article for the newsletter, "Don't Let a Question Become a Problem":

> It looks like this might be the last issue of **THE VOICE OF LOCAL 306.** If it is, I would like to thank everyone for their kindness and understanding the past number of years. One person I would like to thank personally would be BIG AL GILBERT. Al took a chance on me more than 10 years ago and made the recommendation to the International Union to appoint me the Benefit Rep. for Local 306. Thanks Al.

Ray thanks a few more men, and then:

> my Dad, Orbie Dishman who taught me from day one that the **Union** is the people. If you don't like what the Union stands for, quit. Go work somewhere else.

"Now back to business," Ray writes. He provides a list of "important numbers to cut and save"—for dental, vision, hearing, for the International Union—and then some common questions that he calmly answers:

"I retired December 1, 2006, can I draw unemployment?"

"I retired June 2006 can I go to work somewhere else without my pension being reduced or stopped?"

"My Sub benefits have been coming in late what's going on?"

"I'm retiring under Mutual Consent when will I be able to

get separation?" The last question provided Ray with a pretext
to say so long:

> **Question:** How long will you be the Benefit Rep?
> **Answer:** I will be the rep until October 1, 2007. I will leave
> the Detroit address sometime in March.
>
> **Remember—Don't Let a Question Become a Problem.**
>
> Until next time, see you in Church.
> Thanks, **Ray**

I'd told Ray, before the meeting, not to say anything about my
being there—that I'd just stay in back and do my best to blend
in. Ray assured me he wouldn't say a word.

"We've got a writer with us today," Ray told the retirees.
"Paul Clemens. He's working on a book on the plant and has
been spending some time there. Paul?"

The above is a close approximation: I was too stunned to
take notes. I walked up to the front of the room, wondering
what I could tell people who'd spent decades at Budd about
my—by this point—handful of visits to the closed plant.

What did I say? I don't much remember, and I don't think
anyone heard. I believe I said something about the upcoming
auction, but can't be certain. I didn't take notes of myself
speaking, of course, but did manage to scribble this about my
speech after I'd sat back down: "Mike didn't work. Not interested." I told myself not to say a word about 16-line going to
Mexico, and am pretty sure that in that I succeeded.

I sat back down and tried to complete the word-search puzzle of Local 306 presidents on the newsletter's back page. One name that I found, running horizontally in the sixth line down, was that of "Ervin Baur." I'd heard it before, and had seen Erwin Baur quoted in the papers. He was a strident old-timer I'd wanted to track down. I'd heard that he'd left Detroit and moved to Berkeley, California, decades back.

I contacted Harley Shaiken, a labor professor at the University of California–Berkeley, hoping that he might know Baur from Berkeley's labor-left circles. Shaiken was an alumnus of Wayne State, my employer, and had been considered for a newly created labor position at the university before making clear his intent to stay at Berkeley.

Months later, Shaiken would be a contender for an even bigger job, this one in Washington. From the December 17, 2008, *Wall Street Journal* Washington Wire blog on the presidential transition:

> **Shaiken Emerges as Top Candidate for Labor Secretary**
> Harley Shaiken, a prominent expert on unions, Detroit and the U.S.-Mexican border, has emerged as a top candidate for the post of secretary of labor, officials familiar with the vetting process say.

Once again, Shaiken remained in Berkeley, where it turned out that he did indeed know Baur. Shaiken helped to arrange our meeting.

Over a year after finding Baur's name in the *Voice of Local*

306 word search, then, I flew out to Oakland and spent two days talking to Erwin and Estar Baur in Alameda, where they'd recently moved into a senior center after selling their Berkeley home.

A nearly seven-decade-old drawing hung on a wall of their apartment. Doodled in Detroit by a Budd personnel manager who sat opposite Erwin at the negotiating table during World War II and brought by the couple to Berkeley in the late 1970s, after Erwin had retired from Budd, the drawing shows a young Erwin, the representative of UAW Local 306, dressed in a white shirt and dark tie and smiling straight ahead. The smile is unsettling. Above it, his nose has been made porcine. He clasps wads of cash and piles of coins to his chest. Mountains of bills and bags marked "$" are scattered all about him. On the negotiating table in front of him is a jug, spilling over red, marked "Bucket of Blood."

Pinned to the table beneath Erwin's arms are papers marked "CONTR." It's the contract between company and union. A sign over Erwin's right shoulder, partly blocked by a barrel of bullion, reads: "This Plant Under New Owner. Now Affiliated with UAW." Over his left shoulder are the smokestacks of the Budd foundry, spewing smoke. "Budd," spelled perpendicularly on the smokestacks, is lined through. Though blurry, the letters *U* and *A* and *W* would seem to have replaced the company name. Erwin's demands aren't done. "Now, one more item," he says, his words captioned in the bubble floating above his head.

"That's Erwin," Estar said, showing me the drawing. "The pig. See?"

"That's the picture of the personnel man of me," Erwin said from the other room.

"That's his view of Erwin. Erwin has taken all the money from the company."

"The last drop of their money," Erwin said.

"He didn't mean for Erwin to have it," Estar said of the drawing. "He was just doodling. I had it framed. I think it's wonderful. It shows how Erwin got along with the management."

I noted Erwin's tie.

"Everybody wore ties when they were bargaining," Estar said. "They dressed like *dudes*. It was a point of pride with the workers that their representative should look as good as the company's representative."

I said that the management man was a talented artist.

"He was," Erwin said. "He really was."

"He was in the wrong field," Estar said.

"He got fired."

"He was a very intelligent man."

"We forced him into a promotion," Erwin said.

On the first morning we met, in what I hoped was anticipation of my visit, Erwin wore a T-shirt that said: "Detroit Newspaper Strike—1995—No Surrender." "That was a rough strike," Erwin said. I gave him a UAW Local 306 button that I'd found in the plant. It said: "I Believe in Budd Detroit."

Erwin was born in 1915 in Düsseldorf. His father came to this country first, working for the Youngstown Sheet and Tube Company. "He was an engineer," Erwin said. "My father got a contract in 1925, and he died in 1930. Fulfilled the contract and that was the end of that—he died. He was here on that contract, and we came here because my mother didn't want to live in Germany alone." Erwin came over in 1929. Nearly eight decades later, he receives pension checks—for $620 a month—with German names on them. "It's got three names on it now," Erwin said, meaning "Thyssen," "Krupp," and "Budd."

Erwin himself "started as an apprentice at the Youngstown Sheet and Tube Company. Even in Youngstown, I worked on things for cars." The job didn't last long. "The Little Steel Strike came along in May of '37," Erwin said, "and I got fired. I was twenty-two. It was hard to get work then." He moved to Salem, Ohio, where he stayed for two years. From there, he went to Cleveland, Estar's hometown, and worked for Fisher Body. "GM," Erwin said. "Local 45."

In 1942, he and Estar came up to Detroit. "I'll show you how you get hired," Erwin said. "In '42, I was very new at the game, and I came to the Budd Company. And I was bold enough to say, 'I want a tool-and-die job, and what are you paying?' And then they had to explain what they were paying. And I said, 'What's the top rate?' They said, 'Well, you'll have to talk to the superintendent, or the foreman.' I said, 'I want to know what the top rate is, because if I can't get it I don't hire in here.' That's how bold we got then. Superintendent came out, said, 'We pay $1.25. That's the highest rate.' 'Well, that's your base rate. What's your leader's rate?' He said, 'That's fifteen cents higher.' I said, 'Well, we'll begin there.'"

Erwin and Estar had lived on Springle near Charlevoix, three blocks over from the Budd plant. "Hudson, it was next door yet, and still operative," Erwin said, recalling the plant's neighbors. "There was Packard, there was Motor Wheel, Midland, and Budd's, and on the other side of town the competitor was Kelsey-Hayes.

"Within a year I ran for president of the local union, and nearly won," Erwin said. "Then ran for the bargaining committee, a six-man committee—six-*person* committee, as a matter of fact we had a woman on at that time. Very interesting place. Very open. And I found it, in the skilled trades, very talented, for a very good reason. They had contracts in so many different fields that just by the sheer number of things they were involved in, you learned. So it was a highly skilled group of people in the tool room. And also in the maintenance, because there were so many changes all the time.

"It was largely war work," he said of the time of his starting at Budd. "Stampings were needed during the war as well. A big part of the work was not a change, except for customers"—that is, the U.S. military rather than the car companies. "The Budd Company worked for all of them, because it was a supplier. Which also meant that its workforce was generally more skilled than other places. Big Three companies were very demanding. And gradually, as a matter of fact, the parts companies all went out of business. Kelsey went out of business, Motor Wheel went out of business, Midland went out of business. The Big Three got very competitive and gradually took in more of their own work.

"The Budd Company was a very innovative kind of company. The first Thunderbird—that was totally designed in that plant. The entire body. The Wixom plant was built from that model. Later on, that body developed from a two-door to a four-door—an open four-door—at which time the Ford Motor Company built a new plant in Wixom. They bought a part of a farm there and put that plant there."

I told him that the Wixom plant had closed six months after Budd.

"Maybe it's back to farming," Erwin said.

"The Thunderbird was the last big job," he went on. "When that went to Wixom, it began the decline of the whole parts industry. Because by that time, the Big Three were able to build their own stamping plants. They'll just build a whole new plant for a new project.

"I don't like to brag, but I did very little," Erwin said of his work, or lack thereof, in the plant. "I was a troubleshooter. When you develop a new project, there's all kinds of problems come. There's maybe twenty different dies of various sizes. So there's all kinds of problems. I was always lucky. I had a little office, telephone in it. In addition to that, I was the most active person in the union. I held all the offices, except for financial secretary. I've been president down to chief steward or just rank and file."

"Erwin had a good job when he worked in a factory," Estar said. "I had the pits when I worked in a factory. Erwin loved his job. I hated my job. I worked in Ford Motor Company and I worked at Dodge. My last job was at Dodge. I worked seven years on a production line. Dodge Main."

"I never had trouble in the plant," Erwin said.

"I used to hate him," Estar said. "I absolutely used to hate him sometimes."

"I enjoyed going to work."

"I could hate him to this minute," she said. "See, I had children. I started working at Ford. I don't think I stayed there more than a month. I had to get help to take care of the children. There wasn't any money left by the time you paid somebody to help you take care of the children. Women have it better now than they did before, but it's still not right. When I went to work at Dodge, my little girl was in school, so I worked afternoons, and Erwin days, and we took care of the children between the two of us. And so I stayed there seven years.

"When I used to go into work in the morning," Estar went on, "the gates would clang behind me, and I'd feel just like I was going into prison. It was the only job I could get that paid money. We needed two of us to work to get the down payment for a house. You could get by on Erwin's income, but I couldn't save anything."

"In other words, a skilled-trades income is not enough to support our way of living," Erwin said.

"Especially when you're active in the movement," Estar said. "You give your money away."

"Estar had the dirty end of the production jobs. I always had the easy end."

"I used to hate him. Absolutely hate him."

"The reason I liked my job—I never worked."

"I'll show you what workers do," Erwin said later, in a similar vein. "They're funny. We had a guy who alleged that he was injured. The company examined him carefully and decided no, he wasn't injured, he was just malingering. He wants to get out on retirement—total disability retirement. So he put on this act, being unable to work, just limping around, complaining all the time. And he knew he could get out on disability and live—he had, personally, enough money and so on. But he wanted that total disability retirement. And the company knew he wanted it, and the company also knew that he was a big faker. But he got so obnoxious about the whole business that the company finally said, 'Get him the hell out of here!' "

You just have to make enough trouble, I said.

"But you have to be a really obnoxious son of a bitch," Erwin said. "This guy was really something. Finally, they agreed to total disability for him. Guess what he did?" Erwin paused. "Ran around the plant like a deer! You can just imagine what that will do to the personnel department. It sure hardens the personnel department against the next malingerer.

"We had a friend," Erwin went on. "Didn't work at the Budd Company, just an old friend of ours. He lived on a street where personnel had one of their people. Fred, one day, was out talking with his neighbors—'Oh, I know somebody over at the Budd Company.' He used my name. And he knew this fella was part of the personnel department. Said he got such a lecture about that son of a bitch, Baur."

"He was thrilled," Estar said.

"Fred was really excited about it," Erwin said.

"So were you," Estar said to Erwin. "Erwin was very flattered."

Estar recalled a daughter's semantic near miss when someone called the house and asked for Erwin. "Do you want to talk to the troublemaker?" she asked. She knew her father's title had "trouble" in it.

"I thought it was the right definition," Erwin said.

■

Troublemaking, troubleshooting: still an eye-of-the-beholder business in the Budd plant.

The two Mexican engineers in the Budd plant from Gestamp, the Spanish auto supplier, were there to observe 16-line's dismantling—to troubleshoot in the future tense, so to speak, when the press line would be reassembled in Mexico. One of the Gestamp engineers, Salvador Sierra Bernal, whose expertise was stamping and welding, spoke halting English, and the other, David Ramirez, whose expertise was electrical, spoke next to none at all. But they smiled, and steered clear, and seemed to enjoy Detroit, inasmuch as this is possible with Budd as your base of operations. They had seen LeBron James and the Cleveland Cavaliers beat the Pistons in a two-overtime epic in game 5 of the 2007 NBA Eastern Conference Finals, a story Salvador told Jeff Jinerson and me over dinner at one of the city's better Mexican restaurants.

Everyone liked them and joked with them. (At dinner, Salvador said that he didn't swim. Jeff: "So you walk across the Rio Grande?") "They're good," Duane, the electrician, said. "They can't be any better than they are. They want to watch. Nothing replaces the human eye when it comes to putting this shit back together."

I asked if he was working with them.

"No, they're working with *us*," Duane said.

What was their role?

"To stand there, in awe, and hope they can put it back together when they get it to Mexico."

Working with Salvador and David were two Germans from Müller Weingarten, the German press maker. They exhibited their people's historic talent for making friends in foreign lands. Troublemakers or not, they were considered such by the rigging crew. When fed up with having them underfoot, Jeff Jinerson, the first crew leader, would let them have it, unleashing a torrent one hoped they couldn't translate. The English speakers on the rigging crew sure couldn't translate the Germans' code. One of the Germans had spray painted the letters VR on the corner of a 16-line press column. Detroiters with no knowledge of *Deutsch* guessed away at the meaning of this marking. Volkswagen Rules? *Vorne rechts*, or "front right."

As we stood together and watched the presses come apart, I sometimes suggested to Salvador that he go down into the pits or up onto the crowns with the crew. Salvador smiled, to say, "No way." There were, it seemed, some jobs that Mexicans wouldn't do.

■

The Budd auction was the only public event to be held in the plant post-closing. If you wanted to see its insides, this was your chance.

Out-of-state license plates were a common sight in the plant's parking lot during the auction's three days. Missouri, Wisconsin, Kentucky, Indiana, Tennessee, Arkansas, Ohio, and Ontario, the Canadian province Detroiters consider a suburb, were all represented. A yellow sign with black lettering sat at the plant entrance:

AUCTION TODAY
ASHMAN COMPANY

The first day was the auction preview, at which prospective buyers were allowed to see up close the equipment that might have caught their eyes in the catalog: mechanical presses, power shears, mills, lathes, grinders, band saws, boring machines, radial arm drills, drill presses, blast cabinets, threading machines, robotic welders, arc welders, radial arm saws, planers, air compressors, cooling towers, boom lifts, forklifts, hydraulic lifts, electric lifts, die lifts, tow tractors, electric carts, oil carts, floor scrubbers, floor sweepers, bridge cranes, jib cranes, calipers, crimpers, conveyors, vises, hazardous waste containers, heavy-duty chains, cabinets, bearings, belts, bolts, tubes, bars, and a whole bunch else—the technical term is "Misc."—besides.

My favorite item, Lot 354, was a mammoth 1979 LeTourneau. A 132,000-pound-capacity diesel forklift, it was taller than a small-town courthouse. Included in the catalog under the section "Rolling Stock"—stuff with wheels, that is, such as forklifts, tractors, electric carts, floor sweepers, floor scrubbers, and fire trucks—the LeTourneau had been used to carry dies when the plant was active, Ray Dishman told me. Whether it sold at the auction I was never sure; in any case, it didn't budge. Too big to move, it simply sat there. Nine months later, as the crew's time in the plant was coming to a close, guys discussed driving it off of the plant property and down the road, an idea that overhead power lines, lower than the LeTourneau's height, would have made tricky. Three years later, the LeTourneau still sits outside the plant, reminiscent of the city itself: a big thing with a French name that no one can quite figure out what to do with.

The preview and auction were like an estate sale for men. Jeff called it a "boys' day out." (I saw one woman in the plant in three days.) Instead of going through the dead widow's jewelry, guys rooted around in the closed plant's presses, mills, and lathes. "Can you imagine what the place looked like in the fifties?" a guy in a gas station uniform asked, of no one in particular, the day of the auction preview. We were standing in the inspection area, checking out Vernier calipers (Lot 144), Starrett bore gauges (Lot 173), and Brown and Sharpe micrometers (Lot 157). The inspection tools were many decades old; a majority came in inlaid wooden cases. "Things were labor-intensive back then," the gas station guy said. "Everything manual. You needed the people."

My companion felt a similar rush of sentiment when we came to a newer, computer-controlled Bridgeport machining center (Lot 208). "On something like this," he said, "you just program the cuts you want into the computer, and it machines it for you. Not like the old days, when you weren't considered a real machinist if you could count past three and a half on the fingers of one hand."

Still posted to the caging above Lot 83—"(8) Carts w/ Contents," the contents being massive wrenches, bars, and clamps—were old Budd Company notices. "Effective immediately to reinforce the current policy," one began. "Gloves will only be given in an even exchange. If you need ten pairs (Die Room), you must return ten pairs. This is due to the massive amount of gloves that are not being returned and thrown around the plant." To further guilt workers, there was a "Did You Know?" sign, listing materials and their costs: "Gloves (Kevlar) $2.95. Gloves (Leather Weld) $2.75. Gloves (Rubber) $1.31." Below these postings, on a shelf above the cart with contents, was a smudged copy of *The 9/11 Commission Report.*

To Jeff, the crew leader, none of the stuff in the auction was of the slightest interest. It was "shit" he wanted "gone." His focus was the disassembly of those press lines, tagged "Not in Sale," that had already sold and were destined for far-off lands. "My job is to get the stuff loaded onto the trucks," he said of his mission.

His lack of interest in the Budd auction did not extend to the Budd plant itself. For Jeff as for Duane, the plant was full of good ghosts. He was sentimental about it, collecting photographs, plaques, buttons, and anything else that had been left behind with the Budd name on it. (No one was touched, for some reason, by the ThyssenKrupp letterhead still scattered about: "Das Beste. Von uns. Für uns.") Jeff gave me, as a souvenir, a Frisbee he'd found on the floor of his electric cart. Covered in decades of grime, it was similar to the button I'd give to Erwin Baur. It carried the logo of UAW Local 306 and, in a red-lettered circle around the Frisbee's center, said: "I Believe in Budd Detroit."

"I got a bunch myself," Jeff said.

The auction started the next morning, which dawned overcast and stormy. Inside the plant, I was given a ride to Lot 1 by Walter, a Mexican from the Ashman Company who had use of a cart. The first of the twelve hundred lots was less than thrilling: "(3) Barrel Cart, Floor Magnet, & Shop Vac." In charge was the auctioneer, Lloyd Ashman himself, whom I'd seen and heard practicing the day previous. He hovered over the action, standing at an elevated podium atop a Motrec cart. While the patter of the auctioneer is ancient, or seems so, the wraparound mike he wore was that of a modern pop star.

There was no skipping ahead. The group moved, en masse, from lot to lot, proceeding absolutely sequentially. In the darker parts of the plant, to better illuminate the auction lots, there was a portable floodlight. Walter, my driver, served as the auction's sighter, acknowledging bids with a quick yep. Another worker stood above or next to the lot being auctioned, holding a sign with a red arrow that said: "This Lot Is Being Sold." To a former Catholic school kid, the process was akin to doing the stations of the cross with a priest who talked terrifically fast and who would walk us through twelve hundred stations rather than fourteen. One obese fellow, not up to all the walking, moved from lot to lot on a rolling chair, propelling himself with his feet like a Flintstone.

A few of the bidders looked flush, dressed in khakis and oxfords and fiddling with their cell phones. It seemed they were professional buyers and sellers, of what it didn't matter—could be hot dogs, could be a Clearing press—so long as they bought low and sold at a profit. More common were the blue-collar guys who had their eyes on an item or two for their machine shop downriver or their tool-and-die place out in Macomb County. They wore dirty work pants and work shirts with their names patched on the front. Their T-shirts said things like "Lincoln Park Boring."

As a kid, I'd spent plenty of time at automotive swap meets with my father, watching stubbly men inspect cylinder heads, crankshafts, and rocker arms for hours on end and attempt to barter the price down until it equaled the roll of greasy bills they had in their front pants pockets. If all went well—meaning that my father didn't end up buying more than he'd sold—we'd return home with a sizable such roll.

The Ashman Company required cashier's checks. I followed along, like everyone else, in the Ashman catalog, which served as the auction's hymnal. "This catalog is meant merely as a guide," it said at the top. "The Auctioneers do not warrant the accuracy, genuineness, authenticity, description, weight, count, or measure of any of the lots specified herein." The hymnals at St. Jude, though touching on the supernatural, came with no such disclaimer.

By Lot 80, it was time to move the cart and podium some twenty yards, for improved proximity to the upcoming lots. Fred Flintstone scooted along; the rest of us walked. By Lot 85—"Rack w/ Assorted C-Clamps"—Lloyd Ashman was cracking jokes. "I don't like anything we've just sold," he said, "but this is a nice lot." For a while thereafter, I'd attempt to keep score, marking my auction catalog's columns with dollar amounts: "$10,000," "50K," "$85."

I soon stopped, too tired to tally. By afternoon, tired bidders were looking for a relatively clean place to relax. Some sat on the Yale and Caterpillar hi-los—Lots 392–420—that had been grouped together north of the press shop and had yet to be auctioned. The selling off of Budd equipment required stamina from buyers and sellers both. The fat man in the chair, it seemed, had been through this before and knew about pacing.

By the time the auction moved to the upper floors on the second day, a younger man had taken over the role of auctioneer from Lloyd Ashman. Lots 991–1,037 (including a Greenlee power bender and an Ingersoll Rand winch) were on the third floor. Lots 1,038–1,189 (including a Powermatic floor-standing drill press and a Cincinnati Bickford twenty-one-inch Drill Press) were on the second. It was oppressively hot on both floors, and I decided to descend not long after making the climb.

It would be this way for much of the summer: a battle to fight the heat and the tropical torpor it engendered. As summer wore on, I worried less and less about my presence in the plant. In a sense this was a negative, as nervousness increases perception and comfort kills it. I no longer called ahead, to let Jeff Jinerson know I was coming in, and I spent more and more of my time in the plant talking with the crew's first rigging foreman, Matt Sanders, an affable fellow in a Stars and Stripes hard hat whom I'd come to consider something of the crew's conscience.

Later in the summer, Matt gave me a spreadsheet, dated July 24, 2007, that outlined the transportation of 16-line's heavy parts. The five weeks from early August through early September were to follow a similar pattern, beginning with the shipment of the crown, then the slide (*émbolo*), then the bolster, then the upright left column (*columna izquierda*), and the upright right column (*columna derecha*). "I think, in our planning, Jeff said he's gonna need 120 loads total," Matt said.

Matt was bearishly, intentionally friendly, going out of his way to talk to me. He'd endeared himself to me right away. "When can you start?" he asked me. He'd sized me up and concluded that I was capable of working on his crew. This was incorrect, but I liked him for it. After Eddie, it was Matt whom I'd seek out after arriving at the plant. He possessed an affability that never flagged. He said he had a temper, but I never saw it and suspected he claimed one only to keep up appearances. He also said his anger disappeared in no time, which I did believe. "I'll motherfuck you and everyone in your family," he said, "and then we'll go get a beer."

It was Matt who'd taken me into the shithouse just off the press shop and showed me what someone had written above a urinal:

Goodbye
Budd 1904–2007

That first date was way off, the second by a month or so, but the sentiment was solid. Matt was touched by it. On the same wall, someone had written: "Fucking Contractor Scab." A later someone responded: "Scab with Money."

Though in some sense a contractor scab himself, Matt bore no ill will against the union guy who'd likely composed the message. One hot Saturday afternoon, I stood with Matt in Budd's old human resources offices, on the second floor of Independence Hall. Matt puffed away at his cigarette, Chrysler's Jefferson North Assembly Plant visible out the window behind him. "I get no pleasure from taking these places apart," he said. He knew that he was here on a crew of a dozen or so because a workforce that over the years had included many tens of thousands, with tens of thousands more dependent upon them, had been reduced to zero. Matt spoke of his wife, a union employee who for two decades ran the deli counter for a local grocery store chain that was now in the process of being bought out. Her counter made money, he said, with solid margins and little waste. Her former supervisor gave her a great review. Still, she worried. "She's only guaranteed an interview" with the new company, Matt said.

At the end of some days, Matt was a walking collection of winces and grimaces, bumps and bruises. He could often be seen with a hand to his opposing shoulder, which he'd move in small, pained circles. Other days he limped like hell, either because he'd taken a tumble ("I went ass over teakettle on 16-line") or due to the whims of inheritance and fate. "It's the Polish curse," he said as he gimped along. "I never met a Polack yet with good knees." He was fragile for a burly fellow. When he thought he had walking pneumonia, Jeff Jinerson diagnosed the cause. "Matt's problem is that he doesn't smoke enough," Jeff said. "His wiring is all fucked-up."

Before becoming a rigger, Matt had worked as a welder for eight years at a place in Hamtramck, then off and on at a machine repair shop a friend owned. He was a youthful forty, despite a certain amount of hard living ("I like hard liquor. With wine, I might as well go straight to shitfaced") that the hard work helped balance out. He knew how to turn a phrase. He observed of a man from whom he wished to extract a favor that he was most profitably approached in the morning, "before he drinks his lunch and grows a dick." Of someone he thought a tad dumb, he said, "I might not accuse him of being the smartest person I know." Matt had brown hair and a bushy copper mustache a week shy of being walrus-like. One of his fingers, years ago, had gotten chopped; he showed me where it had been reattached. The stitching was nearly unnoticeable. "The doctor did a good job," he said. Matt had just bought a new truck, a maroon Dodge Ram 2500 Heavy Duty, to replace his 2005 Ford. The Dodge was a diesel and got seventeen miles per gallon as against the Ford's twelve. He hadn't minded the Ford's mpg rating so much when he bought it two years back, "but that was before gas got stupid."

Matt was constantly beleaguered—a blue-collar Thurber husband. He talked of "ten thousand problems that come up every day, like Germany don't know how to order fuckin' trucks." This was a reference to the engineers from Müller Weingarten, Uli and Johan. I said that since he was the rigging foreman, this didn't sound like his problem. "It is when I gotta move the shit off the floor," Matt said. The shop floor was packed with parts of disassembled presses. Spray paint typically marked what was what, but things could get confusing still. "I gotta yell at them," Matt said, "and then they yell at whoever, and they yell at whoever, and then it comes back to me, 'cause they're all yelling at me again."

I asked if he was getting any better at yelling.

"I've always been real good at it," he said. "My problem is I've got such a short fuse I just keep it under control. Because I can go from zero to very loud to just choking you in about five seconds."

The Budd job's first big rigging maneuver, the heavy lift of the crown of 16-1, was scheduled for the morning of August 5, a Sunday. It had been two months since major disassembly work on 16-line had started—the same day I first set foot in the closed plant. The day before the big lift, Matt and I toured the press shop. We passed a crew in Machines International jackets taking down a crane bought at the auction.

"It's a big place!" one of them yelled.

"Yeah, it is," Matt said. "Biggest job I ever worked on."

"When they start taking apart these old shops . . . ," one of them started to say.

"I haven't put a new machine in in *years,*" Matt said.

The rigging crew's headquarters had recently moved down from the second floor of central maintenance to a large tool crib on the first floor. "It was too hot upstairs," Matt said. There were dozens of magazines that had been left behind and were now spread out on a table. Matt inspected the stacks of *Playboy*s. "That amazes me," he said, picking one up. "This fucker looks almost brand-new. That's a '94."

I said I couldn't believe the crew had taken the trouble to move such stuff down.

"Yeah, I know," Matt said. "It kinda makes you wonder. Like this here—this fucker's in new condition, and that's a fuckin' 1988. It's like a little time capsule in this place, right down to the fuckin' magazines."

It was quiet in the plant. Most of the crew had gone to lunch. One of the younger guys—"glasses, ponytail, real tall dorky kid," Matt said—was picking up his lunch for him. I asked Matt if any of the kids were any good.

"Some of 'em I can work with. Some of 'em I just wish they wouldn't show up to work every day. A couple of them guys are so fuckin' burnt, you give a direct order, and the minute you turn your back they forgot what you said."

To illustrate, he picked up a copy of *Heads* magazine from the pile.

"Here's the mentality of some of the idiots I have working for me," he said. "The one magazine somebody fuckin' actually paid money for and brought in is about fuckin' pot." Matt impressed upon them the need to refrain while in the plant. "I tell them all the time—'If you want to kill yourself, that's fine. But if you do it on my time, I got too many questions to answer.' "

Matt saw a falling off not only in the country's industrial production—his presence in the closed Budd plant testified to that—but also in its capacity to dismantle the plants that were no longer producing. It was industrial decline in its second declension. "The shit me and Jeff do, it's a dying trade," he said. "When we're gone, you're not gonna find a good rigger, you're not gonna find a good welder, you're not gonna find a good machinist. Nobody wants to do it anymore. 'I'd rather sit at a computer at my desk all day. Wear a white shirt.' Guys who don't mind getting dirty and actually want to throw their back into their job, they're getting to be few and far between. At the end of the day most days, I got a sense of accomplishment. I walk outta here, and you can physically see—'That big son of a bitch was in the air, and now it's down on the ground. I had a good day today, look at that.' You're sitting at a desk all day, well, you walk away, come back tomorrow, and it's the same damn thing again." If he had a desk job, he said, "I'd go crazy. I could probably make it to lunch, if I had enough pencils to break."

Speaking of lunch, I asked Matt where his was. "I don't know," Matt said, looking around for his gofer. "I was just gonna start motherfucking him."

■

I'd told Matt the day before that I'd be in around 7:30 in the morning to see the crown of 16-1 come down. How long would it take? "If everything goes real well, two hours," he said.

It took longer than that simply to set up. I sat on an I-beam on the shop floor and doodled in my notebook, drawing what I saw. During dull stretches in the plant—there were plenty such—I sometimes pretended that I was a location scout who had just stumbled upon the ideal setting for a dystopian film set in the postapocalyptic near future. If Ridley Scott ever decided to film a *Blade Runner* sequel, I knew a place.

"There's never a need to be in a big hurry," Matt said. "This shit takes time."

It was a Sunday morning, and I had missed Mass to witness the crown coming down. I wandered around the plant to kill time. I'd long since learned not to kick any of the junk—bolts, nuts, screws, bits of this and that—with which the shop floor was cluttered. You found that items that looked light didn't budge when nudged by the end of your foot. Without boots, you'd have had a badly stubbed toe, if not a broken metatarsal. I kicked bolts that felt like fifty-pound dumbbells. After a time, you learned to step over and around most everything.

On one of my wanderings, I'd picked up a discarded set of "commitments" signed by the twenty-five Budd Detroit press shop workers who had been part of the 16-line "natural working group." In the Budd cafeteria there was a ThyssenKrupp poster—"Natural Work Groups: The Power to Secure Our Future"—that showed all hands in, as in a football huddle. In honor, I presumed, of Krupp, some patriot had penned in a swastika.

Seeing such corporate claptrap in a closed plant was a little like looking at a deceased person's to-do list. What's the point, you wonder, when it's all bound to end anyway? Framed as a set, the four 16-line "commitments" were signed by all twenty-five members of the natural working group. The commitments were to "Group Purpose," "Vision," "Goals and Objectives," and "Standards/Norms/Expectations."

The workers were simply parroting the plant's German parents. I'd sometimes snatch up a stray bit of company correspondence from the plant floor and read what I could stomach. From the *Handbuch* "THYSSENKRUPP BEST:" "Against the background of a visibly weakening world economy . . . It is vital to identify internal value-adding potential . . . This corporate value-enhancement program takes an integrated approach with a self-supporting dynamic to achieve a sustainable increase in value . . . The success of 'ThyssenKrupp best' is very much in the interests of the workforce: only a successful company can offer its employees secure and challenging jobs with good prospects." And, here, there, everywhere, the ThyssenKrupp letterhead: "Das Beste. Von uns. Für uns."

In the cafeteria, where windows were broken and playing

cards still sat on a tabletop, there was another ThyssenKrupp poster still attached to the wall. Its title was "Quality Attitude." The poster was divided into two columns. The left column, in red, contained examples of "Supportive but Not Committed" attitudes toward quality; the right-hand column, in green, contained "Committed" attitudes toward quality.

Supportive But Not Committed	*Committed*
Agrees We Need Quality Products	Quality First Attitude
Onezy-Twozy Rejects Acceptable	Zero Defects at Customer Plant

And so on. "Sense of Urgency Is Calling a Quality Manager on a Quality Issue": this was deemed a supportive but not committed attitude. Committed, by contrast, was: "Has a Sense of Urgency Where Customer Complaints Are Reacted to and Treated Like a Near Fatal Injury." The prose and sentiment worked in tandem to depress.

It was raining outside the morning of that first crown lift, which meant that it was raining inside as well, with water dripping down through the holes in the roof. The plant exaggerated whatever the external conditions, making warm weather hot, cool temperatures cold, and converting humid conditions outside into the primordial soup inside. On such days, it seemed as if someone were staging the opening scene of *Macbeth.* Pizza boxes from the auction a month and a half before were still scattered about, getting soggy from the ceiling's precipitation. Trash piles dotted the plant. In one pile, among much else, I spotted empty Twix wrappers, Snickers wrappers, Newport packs, Marlboro packs, Doritos bags, Detroit Donut boxes, assorted beer bottles, Coke bottles, Pepsi bottles, Mountain Dew bottles, Gatorade bottles, Popeyes bags, Wendy's bags, and McDonald's bags. As the plant's equipment would disappear over the months, these piles would grow.

Outside the press shop's bay door, red Cassens Transport trucks drove up Conner Avenue, carrying Jeep Cherokees and Jeep Commanders from Jefferson North Assembly to the Ford Freeway and, from there, to Chrysler dealer showrooms. It was nice to remember that some plants, for the time being, were still producing.

Budd, by contrast, was just about ready to begin some serious disassembling. To make the lift, the crew had "trucked the gantry up from Sandusky," Matt said, referring to the Tower Automotive plant in Upper Sandusky, Ohio, that a splinter crew was taking the presses out of. A four-hundred-ton lift system with four hydraulic "legs" that looked like large jack stands and functioned like powerful floor jacks, the gantry would be going back to Ohio the next day.

"It's like working for the carnival," Jeff said. "Set it up, tear it down. Set it up, tear it down."

Working with Matt and Jeff were Nedzad, the Bosnian, and Z., the black woman who left the crew shortly thereafter. The fifth member of the heavy-lift team was a guy named Guy. "Been to church yet?" he asked as I sat and watched nothing happen. Matt said that Guy had worked in the "press shop in the Rouge," and that "though he doesn't know much about rigging"—there was a "yet" implied—"he knows his way around a press shop like nobody else." A tough-looking customer, Guy took pictures. Matt and Jeff gave him the finger.

"I'm in the Witness Relocation Program," Matt said.

One of the bigger presses in the Budd plant, 16-1 was the Danly QDC D4-2000-180-108, the tonnage rating and decapitating powers of which have already been described. Twenty-six feet tall, it weighed around a million pounds. About 400,000 of those pounds were in the crown, but that figure had been reduced by 75,000 since they'd taken "some shit off" in preparation for the lift, Matt said.

Two beams—the "headers"—ran across the crown length-wise and rested on the gantries' pads. Two more beams, atop the others, crossed the crown widthwise, forming a rectangle, for what Matt called a "box lift." The gantry then pushed the beams and, with them, the crown up from below, in what resembled an industrial bench press.

The crowns of all of the presses in 16-line were lifted with the gantry. Matt assumed, however, that about two-thirds of the crowns in the press shop were small enough to lift with an overhead crane. Where a gantry pushed the crown up from below, a crane pulled the crown up from above. Each bay in the press shop—there were five bays in all—had an overhead crane, and for the press shop's smaller lines, which had smaller presses with smaller crowns, a gantry, which could handle more weight, wouldn't be necessary. The overhead cranes, which tended to have 120-ton ratings, would suffice. Lifts with overhead cranes were less dramatic: they pulled the crown up with a set of spreader chains and suspended it in midair before moving it this way and that. The crane looked like an industrial Geppetto pulling a heavy puppet's strings.

To hear Matt tell it, disassembling a press and taking it

down just wasn't that difficult, however it was done. Take care of the electrical, the plumbing, and a bunch of other tedious stuff, and then "you just start unstacking it," Matt said. "You pull the crown off. You pull the ram next. You pull or drop the side columns. You pull the bolster. You pull the base." And, just like that, a million pounds of press was on a truck, bound for central Mexico.

The lift of the crown of 16-1 would begin this heavy rigging process. Tape measures ran from the base of the lengthwise beams down to the gantry legs below. During the crown's slow descent, the crew constantly checked the tapes to see that all four sides were level. "One's going to run a little faster, another a little slower," Matt said of the legs. "That's the nature of the beast." Jeff, who ran the controls, constantly stopped and started. The others—Nedzad, Guy, Z., and Matt—went up on lifts to make sure that they had clearance. Gantry 3, Jeff said, was "fast on the down side." Everyone, Nedzad excepted, constantly picked up cigarette packs and shook them.

"It's a game of inches," Jeff said to me.

Six hours after they started—and two months and a day after work on the line began—the crown of 16-1 was down, setting securely on blocks. Jeff brought out a case of beer to celebrate. The first big slab of Budd's industrial Stonehenge had come back to earth, bound for south of the border.

CHAPTER 4

■ ■ ■

Surplus
Industry
Service
Providers

Left to right: Arkansas Dave, Arkansas Terry (Sr.), Josh, Arkansas Rick

WINTER IN THE closed Budd plant ran from mid-October through the job's conclusion at the end of April. In my memory, it's always winter in the plant, not only because winter arrived early and overstayed its welcome, but because my cold-weather visits were more frequent than their warm-weather counterparts, and usually lasted longer. The colder the conditions, the more I wanted to be at Budd. When the temperature in the plant was below zero, I couldn't seem to keep away, or leave once I got there.

The end of summer and early fall had been rough for the crew. Morale was low, turnover was high, and I kept my distance, clear of the crew's internal dramas. For one reason or another, every crew member in the preceding pages—Eddie, Nedzad, and Guy excepted—would be off of the crew come winter. Jeff, the first crew leader, would be the first major departure, in mid-August. Crew members walked off in protest—a strike, in effect, for the nonunionized—and for a few days thereafter a new crew took over. Jeff would return a couple weeks later, then be gone again, this time for good.

Matt was promoted from rigging foreman to crew leader to replace him. It wasn't a role Matt cared for. The complications were constant. "Most people are, 'Hooray for me, fuck you!' " he said one day, lamenting his new lot in life. He spent much of his time on his cell phone. While 16-line was still in the middle of its disassembly, other lines had to go. Matt told me that 4-line was a "rush job" and needed to be on a boat to

India, having been bought by a company in New Delhi. By September, presses 4-2, 4-3, 4-4, 4-5, and 4-6 had to be out of the plant. Then 3-line, too, was headed to the subcontinent. Matt talked to a dispatcher in Toronto to get trucks to Detroit to haul the presses to Baltimore to get on boats to New Delhi. His company contact was "Wilma," who Matt said sounded a lot like Apu from *The Simpsons*. "Hello, Mr. Sanders," he said, quoting their conversations. "How are you today? How many trucks will you be needing?" Matt said that they were scrapping a press a day in those India-bound lines. "We started taking 'em apart civilized," Matt said, "and then just started cutting." Matt would leave the crew in mid-October.

It was a bad time outside the plant, too, and bound to get quite a bit worse. Weeks after the UAW strike of GM that had taken me past Poletown, Chrysler workers struck. Though the strike excluded Jefferson North, then idled, and the Mack Avenue Engine plants, I drove by them and by Budd anyway, to see what was what. It was October 10, 2007, and guys stood in front of Local 51 along Conner Avenue with "UAW on Strike" signs. On the site's other side, along St. Jean, workers had dropped by to lend support, parking their trucks—Dodge Durangos, Dodge Dakotas—on the grass across the road from the Mack Avenue plants and holding picket signs.

The new UAW contract, which made concessions on the backs of future hires, would mark a new manufacturing moment: you could now make more money taking an auto plant apart than you could, as a new hire, working in one. Based solely on the dollar per hour, you'd be better off working at Budd and taking it apart than being newly hired at Jefferson North and assembling a Jeep Cherokee. "I got the factory job I always wanted," a young guy on the crew said to me. He wanted that quoted. The men in his family had worked for the Big Three for decades, building things, and here he was at Budd, breaking it down. He was making the best of a bad lot.

With Matt's departure, I worried about my continued access to the plant and crew and confronted the real possibility—despite a year and a half of digging—that this book wasn't to be. I'd passed through several sets of hands to get where I was, and several more again to stay there, and at some point, it seemed, this run of good luck would run out. I stayed away for longer stretches, unsure of my status, not wanting welcomes to get worn.

Counting by the calendar, the rough midpoint of my time in the Budd Detroit plant—December 2007—marked the beginning of the Great Recession. The beginnings of recessions are identified in retrospect, but no one around these parts would have paid much mind if it had been a recession foretold. In Michigan, a steep recession has hung around as long as the new millennium. In Detroit, a recession, or worse, has been part of the urban weather for decades. What marked this moment in my mind, then, wasn't the national economic cataclysm that had just officially begun. It was the fire that broke out at the Budd plant, one year to the day after its official closing.

I initially attributed the fire to the appearance of the fire barrels, which I first saw burning on the shop floor a few days before, on the first of December, a sixteen-degree morning. The black smoke that darkened the sky made the fire appear worse than it was, as if the entire building were burning down, an impression not at all dispelled by the message on my machine when I'd gotten home from work that evening. That message, then a few minutes old, was from Guy Betts, the former worker at the Ford Rouge who had taken a buyout from Ford in the previous wave and who, with the departures of Jeff and Matt, had been promoted to crew leader. "Turn on the TV," Guy said. "The plant's burning down." There was no concern in his voice, just the ground-down sound of vocal cords cured by cigarettes, alcohol, and decades of communicating over industrial din.

I drove the four miles to the plant and found, for the first time in six months, my entry blocked: Detroit police cruisers, lights flashing, were parked in front of the entrance gates on Charlevoix Avenue. I drove north on Conner Avenue, along the eastern edge of the plant, and turned west onto Mack, slowing to a near stop at the crest of the bridge that bisects Budd from Chrysler's Mack Avenue Engine plants. From the bridge I could see Detroit Fire Department trucks along Conner Lane, an old road, long closed, that runs parallel to the Conrail yard, and down which the tire crooks and copper thieves tended to come.

The black smoke filling the sky was from an oil fire in the western part of the Budd plant. It had nothing to do with the fire barrels, and likely didn't merit the level of emergency response that it'd received. The fire did succeed, however, in scaring me straight. It's impossible for unwritten pages to go up in flames, but that's exactly what I saw in the smoke that night: a book that didn't yet exist being burned out of existence. That moment marked the beginning of my second, more assertive phase in the plant. From that point forward, I'd be at Budd every chance I got. I didn't know how much longer it, or I, would be around.

A few nights before the fire, Guy Betts and I had met at a bar by his house. It was loud, but Guy's voice rumbled as if internally amplified. It sounded as if he had a microphone in his larynx. He greeted me, as in the plant, as if I were multiple. "How we doin'?" he asked. In the plant, this was always followed with "Where's the coffee?" Sometimes the order was inverted, in which case he didn't concern himself with how we were doing, since I always arrived empty-handed. "Put that in the book," he'd say, meaning my lack of consideration.

To him, I was "the writer." The guys on the crew were "the girls." "The girls don't want to work today," he'd tell the writer. On terribly cold days during the winter this was often true, and the writer had a hard time blaming the girls for wanting to huddle by the barrel fires or go on home. None of them was as tough as Guy, who never wore a hat, covering his head with only a Harley-Davidson bandanna. He rarely wore gloves and wore cowboy boots instead of insulated or steel-toed work boots. The boots click-clacked on the concrete but had practical benefits for a rigger atop a couple-story Danly or Clearing press. "These things will save you if you're sliding," he said of his cowboy boots. "You're slipping—boom. Hook on." Later in the winter, it looked as if exposure to the cold had caught up with him: he had what appeared to be frostbite where his hat should have been. No, Guy said. He had just got a new puppy, and it had nibbled his ear.

Despite his toughness, Guy got sick from time to time.

Eddie attributed these winter sicknesses to Guy's height. "It's hard for him to keep his head above snow level," Eddie said. His stature aside, Guy walked incredibly fast, with terrific leg turnover. I had a hard time keeping up with him as we criss-crossed the plant. Crew members required nicknames—there was Stutter, and Big Bird, and before I knew Guy as Guy I'd known him as Kickstand, after a parking lot incident involving an unsteady motorcycle and the earth's pull. Cornbread Eddie decided to come up with a definitive nickname for Guy, who sported a Fu Manchu. "Who's the fella who tried to shoot them rabbits with the shotgun?" he asked me.

"Elmer Fudd?"

"No. The Mexican guy."

"Speedy Gonzales?"

"No." Eddie turned to some guys on the crew. "Who was the cartoon character who shot at them rabbits?"

"Elmer Fudd?"

"No, with the mustache."

"Yosemite Sam?"

"That's it!" It didn't stick. Guy stayed Guy.

Years earlier, at the *Detroit Free Press*, Guy had repaired printing presses. He left the job in 1994, anticipating the Detroit newspaper strike a year later. "I don't need the headaches," he said of his thinking at the time. He drove a tractor trailer for a while. Then "a buddy o' mine told me that they're looking for drivers at Ford," he said. "I went to Ford's, and I says, 'I got a CDL license' "—a commercial driver's license—"and they says, 'Well, what do you want to do—drive a truck or be in machine repair?' I says I didn't care—'just work for Ford's!' They said, well, we got an opening for machine repair. By the time I got home, they called me and said, 'Can you start tomorrow?' "

Just work for Ford's: a desire of Detroiters for more than a century. Guy ended up repairing presses for twelve years at the Ford Rouge. "When I started hearing about buyouts," he said, "I didn't think there was going to be a future for the auto industry." The math for remaining at Ford was brutal. With only a dozen years beneath his belt, he worried about being bumped by a more senior Ford worker who had come over from a closed plant. In the past, he said, bumping had been in-house; with the round of buyouts that were part of Ford's "Way Forward," anyone could bump anywhere. Guy figured, "They're closing the Norfolk plant"—the Norfolk Assembly Plant in Virginia, one of sixteen Ford plants, including the nearby Wixom Assembly Plant, to be closed as part of the company's turnaround plan—"and they're coming to the Rouge plant to finish off their pension." Being fifty years of age and having ten years of service got one a buyout of a hundred grand. "I *just* turned fifty," Guy said.

His old boss at the Rouge gave Guy's name to Jeff Jinerson, who—as he'd told me the first day we met—was looking for skilled people to work with him at Budd. Guy got into the plant in late spring "as a machine repair laborer, a workingman." Much of his early time on the crew was spent away from Detroit, at the Tower Automotive plants in Indiana and Ohio. Several months after his start, with Jeff and Matt gone, Guy found himself boss back in Detroit. It was mid-October.

Guy introduced me to the crew one day in late October. He explained who I was and what I was doing, and let them know that I had his blessing to be there. I appreciated the intro, but it struck me as backward: the crew members, almost all of whom had gotten into the plant after me and would leave before me, should have been introducing themselves to me. I'd acquired, in my own mind, something akin to squatter's rights. A week before the Budd job's completion, newer guys on the crew would still be coming up to me. "So, you're writing a book?" they'd say.

THE MANAGEMENT

After Eddie's, the truck I most wanted to see when I pulled in to the plant was Guy's. It was a white Chevy 1500 4x4 with a memorial sticker for Dale Earnhardt in the rear window. Guy and Eddie were now the men in charge, a fact borne out by the message tacked up in Eddie's shack:

NOTICE TO ALL EMPLOYEES

Anyone caught going through my paperwork or any other confidential paperwork or taking anything off the property including scrap, tools, equipment, etc. belonging to management or ___ ___ will be terminated on the spot and prosecuted if necessary unless they are given prior authorization from management to take equipment out for repairs. (Management: ___, Eddie, or Guy only. No exceptions.)

I have read the above and agree to the above terms.

Eddie said of crew members who stole, "It's tempting. It's just plain tempting." He had no worries about his ability to detect such theft. "I was born yesterday, but I wasn't born last night," he said.

Not that crew members did all that bad. Guy said that he started them out at sixteen dollars an hour, with a bump up to twenty dollars an hour after thirty days. It was better than a new hire would get at Ford.

The management team of Eddie and Guy helped hire and fire. Standards weren't terribly stringent. "He's done," Guy said of a new hire who'd gone to jail. "If he had come to me and said he had probation, that would have been one thing. Half the guys on this crew do. But this . . ." I once asked Eddie—whose position had evolved from simple security to more of an "operations-manager"-type position—why a guy on the crew had landed in court. "He tried selling Amway and got caught," Eddie said. Eddie kept me up-to-date on the comings and goings of crew members. "Two guys quit on us today," he told me one morning. "Said the pace of the work was too slow. Myself, I don't buy it."

No two crew member CVs were the same. Bill Bonner, a big guy with a bald head whom I considered excellent company, had been previously employed as a bouncer at a strip club, the Atlantis in Lincoln Park. "A *lot* of pussy," he said. He was now a "retired bouncer." I asked why this was. "Shot three times," he said, lifting up his shirt. He had two scars in the belly and another up by his right nipple. It looked as if he had five nipples.

"It's safer here," I said.

"Not much," he replied.

One Friday, his mom and his girlfriend, six months pregnant, pulled in to the plant to go to lunch. This was an odd sight, and I gave him a look.

"It's payday," Bonner said, shrugging.

Payday was every Friday and an event unto itself, although Eddie tried to feign indifference.

"Checks arrived yet?" I asked him one Friday noon.

"Don't know," Eddie said. "Don't need money. Got plenty."

Despite its other lacks, there is no shortage of check-cashing places in Detroit, and many of the guys on the crew, after getting their checks, would drive to a nearby party store, which took a percentage off the top for cashing it.

"Why don't they get bank accounts?" I asked.

Eddie and Guy were sitting on Eddie's fire truck. They laughed. Guy gave me a look that questioned my basic comprehension.

"If they had bank accounts," he said, "the child support would come out automatically."

Always buzzing, Guy never gave the slightest hint of slacking, whereas Eddie presented a common working-class paradox: the man who, without seeming to do overly much, is nonetheless absolutely indispensable to the undertaking. A friend of mine from graduate school, a shy, retiring sort, used to describe himself, at gatherings of friends, as "the fulcrum," which I found to be a winning tribute to his hard-to-perceive centrality. That was Eddie's role at the closed Budd plant—he was the fulcrum.

He was also envied by the crew members, who knew that he'd gotten in his thirty before the plant closed, a career path pretty well closed off to them. Perhaps because his position was secure, Eddie had a talent for holding himself above things even while he was in the middle of the mix. He considered himself a calculating man amid a sea of hotheads. Eddie preferred the dispassionate approach. His politics, for instance, were entirely pocketbook. "Eight years under Clinton, people was working good, things were going good," Eddie said. "Eight years under Bush ain't been so good." His views on the presidential campaigns had yet to fully cohere but were articulated with perfect parallel construction. "I'm not an Obama favorite," he said, "I'm not a Clinton favorite." He complained that Republicans were for the rich but was fond of the war hero. "McCain's my top notch," he said. Months later, he'd ask me if I'd seen the Clinton-Obama debate. I hadn't, and neither had he. I asked him whom he'd vote for. "I'm an undecided," he said, "but it looks like Obama. I can't see putting another Republican in there."

At present, he had more pressing concerns. "One year ago I retired," Eddie said the day after the fire. "I was putting the locks on the place." One year later, on a twenty-degree December morning, he was at a plant with no production and, except for the fires in the oil barrels, no heat. The fact that the fire occurred at all Eddie attributed to his absence at the time it broke out. "I go away, everything goes to hell," Eddie said. He was warming himself by a fire barrel north of the plant's press shop when I arrived at 7:00 a.m. "Looked worse than it was," he said of the fire, adding: "I was here all night." One of the torch men from the scrap company, RJ Torching of Flint, had been cutting too close to a pit of oil on the plant's western side, sparking the fire. The workers got out of the plant to the east, and Guy called from the parking lot to tell me to turn on the TV.

Eddie wore a red, white, and blue Budd winter hat missing the ball atop. Guys kept hitting it, so he took it off. His brown work gloves, which he'd wear most of the winter, had silver duct tape at the tip of the left index finger to cover a burn hole.

To warm themselves in winter, workers would walk to the fire barrels, extend their hands, and flip them back and forth before turning around bodily and approaching the fire backward, palms down, like mimes backing up to an invisible wall. They sometimes repeated this several times—front, back—like sunbathers in search of an even tan. Each worker had his own procedure, just as every pitcher has his own windup. It was so cold in the plant through so much of winter that I was all too often content to sit around the fire and jot similes of this sort in my notebook.

Temperatures ran ten to fifteen degrees colder inside the plant, where the steel and concrete created an industrial icebox of considerable dimension. Guys on the crew began to complain of the cold in the plant as early as October. The first sticking snow had fallen a few days before the fire, on the first of December. Wintertime cell phone conversations—to check on the whereabouts of a truck, or the arrival of a propane order—were often cut off before fingertips went numb. "Gotta go—my hand's freezing" was a frequent sign-off.

Snowflakes fluttered down from the holes in the plant's

roof. It could be hard to distinguish falling snowflakes from ash that had shot up from the flames in the fire barrels and then floated back down. The leaky roof had been letting in rain for months. With time, puddles became ponds. With winter, ponds became ice rinks. On snowy days, guys made snowballs from what was brought in on the backs of the trucks hauling the press pieces out. Held over the flames for a few seconds, snowballs became ice balls. "Bombs away!" someone would holler.

The pace of work slowed. The fires required tending. They were fed with pecan squares, a little less than three feet by three feet, that workers had pried up from the flooring around the presses. The squares were heavy enough to require two men to heave into the flames, and so soaked with oil that it would bubble out in the heat. It smelled as if (another notebook simile) someone had a fireplace going in an old gas station garage. One's clothes came out smelling cured. The plant provided comfort to the crew dismantling it the only way it could: by consuming itself. The American working class was mopping up after itself in a plant that was burning itself up as fuel. "That fire's too hot," Eddie sometimes said, jokingly. "Turn the thermostat down." There was no mechanism for this except time. Turning the thermostat up, on the other hand, simply meant putting on another pallet.

These fires were the center of the plant's social life for winter's six months, a place of communal thawing where four, five, fifteen guys would huddle, shiver, and shoot the shit. One especially bitter day, a trucker from Texas complained.

"It's so cold in here," he said, "you gotta take a Viagra to take a piss."

Keeping out the cold with layer after layer created its own problems. "Hard to piss through six inches of clothes when you got three inches of dick," Guy agreed.

"It stays this cold much longer," Eddie said, "and I might just start wearing Depends."

You warmed up just enough to get cold. For a time, propane heaters were brought in, but Guy didn't like them. "We don't need no heaters," he said. "There's plenty of stuff to burn in here." When guys got sick of the fumes from burning what the plant had on offer, they improvised. Once, as Guy and I went down into the pits below 9-line—where, a pit worker joked, he expected to find Hoffa—I noticed twigs and fresh-looking leaves scattered about. Sick of the fumes from the oil-soaked wood pallets, a crew member pulling tie-rods atop the 9-line presses had chopped down a small tree and brought it into the plant. He wanted clean wood to burn in his barrel.

THE GUARDS

By December, roughly half the presses that had stood in the press shop in June had been trucked away, opening up new sight lines. The crew surrounded the exposed press pits with angle iron, along which they strung yellow tape, as at a crime scene. Eddie called this process "railing it off." Later, the crew would surround exposed pits with chicken wire. With the departure of the Mexican engineers observing the disman-tling of 16-line, there was no more Spanish to be heard in the plant. Among Romance languages, it had been replaced by Portuguese, spoken by workers from Delga, the Brazilian sup-

plier that had purchased 2-line. The side jobs at the Tower
Automotive plants in Ohio and Indiana were complete, and
splinter crews would begin to depart Detroit for a new job out
of state. Its plant auction was upcoming, just before Christmas, and it, too, would be handled by the Ashman Company
of Walnut Creek, California:

PUBLIC AUCTION
On the Premises of
MAYTAG
927 North 19th Avenue East
Newton, Iowa 50208

Included in the Maytag auction, among much else, were complete assembly lines, stamping presses, stackers, de-stackers,
mills, lathes, grinders, saws, semis, semi trailers, trucks, and
forklifts. Guy said that the rigging company owner was order-
ing Carhartt jackets for the crew; he'd come up with a slogan
for the back: "When We Come to Town, Jobs Leave." By the
time the crew got to town, of course, the jobs had long since
left.

The Maytag job's beginning coincided with the buildup to
the Iowa caucuses, and the Maytag closing became shorthand,
to presidential candidates, for tough times in the industrial
heartland. The next month, there was a small controversy during Michigan's Republican presidential primary in January.
John McCain, with ill-advised candor, said that many of the
state's lost manufacturing jobs "are not coming back." His

Republican opponent Mitt Romney—whose father, George, was president of American Motors—said he'd "fight for every single job." The correct campaign position was Romney's; the accurate economic assessment was McCain's.

But their proposals to retrain workers "who lose their jobs because of the foreign competition unleashed by free trade" were similar, and similarly misguided, according to a *New York Times* editorial by the University of Rochester economist Steven E. Landsburg. Landsburg wrote:

> All economists know that when American jobs are out-sourced, Americans as a group are net winners. What we lose through lower wages is more than offset by what we gain through lower prices. In other words, the winners can more than afford to compensate the losers. Does that mean they ought to? Does it create a moral mandate for the taxpayer-subsidized retraining programs proposed by Mr. McCain and Mr. Romney?
>
> Um, no. Even if you've just lost your job, there's something fundamentally churlish about blaming the very phenomenon that's elevated you above the subsistence level since the day you were born. If the world owes you compensation for enduring the downside of trade, what do you owe the world for enjoying the upside?

Landsburg describes the benefits of free trade and the myriad, daily ways we maximize our purchasing power without resorting to sentiment or feeling remorse. His conclusion: "If you're forced to pay $20 an hour to an American for goods you could have bought from a Mexican for $5 an hour, you're being extorted. When a free trade agreement allows you to buy from the Mexican after all, rejoice in your liberation—even if Mr. McCain, Mr. Romney and the rest of the presidential candidates don't want you to."

Well put. Spoken like a man with tenure—at a university that extorts parents to the tune of fifty thousand dollars per year. Perhaps parents might send their college-age kids to school in Mexico semester after semester, year after year, allowing them to earn a degree for a fraction of the cost that supports Professor Landsburg's teaching load and research agenda?

This is unfair. But whatever the merits of such argumentation in the seminar room, it was damn near impossible to assent to such conclusions in the closed Budd plant during that dark winter. The economic collapse was a frequent topic of conversation between me and Dave Scarlin. "Dave's sleeping," Eddie informed me that post-fire morning. "He's seventy-six years old."

Dave Scarlin was not quite sixty-six and had begun working security at Budd a year before the riots, in 1966. A handsome gent, he had silver hair, short and squared-off. When he was first hired in, the Budd plant had twenty-nine guards. "I was number twenty-nine," he said. He said that, back when, the Budd Company used to clean the guards' uniforms and provide them with a shoe allowance. He had retired a few years before, but returned to work after the closing at Eddie's invitation. His family name had been changed, in the mists of time, from Scargalino, a fact Eddie often noted. "What sound does spaghetti make when you throw it against the wall?" Eddie asked. "Wop!" I shared a joke that my Italian grandfather used to tell. Question: "Why are Italians like shoes?" Answer: "Wherever you go, dago." Eddie loved it. "My little dago buddy ain't shot nobody in about three weeks," Eddie once complained on the phone to the boss. "I've been trying to train Dave for thirty years," he told me on another occasion. "He's untrainable. Italians—can't teach 'em nothin'."

Dave would do security work at both Budd and Maytag during the winter, driving between Detroit and Iowa. He drove a dented Pontiac Trans Sport that he acknowledged wasn't much to look at but that was perfect for hunting and fishing trips, which he took plenty of. Push come to shove, he said, he could sleep in the back of it.

Dave's son, Tony, a Detroit fireman, would help with security near the Budd job's end. Tony's son, Rob, also worked security, making three generations of Scarlins and providing Eddie plenty of dagos to disparage. Tony had written an account of a deer-hunting trip that he and Dave had taken in the fall in the south-central Nebraska River bottom basin. Handwritten on yellow legal sheets, the piece was 550 words. Dave asked me if I could help get it down to 500 words, for submission to a hunting magazine. It told the story of how Tony had taken down, with a bow, an award-winning buck.

I told Dave that I didn't know anything about bow hunting, but that I could perhaps polish it a bit.

"That's the word," Dave said. "Polish."

Dave was a runner as well as a hunter, and our security sweeps of the plant were taken on foot. Sometimes, we'd walk the plant's perimeter. One slow Saturday afternoon, Dave and I toured the floors of Building A and Building C, the Budd plant's tallest.

Detroit's East Side was not the south-central Nebraska River bottom basin, and Dave carried a gun with him rather than a bow. With the elevators out, we climbed steps. The internal stairwells, even in daylight, were dark to the point of sensory deprivation. When we got to the fourth floor of Building A, I saw huge piles of black-and-white goo that looked like candle wax. It was pigeon shit, dropped down from perches in the beams and piping above. There were piles of it—that, and porn. Dave noticed something else.

"See anything unusual here?" he asked.

I didn't, though I heard a loud humming. Looking up, I saw that we stood beneath two rounded fluorescent lights. One, plugged into an outlet above our heads, was on.

"Which means there's a line up there in the ceiling," Dave said. "Which means there's copper."

We walked on, and Dave discussed the tools of his trade. When he did his sweeps of the plant at night, he said, "my pistol's here"—in his right hand, resting in the crook of his left arm—"and my flashlight's here," in his left hand. He said that Jeff, the first crew leader, "used to call me Wyatt Earp." Dave laughed. "I don't want to shoot anyone," he said. Back in the summer, Dave had seen three guys come into the plant while he was on night duty. He shot three times, in warning, and shined his light. He fired two more warning shots, then saw them run under the viaduct and off plant property. Dave never shot except in warning, a habit as practical as principled.

"I don't want the hassle and the lawsuits," he said.

We climbed back down the dark stairwell to the shop floor, crossed over to the stairwell of Building C, and started up more dark steps. On the building's half floors were locker rooms and bathrooms with old-style urinals—a big circle, with everyone pissing toward the same center point. On the west end of the second floor, near elevator 5, we saw a crated Ford part. It was dated February 10, 1988. "Panel for a van," Dave said. On the third floor, parts still hung on the wall. One, marked "82 ST Truck," was an old floor panel for the Chevy S-10.

We got to the top floor. "The fourth floor of C Building used to be the brake shop back in the sixties," Dave said. "They made brake shoes." Work cards from old jobs were still scattered on the floor. Glass crunched underfoot. Dave found a fire extinguisher, tested it. "Still works," he said, and set it in the stairwell for our trip back down.

All the windows on the floor's west side were knocked out. Here and there, as a result of such holes, strips of dangling aluminum siding twisted in the wind. The creaking created a horror-movie soundtrack, unnerving even at two o'clock on a sunny Saturday afternoon. Though we were not far from the center of a once-immense city, our isolation felt intergalactic.

The feeling intensified after we'd climbed another flight and stepped out onto the roof, where a tree was beginning to grow. Trees are a common sight atop abandoned Detroit plants, and Budd's rooftop growth seemed to be proceeding on schedule. Nature will take this place back over. Eddie said he once had to pull a pheasant out of the skimmer pit with a bucket. "He flapped his wings and covered me in oil," Eddie said. Who was to say that Detroit's East Side couldn't, someday, be the south-central Nebraska River bottom basin? People couldn't stop talking about urban farming in Detroit as a use for all the empty land. But why stop at farms? Why not extend the oxymoron to urban forest? Maybe, then, a bow would be the thing to bring up to the Budd plant roof.

Unlike Eddie, Dave felt sympathy for the other guards—the Pinkertons, so-called, who sat at the plant gate. Dave once told me the story of one of the male guards. The guy made nine dollars an hour after seven years, Dave said, and had just worked a sixteen-hour shift, as the guard who was to follow him had called in. He wanted to quit but couldn't. Neither, really, could he continue working: he didn't have enough gas in his car to get home, or, once there—if he made it—to get back to work. Dave said that he gave the guy five bucks. "I wish it'd been ten," he told me. A few weeks later, Dave said, the guy paid him the five dollars back.

That the man had settled his debt despite all drove home to Dave just how desperate the situation in Detroit was. That a seemingly honorable man who'd worked a double shift would be reduced to begging gas money—well, the ironies were hard to wrap one's head around. A Detroit man, willing to work, who could only find work guarding a Detroit plant where work had ceased. A man who had a hard time getting to work because the work he had paid so poorly. A man who . . . "These people are fucked," Dave said.

Things weren't much more hopeful for the crew inside.

The wintertime sight of the workers huddled around the fire barrel brought out the same sort of sentiment in Dave. "Next year," he said, gazing upon such a scene, "people will be doing this in front of their homes."

■

Eddie's security style was different. It was more didactic and involved less exercise. He used one of three vehicles to tool around the plant and its property: a white golf cart ("Please Repair Your Divots and Ball Marks. Thank You!!" the sign on its steering wheel said); a small red fire truck, with a sign on its side that said "Empty Extinguishers Could Put You Out of Work. Please Report Them"; and a green John Deere Gator.

"Get in my Cadillac," he'd say, whatever the cart, and off we'd go.

During the winter, ice crunched under the tires, making it harder to catch crooks unawares. Dangers lurked above. "Be careful," Eddie warned. "Pipes are bursting and coming down." On one tour he pointed out with his flashlight a large water shutoff valve that had popped off the end of a pipe. I hopped off the cart and picked it up. No faucet handle for your garden hose, it weighed a good ten to twelve pounds. "That falls on you," Eddie said, "it'll give you a headache."

Eddie always had to have his flashlight on him as he conducted his rounds. The quickest way to anger him was to take his light and not return it. "I'm going to shoot him," he once said, with convincing seriousness, of a kid on the crew who'd mistakenly made off with his flashlight. When Eddie retrieved it the following day, his world improved on the spot. "I'm feeling pretty good," he said, "since I got my flashlight back."

As we toured, Eddie narrated, and as he narrated, he'd stop, hopping in and out of the vehicle, inspecting this and that with his light before driving off again. "This is the ultimate way that you do security," he said. "People don't understand about security. You drive slow. You listen. You have time to feel, you have time to sense, you have time to see. Most people, when they drive in security—'Yeah, I did a patrol.' *Rrrrr-rrrr*," he said, mimicking the sound of unheeding speeding. "You didn't do nothin'. You ain't heard nothin'.

"Drive slow, observe," he said. "It ain't about speed. Now, at nighttime, it's kind of spooky. 'Cause you gotta use your light—then you blow your cover. I usually try to work myself in from a lighted area, and then just sit in certain spots. Sometimes, if I'm working here, I crank that light up"—he pointed to a generator—"and I'll crank that light up"—another generator—"and let 'em run, and that way I got a little light around four in the morning. I can see if anybody's walking around. Get these dudes out of here. Keep 'em out."

Sometimes, in a garbage pile, he'd spy empty pop bottles, pick them up, and throw them in the back of the cart. "Twenty cents is twenty cents," he said, picking up a twelve-ounce Coke can and a twenty-ounce Sprite bottle. Sometimes we drove from spot to spot in the plant, and Eddie would stop and set booby traps to track the routes critters were taking into the plant. "I don't know if I want to block it or bait it," he said of one door. Some doors he blocked with bits of heavy metal. Others he left open. Some he welded shut.

"Hmm," he once said on a sweep.

"What?"

"I don't see nobody. That's bad for business."

Winter increased his difficulties across the board. Sometimes, Eddie's carts wouldn't even start. When I arrived on the morning of the Martin Luther King holiday, Eddie was pouring water into the batteries of the golf cart. The water inside the plant had been out for a while, and most of the plant's power had gone out the week before.

"The carts ain't runnin' good," Eddie said. "They're froze."

Eddie and I took the Gator, which was nearly out of gas, and filled bottles at the leaking fire hydrant along Charlevoix Avenue near the front gate. In the back of the Gator was a bag of rock salt, along with three fire extinguishers. "It's almost like prehistoric times—I need H_2O!" Eddie said as the bottles filled up. "You gotta have survival skills in this line of work. As long as water runs, it won't freeze." The hose was hooked into the fence that separated the Budd plant from Jefferson Avenue North; as it ran, it drained into the Chrysler ditch. Eddie said that the Detroit Fire Department had left the hydrant running as a favor. "They know what we're going through," he said. Back in October, I'd seen Eddie at the same leaking hydrant, washing his hands with soap. The Pinkertons at the plant gate got buckets of water from the hydrant for the toilet in their shack.

Eddie was annoyed that someone had left the hose pointing up, making it more likely to stop flowing and freeze. After he'd finished filling the bottles—a two-liter Squirt and a twenty-ounce Vernors—he put the hose, pointing down, back through a hole at the base of the fence.

Eddie needed the water for more than just the carts. He needed it so that he'd be able to wash his hands after using the facilities. A few days before, Eddie had excused himself from our discussion, saying he'd had too much coffee that morning. Like brides before their weddings, some guys on the crew tried not to eat or drink too much before coming into work in winter, so as to avoid certain necessities. Relieving oneself in the cold required administration, the removing of more layers of clothing than a Victorian lady. Luckily, the cold seemed to slow down, if not shut down, certain bodily functions.

The plant closing frequently led Eddie to lamentation—to reflect on the last things, and the first things, and how in the mind of man it was all muddled but clear, crystal clear, to God the Father, who gave us the life of his son, Christ Jesus. "From Adam's rib God created Eve," Eddie said, "and from them come all men and women, and they prophesy that, at the end of days, there'll be one man and one woman left, just as it was in the beginning." He paused. "That's something I think about."

Our dorm room for these bull sessions was Eddie's guard shack, which served as our warming hut as winter wore on and temperatures continued to dip. In the cold of winter, the heat of the shack—provided by a small space heater pinched from the plant—made Eddie sleepy. His motto: "A good guard is a rested guard." I never rested, lest I miss something to put in my notes. Eddie appreciated my attentiveness. "You can't go," he said to me more than once as I prepared to leave, leaning back in his chair and closing his eyes. "Damnit, this is a two-man operation."

Because it was Eddie's castle, the shack was where I went to announce myself after arriving at the plant in the winter. Parked next to it was usually his truck, a GMC 4x4, which had a bumper sticker in the back window:

Protect Your Future
Buy

Our conversations were interrupted from time to time, as trucks pulled up on the scale alongside his shack. Eddie had to tend to the scrap and transport trucks that came in and out of the plant, hauling bits of it away.

"A hundred and forty-three thousand four hundred and eighty. How's that sound?"

"Just a little over, but that'll work." This driver and load were headed to the OmniSource scrap yard in Ecorse.

"You be back tonight?" Eddie asked.

"Don't know," the driver said. "Just following the guy in front of me."

"You'll be back," Eddie said.

Eddie's talk was capable of shifting back and forth between a bill of lading and, for instance, the problem of evil, which preoccupied him. Keeping Ivan Karamazov out of it, I once suggested that the matter of theodicy was complicated, but Eddie claimed to know where the answer could be found. "I just lean back in my chair," he said, "and look up at them stars." During one of his soliloquies on man's fall, I quoted, like an ass, the opening of *Paradise Lost:* "Of man's first disobedience, and the fruit of that forbidden tree . . ." "What's that from?" Eddie asked. I told him. "I might have that book at home," he said. "Does it got a yellow cover?" Eddie, a born poet, had no need of the book. I much preferred his exposition to Milton's. "In the beginning," Eddie said, "life was good. Then the fruit comes into the picture."

As we talked in the shack, Eddie often worried aloud about the younger guys on the rigging crew, a few of whom seemed, to him, too eager to assume the role of the hard-living autoworker that their fathers, grandfathers, and uncles had inhabited without effort but that they, doing the cleanup after auto production disappeared, had to aspire toward. This concern expressed itself in religious terms. "One of the young guys showed up drunk," Eddie said one morning. "Showed up drunk" meant that the kid was soused at 7:00 a.m. "Didn't know where he was or what he was doing. Couldn't walk, couldn't talk. I sent him home. I tell these younger guys, who are making a thousand dollars a week, 'Don't spend that money on booze. Go to church. Put money in the basket, giving back to God what God has given to you. Read the King James Bible.' There's great consolation in the King James Bible. God knows I've backslid in the last year, working here, but I still go to church, put my money in the basket, and try to get closer to God."

Among the younger guys Eddie worried about were his sons, Greg and Brad, both of them in their twenties and helping with security at the plant. "Your mom had two affairs," Eddie once said to Brad. "Neither of you belongs to me." At other times, he asserted his paternity more strongly. Brad once asked Eddie, as Eddie was leaving the plant, what he was going to do that night. "I'm gonna go home and screw your mama!" Eddie said.

The generational decline in Stanford employment at the Budd plant—from father to son to grandsons—made Eddie morose. "There's nothing in Michigan now except this kind of work, tearing places down," he said. "Greg and Brad don't have no shop experience. Right now, they're on my wings, being here. I can torch, weld—if I have to nitty-gritty, I can do it. They haven't done it. I don't know what they'll do."

I don't mean to suggest, with these snippets of talk, that no security work was done as we sat in the shack. It was less security work than spying, however. Eddie sometimes saw unknown trucks—delivering Porta-Johns, or diesel for the generators, or propane for the torches—pull onto plant property. At other times, he was seeing who on the crew was returning from lunch, and when they were returning, and—based on their driving—in what condition they were returning. One winter afternoon, Eddie pulled out his Bushnell binoculars—he looked as if he were bird-watching—and spied some pickup trucks with Razorback license plates returning from lunch.

"One o'clock and the hillbillies are back," Eddie said, impressed, for once, by their punctuality.

THE BOYS

The only crew members not called "the girls" by Eddie and Guy were the Arkansas Boys, a team of traveling Razorback riggers for hire granted the masculine honorific by Guy. Eddie called them "the hillbillies." Terry senior, Terry junior, Josh, Jeremy, and Arkansas Dave were likened by others to Gypsies, carnies, and Irish tinkers, and were held in considerable esteem by the others on the crew excepting Eddie, whom the hillbillies annoyed. "They're from so far back in the woods they have to pump sunlight in," Eddie said. The Arkansas Boys got Cornbread Eddie's goat—for instance, when their pickups befouled the fresh fallen snow out in the scrap yard, which was perfect terrain, in its pristine state, for Eddie to track critters in. "The hillbillies messed up my snow out back doing donuts," he complained in March. From time to time, on their way into the plant, the Arkansas Boys fishtailed in piles of what was to them unfamiliar precipitation. "I wouldn't let them pull my little red wagon," Eddie observed. Though Eddie didn't care for Michigan winters and felt the pull of his southern roots, he couldn't settle down South. "That's why I stay up here, in Michigan," he once said after seeing the Arkansas Boys do donuts in their pickups. "Keep away from the ignorance." After they'd been working the Budd job many months, the Arkansas Boys grew homesick. "They're not used to Michigan women," Eddie said. I asked why Michigan women took getting used to. "They got teeth," Eddie said.

The older Arkansas Boys did not. Dave and Terry senior had dental outcomes consistent with the nineteenth-century English Midlands. Arkansas Dave once offered Eddie and me a bag of peanuts, explaining that he'd had the peanuts for two days and couldn't do much with them since he had no top teeth. This lack, coupled with their accents, could make the older Arkansas Boys difficult to understand. As Guy put it, you needed an interpretator.

Quiet and competent, the Arkansas Boys formed a self-contained unit, a crew within the crew. "They keep to themselves," Dave Scarlin said to me the Sunday afternoon after Thanksgiving, when I'd first really watched the Arkansas Boys work. The plant was empty, dark, and dank, and Terry senior and Terry junior, sitting silently by a row of old lockers, were getting ready to go home—their Detroit home—the Extended Stay motel at I-94 and Gratiot, where the Mexicans had put up as well. I'd told Dave that I wanted to introduce myself to the Southerners and see if they had anything to say.

I'd first crossed paths with the Arkansas Boys, some of them, back at the beginning of August, when they were working for Machines International of Wichita, Kansas, and were in Budd to take down an overhead crane in Bay 1 that had been bought at the auction. They hired on in Detroit not long after. A few months and several departures later, the Arkansas Boys had become the rigging company's first string. Terry senior, Terry junior, Josh, Jeremy, and Arkansas Dave were now primarily responsible for clear-cutting this section of forest. A Razorback reinforcement, Arkansas Rick, would arrive near job's end.

Like Indians on a construction site, the Arkansas Boys possessed an innate something, and were considered, rightly, a cut above. Terry senior, a slight man modest about his abilities, called the heavy lifting the Arkansas Boys did "moving furniture." Just tell him where you want it. They seemed a throwback to Detroit's roots—to the country's roots—a time when guys good with their hands didn't have to worry about being good at much else, up to and including speaking. It was inconceivable to think of the buzzwords of modern labor—"grievance," "COLA," "job classification"—coming out of their mouths. They weren't something out of the modern, corporatized union hall; they were something out of Faulkner, and put me in mind of the Bundren family in *As I Lay Dying*, carrying the corpse of their decaying mother across rough country. The closed Budd plant was the body of Addie Bundren, and the Arkansas Boys were in charge of the burial.

Over time, I'd come to the conclusion that the Arkansas Boys were a collection of intuitive geniuses of a kind. Not everyone agreed, and I'm open to the charge of romanticizing. But when I watched them work, I recalled a passage from that 1978 article by Stan Grayson in *Automobile Quarterly*, "The All-Steel World of Edward Budd," which quotes a passage from a 1930 article by Rex Beach about the all-steel body. "Beach," Grayson writes, "noted that some of Budd's workmen had developed a Stradivarius-like feel for how steel would act, and could adjust a huge press the hair's breadth necessary to correct a fault. 'Not infrequently,' [Beach] noted, 'some grimy fellow who can scarcely read and write will look at the blueprint of a new die and declare that it won't do—this may excite the ire of the technical staff, but nine times out of ten he is right.' "

Grimy fellows, the Arkansas Boys had a batting average that was better than nine for ten. "One would assume," Beach wrote, "that a highly mechanized business of this sort"—that is, the stamping of all-steel auto bodies—"would quickly reduce itself to a purely automatic process and that the mill hands would become merely robots, but the opposite is true . . . A peculiar artistry enters into it."

Peculiar, artistic, impervious to criticism, the senior Arkansas Boys, Dave and Terry senior, exuded a rough competence that cut through their grime. Dave was louder than Terry senior, more prone to fits of temper, and possibly the group's leader. I've always been impressed by people who know their craft so well that they can discuss it in colorful phrases absolutely inscrutable to the uninitiated. A prominent boxing trainer, encouraging his welterweight between rounds of a recent bout, knelt before his charge and said, "Knock the grease off this dude, and then swim without gettin' wet." He was telling the fighter to stick and move—perfectly stock advice—but his phrasing was unimprovable. Likewise, Arkansas Dave, when imploring a rigger to lower equipment slowly, would holler, "Milk that motherfucker! Milk that motherfucker!" It was only when you stripped away the phrase's Freudian reverberations that you realized that Dave was—I think—issuing safety instructions. I liked listening to the Arkansas Boys talk, even if—and this was often the case—I didn't have a clue what they were talking about.

Like the best boxing trainers, both Arkansas Dave and Terry senior looked their part, and it's possible that, in a bit of inverted snobbery, I'd have been less impressed by their work if their appearance had been more presentable. At the end of his introduction to Barbara Mensch's *South Street,* her book of photographs of the waning years of New York City's Fulton Fish Market, Phillip Lopate writes of the men, mostly Italian, whom Mensch depicted: "They bring with them a drama and a dignity, an understanding of who they are that is, for want of a better word, archaic. Mensch's photographs sometimes give the impression of dating from another, much earlier era, although she used no antiquing tricks to achieve that effect: it is simply that the tribe she portrays seems a throwback. Their faces and bodies express an almost ancient awareness of the price that must be paid to be a man, to hold one's ground, especially in a society less and less respectful of working-class culture." Precisely.

■

There were still places in Detroit that respected working-class culture. The Arkansas Boys' pickups could be seen, most lunchtimes, in the parking lot of the Texas Bar, about a mile southeast of the Budd plant on Kercheval. The bar's demographics contrasted strongly with those of the surrounding area. In one of the bar's front windows, near the door, was a handwritten cardboard sign:

No Public Restroom or Telephone's.
No—Bum's.
No—Hooker's.
No—Thieve's.
No—Selling of Anything.
We Do Call the *Police*.

The lunch special at the Texas was a cheeseburger, fries, and beer for $5.50. I asked the barmaid, on a snowy Friday in February, to substitute a Coke for the beer. I might well have asked for water instead of wine at Canaan. Despite its being a Friday during Lent, I ate the burger, having already forgone the beer. I was waiting on the arrival of the Arkansas Boys—whom, despite months of observing, I'd spoken to only in small snatches. Our dialogues had been nothing to write home about, or even write in my notebook about.

There was honky-tonk on the stereo. A woman down at the end of the bar was holding court. She was in her forties and fat, with a terrific memory for song lyrics. In between laments, she sang along. "I know my kids are bad," she said, "but I don't need no one to tell me they're bad. I don't like my children sometimes, but I love 'em. I had my first child at nineteen. I'm going to get drunk," she said, for some reason employing the future tense.

Behind the bar were stickers: "Union Roofers Local 149." "Proud to Be a Union Sheet Metal Worker." St. Patrick's Day was six weeks away, and behind the bar, too, were one-dollar shamrocks that had been sold on behalf of Jerry's Kids. After purchase, the donor signed his name or that of his organization, and the shamrock was taped up. "From the Heart of _____ Comes a Shamrock to Help Fight Muscular Dystrophy." Local 58 had bought a shamrock. Local 299 had bought a shamrock. So had several individuals, though some used pseudonyms. I doubted the existence of Dr. Felter Snatch.

By the time the Arkansas Boys had walked into the bar and seated themselves at a table, I'd lost my nerve to approach them. This was their habitat, not mine, and I was out of my depth, sipping my Coke. I continued to observe their work from a distance, as I had for months.

My next close brush with the Razorbacks came a couple weeks later, when Arkansas Dave pulled up on the scale alongside Eddie's shack. It was nowhere near quitting time, but Arkansas Dave said that they were going home to the motel "to do laundry and shit." Dave said that they'd come in around 10:00 the next day, a Sunday, to drop the side columns in 9-line. After they'd pulled away, Eddie said that they were angry that they didn't have any lights down in the pits. "Bring a flashlight," Eddie said he'd told them. " 'Do what you have to do to get the job done.' They know we have no electricity. I don't have a charge card. I can't just send them out for whatever they want."

The majority of the plant's power had gone out in mid-January. Generators and floodlights had been brought in, and Eddie and Guy, as management, would often go around at lunchtime, turning off the lights to keep down costs—parents following after forgetful kids. The lights would click off in this part of the plant, then that, with Budd looking more and more like a movie studio where filming had stopped.

I arrived at the plant around 11:30 on Sunday, hoping to see the Arkansans. When I walked into the press shop, I didn't see a soul. The fire in the basket above 2-line was nearly out— a clue in itself as to how many people might be about. The Budd plant must have been one of the few places on earth where fire's presence or absence was still a predictor of human habitation. In the absence of people, the barrel and basket fires resembled the smoldering remains of a sacked village.

In the distance, down by the base of 9-line, I saw the

flames of a fire barrel that was serving as the furnace for the Arkansas Boys—who, good as their word, were working to drop the side columns of the line's fourth press. Three fire extinguishers were by the fire barrel to prevent freezing. Their pickups—a 2005 Chevy, a silver Ford F-150, and a white Ford F-150—were parked nearby. Shafts of sunlight came in from the coated windows above, producing something of the effect of stained glass.

Their task for the day wasn't a big deal, rigging-wise, which was just as well, since it gave us time to talk. They were at the rough midpoint of what Matt Sanders called "unstacking" the press. Its crown and ram had been removed. They were, now, working on the columns. After that, they'd pull the bolster, then the base, and that'd be that: another press down.

Jeremy was atop the left column of 9-4. Dave and Josh were down in the pit, the darkness of which Dave had complained about the day before, where Dave was torching off a nut. Terry senior and Terry junior controlled the P&H overhead crane, above us in Bay 5, with the pendant controller that dangled down. I stood next to them. Father and son had a habit of sticking their gloved hands *into* the barrel fire, both to warm their hands up and to burn the grease from their gloves.

"They heated it," Terry senior said, explaining their problems with the stubborn nut. Heating it had caused it to expand, and "they" were some guys on the crew who weren't from Arkansas and who, as a result, didn't have the slightest idea what the hell they were doing. Dave knew damn well what he was doing down there. I asked the two Terrys how big the nut was that Dave was cutting. They both extended their arms in a circle, as if making to pick up a big dog. They figured it weighed three hundred pounds.

As we waited, Terry junior provided me quick biographical sketches of the Razorback crew. He himself was eighteen, from Atkins, Arkansas, and was sending some of the money he earned in Detroit back home to his grandfather. With the money he kept, he wanted to buy a truck or a "crotch rocket"—a motorcycle. I said a truck was more practical. "A bike is cheaper on gas," he said.

So far, he'd gotten a thousand dollars' worth of tattoos done in Detroit; he showed me a picture on his cell phone of the tattoo he had done on his upper back. He'd also bought a TV/DVD player for his dad's Ford F-150. He considered this an investment in the future, as he thought that he might want to buy the truck from his father. He'd started at Budd back in September or October—couldn't recall exactly. At the moment, he was waiting on Dave to cut the nut so that, with the overhead crane, he and his dad could pull the tie-rods that ran the length of the press's columns.

Jeremy, atop the columns to handle the hookup between rod and crane, was twenty and from Fort Smith, Arkansas. Dave, in his forties, was from Cabot, Arkansas, but now lived in Indiana. Josh, down below, was twenty-one, looked twelve, and was also from Fort Smith. The women in the plant, if there'd been any, would have considered him "cute." He laughed the most, was the quickest to smile, and had curly hair. Terry junior and Jeremy were more withdrawn, intent to learn a craft and draw a check. All three of the kids had started rigging at eighteen, Terry junior told me.

"After high school?" I asked.

"None of us graduated high school," Terry junior said. "My old man did, and Dave." He said he had dropped out in the ninth grade.

"Aren't you supposed to stay in longer?" I asked.

"Supposed to, I guess, until you're sixteen, or whatever." His main concern was staying in school long enough to get his driver's license, which somehow he secured. His youth freed him from concerns about future employment. He said his dad "knows everyone in Arkansas. If this goes south, he can always get a job in Arkansas."

Terry senior, who stood with us near the barrel, didn't like the weather in Detroit and wanted to go south in the literal sense. He said that it didn't get this cold in Arkansas—down to the single digits—and that it didn't stay this cold this long. There might be some freezing rain in Arkansas, he said, but there was nearly no snow. Terry senior had graduated from high school in 1980. When I talked to him up close, it looked as if he had more teeth missing than remaining. He was even leaner than he looked, with prominent cheekbones and a bit of gray in his beard. On his head he always wore a green hood, which looked to be the lining from a racing helmet. None of the Arkansas Boys ever wore hard hats—another of their distinctions.

"This is scrapping," Terry senior said of the work that they were doing. I said that 9-line wasn't getting scrapped, but had in fact been bought by Gestamp, the same Spanish auto supplier that had bought 16-line for Mexico. Terry just laughed.

Uli, the German engineer from Müller Weingarten who was overseeing the 16-line and 9-line dismantlings for Gestamp, had been around the plant earlier in the day. Uli—short for Ulrich—had been in Budd since May 2007, back when work on 16-line began. He spent November and December back home, outside Mexico City. "We call Uli 'Schultz,' " Terry senior said. "Sergeant Schultz. *Hogan's Heroes.*" For Christmas, he said, "We got Uli a quart of moonshine."

We looked down into the pit where Dave, an American flag bandanna on his head, was finishing torching the nut off. Josh stood with him in the smoke, oil, and water. When Dave came up from the pit, job done, he explained his technique. "I cussed it more than I cut it," he said. The nut sat smoking in the grease of the pit, cut in three equal pieces. Dave's glasses were covered in grease. He wiped them, and said something I couldn't quite catch about having "the biggest rod and nuts around."

■

A week or so after Dave's assertion of rod-and-nut supremacy, he and Jeremy got into a fight in their Macomb County motel. It was probably bound to happen: five grown men living in close proximity in lousy conditions for months on end. Guy Betts told me that Jeremy had gone to jail, but was out now. Whatever the story, Dave's left eye, swollen and discolored from a right hand, told it.

"How you doing?" I asked him when I saw his shiner.

"Could be better," he said. "I'm going home. Fuck it."

By home, Dave meant *home,* not a Macomb County motel. Terry senior would be dropping Dave off in Indiana while on his own way to Arkansas. This was just a quick vacation, Terry senior told me, not a permanent departure. I was greatly relieved: a Budd plant without the senior Arkansas Boys would be a badly diminished thing.

It was early March. "This might be the ugliest I've ever seen the plant look," I said to Guy. It was cloudy and smoky inside the plant, with fog all over the press shop. I could actually see a *cloud* line above the pits to 3- and 4-lines. "Be careful walking around," Guy warned. "Pipes are bursting right and left." Though it wasn't a Friday, Terry and Dave were waiting on their paychecks to arrive from the rigging company before departing Detroit on their trip.

While they waited, there was some excitement: the plant was invaded. Two crew members, working by the light of a fire in an area outside the press shop, said they spotted the wannabe crooks sneak past them wearing parkas. Once they knew they'd been spotted, the crooks began to run, and the crew members came into the press shop to sound the alarm.

I asked if the invaders might not have just been guys on the crew.

"No guys on the crew run that fast," I was told.

Crew members picked up whatever tools were to hand— crowbars, heavy rods, wood boards, big wrenches—and tore ass thataway, into the plant's darkness. Eddie, who'd been summoned from outside, walked in with a shotgun over his shoulder. I stood by a fire barrel at the base of 8-line with

Terry senior and Terry junior. The other two Arkansas young-sters, Jeremy and Josh, had joined the chase, only to return soon thereafter.

"Here comes one dumb ass," Terry junior said, seeing Jeremy reemerge from the darkness, rod in hand. Behind him was Josh, also carrying a rod.

"I stabbed his ass right through the heart," Jeremy said, jokingly.

As the manhunt continued, Guy Betts came over for a chat. "See what people will do for scrap metal?" he said. "They figured we wouldn't be able to hear them during the day, with all this noise."

The search turned up nothing, though later that after-noon, two guys were seen running out of the plant onto Con-ner Avenue. Eddie, for one, wasn't the least bit surprised that the guys hadn't been caught. "There's lots of places to hide in here," he said.

■

I talked to the Arkansas Boys every chance I had from then on. Arkansas Dave's good cheer was a constant. When he'd returned from vacation, I asked him how it had gone.

"What vacation?" he asked. His black eye was healing but still showed traces of trouble. "That was no goddamned vaca-tion. And then I gotta come back to this goddamned place." He yelled at the boys among the Arkansas Boys, who were using a crane. "They don't listen, they don't learn, I'm getting goddamned sick," Dave said.

Around the fire basket a month later, I chatted him up again. His eye had long since healed. "How much longer you here?" I asked.

"Until they're kind enough to tell me to go the fuck home."

I had nothing against Arkansas and wanted to hear from the boys some kindness about the city of my birth. I asked Josh, since he was the sunniest of the Arkansans, if he'd miss Detroit when the Budd job was done.

"No."

"Won't you miss the Texas Bar?"

"No," he said. "I don't even drink." He considered the dubious accuracy of this, then added: "I drank thirty-two beers the other night, between six o'clock and one in the morning, but that was the first time in a long time." He wasn't entirely sure how he got back to the motel, but said, "I remember pissing on a Dumpster on 9 Mile Road."

I asked Josh if his real name was Joshua. "Naw, it's just Josh. I mean, it might say Joshua on my Social Security card, or something. I don't know." He asked about the pictures he'd seen me taking around the plant. I said that I could e-mail them to him. "Hell, I don't even know what e-mail is," Josh said. "I think my girlfriend's got a computer, though."

Now that we knew each other, Terry senior had his own way of greeting me. "Asshole of the earth," he said whenever he saw me.

"It's my hometown," I said, defending Detroit.

"It's my hometown, too, last five or six months, and I fucking hate it."

"Where you going after this?"

He shrugged. "Unemployment office, probably."

THE SCRAP

Employment wasn't a problem for America's scrap crews in 2007–8. The scrap crew in the Budd plant, RJ Torching, was out of Flint. Of the various surplus industry service providers in Budd, RJ had been in the plant the longest, preceding the rigging crew into Budd by many months. RJ's arrival, in fact, preceded the closing itself. Its torch men were often outside, cutting scrap in the Budd yard. Inside the plant, I'd watch RJ torch men cut up the presses that hadn't been sold overseas, but were instead being scrapped out.

The RJ torch man held in highest regard among the rigging guys was James, a broad-shouldered six-footer with a light beard and goatee. I'd watched James work for several months before talking to him. When I finally did, he was friendly; when I told him what I was up to, he joked that he'd help me write it. Though a few years my senior, he addressed me as "sir," as if he'd recently stumbled and was doing his best to stave off the next slipup.

I asked him if he was in charge of the torch men.

"No, sir," he said. "I'm just a peon."

I hadn't seen James around on the weekends. For the previous few months, he explained, he could work at Budd only on weekdays. On weekends, he drove to Jackson, about an hour's drive from Detroit, and home to one of the state's big prisons. There, by eight at night on Friday, James had to report to Jackson County Jail. "I told a cop to leave me the fuck alone," he said. He was allowed to serve his sentence on the weekends. At eight o'clock on Sunday night he was released and drove back to one of the Macomb County motels that served as dormitory for the non-Detroiters—Arkansans, Mexicans, assorted torch men—dismantling Budd.

As part of his sentence, James had to attend meetings in Detroit during the workweek. At one, James shared with the group that he was "cutting up the Budd plant." At this, another group member ceased to be nonjudgmental. He got "fighting mad," James said, and started to scream at him. "You're shipping all that steel overseas! I got twenty-five years in that place!" James took the tirade from the ex-Budd worker in stride; it was in keeping with his recent run of luck. "I can't wait for next weekend," he told me on a drizzly, forty-degree day in mid-January, looking forward to his sentence's end. "I'm going to make up for lost time." Where some men in jail cells fantasize of tropical locales and friendly ladies, James dreamed of Detroit, his torch, and long hours in a closed auto plant in the winter cold.

Not everyone on the rigging crew was impressed with the cutting of scrap that went on. "They did their job in great fashion," Duane Krukowski, the electrician, had said of the RJ torch men, "but you have to understand—there's not much fashion to taking a big-ass crane and grabbing something and cutting it apart with a torch and hauling it out." Some of the torch men were still better than others. The worst, the riggers joked, didn't cut—they melted. Employing a rhetorical device known as hyperbole, they implied that, rather than use a combination of skill and muscle to cut the press into transportable scrap pieces, subpar torch men used their torches merely to heat the steel of the presses to the point that it liquefied. The effect—again, hyperbolically—was similar to that of the wintertime sun on a snow pile of a million pounds: the process would take a while.

James cut. He estimated that he'd cut about 7 million pounds in the last three months or so, and said that it had taken him just six days to cut a 900,000-pound press by himself. He'd had his doubts initially. His first reaction, upon seeing the Budd plant's presses, was "I don't want nothing to do with them big bastards." Of his first view of the plant's exterior, the replica of Independence Hall, he said, "It takes your breath."

We stood that day in a dark part of the shop floor, near the end of the railroad tracks that cut into the plant. Before us was a pile of bricks and mortar. Above us, on the second and third floors, were gaping holes where the bricks and the mortar had been. Some of the equipment on the upper floors came down in elevators; for other pieces, they'd just "take up a hi-lo" and push the presses down through an internal wall. "It's faster this way," James explained. Other upper-floor presses were pushed out external walls, with such spots marked from the outside by loose aluminum siding dangling in the breeze. As time wore on, aluminum siding would peel off in strips.

"They want me to go to Iowa," James said, speaking of the Maytag plant, where RJ Torching scrapped out equipment from mid-December 2007 through early June 2008. "I don't like being away from home." His hometown was Fort Wayne, Indiana, where his grandfather had worked for International Harvester. "My grandfather taught me to cut steel when I was ten years old," he said. James had turned forty two days before, "so I've been doing this for thirty years," he figured. I asked him what other plants he had been in lately. "We took down the Rockwell plant on Fifth Avenue in Columbus, Ohio," he said. That was in the spring of 2006.

James had suggested that I speak to his bosses in Flint, and several months after the Budd job was done, I did so. To get to Flint, I took all highway—the Ford to the Reuther to the Chrysler to Dort Highway—and ended up in the birthplace of General Motors. A stretch of Dort Highway, named after Josiah Dallas Dort, onetime partner of GM's founder, Will Durant, is the "UAW Sitdown Strike Memorial Highway." One can drive all day in Detroit and its surround without hitting any stretch of road that isn't named after someone in the auto industry or the unions it gave rise to. Along Dort Highway, I'd passed the GM-Delphi-AC Delco plant, much of it demolished since the previous March. Bricks were being sold through the union local. The final mile of the drive took me past a row of Flint scrap yards. I'd come to discuss what Jason Roughton, the owner of RJ Torching, the last of these yards, called "the scrapping of America."

Though I'd returned from a train trip to Montreal and Quebec late the night before, I was more excited about my drive to Flint, which I hadn't visited since high school. I had no literary or linguistic connection to Canada, but I loved the language of Ben Hamper's *Rivethead,* the story of his and his family's life on the line in Flint's General Motors plants. Published as I was leaving Detroit for college, the book appealed to the budding writer in me, who saw writing as a matter of accumulating good lines loaded with attitude. That it was about plant life, and that I was from Detroit—this connection mattered less. Campus life would be putting psychic as well as actual mileage between me and any future in a factory.

I read it, then, not as a blue-collar co-conspirator but as a literary critic. The craft I was interested in wasn't the proper handling of a rivet gun but the proper construction of a book. The beauty of Hamper's book is that it makes no attempt to smooth over what seem to be contradictions. *Rivethead* is about a hardworking guy who spends a lot of time sitting on his ass, drinking and drugging on the job; a guy sinfully overpaid ("Generous Motors") for work most of us wouldn't do for any sum; a guy who writes for a progressive paper and who hesitates not a second before using terms like "fags" and "dykes." He has nothing but impatience for do-gooders and yet is desperate, in his own way, to do good.

The bedrock ambivalence Hamper's book dramatizes is this: working the line is terrible, and the passing of such work is a goddamned shame. In the book's best turn of phrase, Hamper says that "working the rivet line was like being paid to flunk high school the rest of your life." Whether this represents salvation or perdition depends on the person.

For Hamper, it's hell. He is a working-class Salinger character: too intelligent, too observant, too able to see through everything into the emptiness beyond to work the line with any chance of contentment. Hamper's problem is that he is temperamentally unsuited for the work that sustained generations of Hampers before him, but he can conceive of nothing else. "There really isn't anything gallant or noble about being a factory hack," Hamper says near his book's conclusion. "The whole operation equals nothing more than lousy prostitution. Thinking tears you apart. Start peering at the walls too closely or leaning on the clock too heavily and the whoremaster reality of all this idiocy will surely gobble your ass up whole." Move Holden Caulfield from the Upper East Side to Flint, send him to work in the city's auto plants, allow a decade or two of corrosion to set in, and that's the sort of sentence you'd get. By his book's end, Hamper has, like Holden, gone crazy.

Anyone reading *Rivethead* without smiling ear to ear cannot be trusted. The book's entertainment value is tremendous. But it is purchased at a price: that of partially explaining management decisions to close down UAW-represented plants in Rust Belt cities. I've read the book several times, and I always finish it feeling a little sorry for the supervisors.

■

Like most scrap yards, RJ Torching of Flint ("Scrap Rats—Portable Processor of Scrap Iron & Metal") resembles an ant colony of tens of thousands of tons. I drove inside the gates of the yard and parked not far from the action of the magnets, trucks, and torches. I asked Ken Brooks, one of the managers, if my car was okay where it was. "If it gets scrapped," he said, "you'll get about six hundred bucks."

Ken took me to the company offices, which were at the

front of the yard, inside a mobile unit of the kind that dots construction sites. He introduced me to Jason, and then left us temporarily.

"Nine scrap yards right down here," Jason said after we'd sat down to talk. He was referring to the road on which he'd chosen to locate his scrap yard, which already had eight such yards before his arrival. "They were all here, and I set up shop. I snuck in the back door." The RJ company logo is a rat clutching a cutting torch. The scrap rat, he pointed out, is meant in a good way, "not the thieving way." At the moment, Jason's mind was on a steel mill—Macsteel, in Monroe, Michigan—that had been sold to a Brazilian company, Gerdau, the previous fall. "I'm looking to meet the new buyer," Jason said. If he was going to continue to sell them prepared scrap, he said, jokingly, "I've gotta make sure their money's good." That meeting was scheduled for after ours.

The RJ scrap yard had security cameras, and Jason said that there were only three hours of the day—from 3:00 a.m. to 6:00 a.m.—that they weren't there. "We're processing all the time," he said. "We have to be. We can't survive if we're not. We'll be out of business tomorrow. If we don't cut all night, we can't keep up with the demand."

As we spoke, trucks continued to arrive at the yard. "Most of the material we're getting right now is from Grand Blanc Stamping and Lansing," Jason said, referring to two closed GM plants. "We're probably handling 180,000 ton a year now. When I started, we were lucky to do 40,000 ton."

I asked if it was a good time to be in their business.

"Most definitely," said Ken, who'd returned. "The best time. Unfortunately."

"You make your own economy," Jason said, quoting a colleague. "I started in '98 with nothing. The market sucked. We couldn't make any money. My dad turned it over to me. We were about four hundred grand in the hole. We had no money coming in. We had seven people, and we hadn't had a job for three weeks. We were sitting around, doing nothing. I went down to Indianapolis, landed a job. I drove up to Fort Wayne, got another job. I tried driving around Michigan to get a job, but couldn't get any. I was making a dollar a ton, I was doing five hundred ton a week, and I paid everybody and made five hundred bucks and hoped to God my crane didn't break down. Ever since then, I've always expanded. This year, I'm going to do four times the amount of business that I did last year."

As with many businesses associated with plant closings, scrap processing is in large part countercyclical. In 1998, when the scrap market sucked, the national economy was solid. The government ran a surplus; inflation was low; employment was high. Now, with the economy shrinking, RJ Torching was growing. The price of scrap steel was high (for the moment— it would crash months later, as the world economy tanked), and there was lots and lots of it out there.

"There's gotta be bottom-feeders," Jason said of his company and the service it provided at closed plants. "Someone's gotta clean up everybody's mess. That's just what we are. Bottom-feeders. That's where scrap rat came from. We do the shittiest job there is in the industry." It was a job Jason was well acquainted with. "I've cut my whole life, since I was twelve years old," he said. "It's *hard*. It's a dirty job. It's hot, it's greasy, it's oily. You get burned."

RJ employed about sixty torch men, and I asked if it was difficult keeping guys on the crews that went to places like Budd and Maytag.

"I fire 'em, and they keep calling back because they can't find a job," Jason said.

RJ Torching had been in the plant "cutting up dies for Ford Motor Company" before Budd's closing, Jason said. "Here's how big automotive plants start," he explained. "The tooling—the dies, the injection molds, the fixtures, some of the machines—aren't actually owned by ThyssenKrupp, or Martinrea, or Magna," by the supplier. "The tooling comes from Ford Motor Company. They"—the suppliers—"might be making Chrysler parts, GM parts, Ford parts. Ford supplies the dies for them to stamp 'em."

I asked how much tonnage they took out of Budd Detroit.

"If you include the Ford dies," Jason said, "probably thirty thousand ton.

"I've been in so many different plants," he went on. Typically, these plants are closed or closing. I noted that Budd's major mid-century plants had been in Detroit, Gary, and Philadelphia. "I did a lot of work in Philly, too," Jason said. "Did the Reading plant—the Dana plant." The Dana Corporation, which came out of bankruptcy in early 2008, closed its truck frame plant in Reading, Pennsylvania, in 2000. Some businessmen knew cities based on their airports. Jason knew places based on the plants that had closed there.

The next plant on his radar was the "3800 engine plant," Jason said, just down the road. The General Motors Powertrain Flint North plant, which made the 3800 engine, a Buick V-6, was rumored to be closing. But because this hadn't been announced officially (it would be, two weeks after our talk), Jason was hedging his bets. "We might be buying all the scrap out of it," he said.

Another big recent job for RJ Torching, besides Budd and Maytag, was "the Guide Lamp plant in Anderson, Indiana," where RJ scrapped out equipment from mid-March through the end of June 2008. Unlike the Budd and Maytag plants, Guide was actually demolished. "North American Dismantling Corporation took it down," Jason said, "and they contracted me to cut all the machines up. Guide's owned by General Motors. It was spun off with the Delphi thing."

According to the North American Dismantling Corporation Web site, "This project consisted of the purchase, environmental decommissioning and dismantling of the approximately 2,300,000 square feet of the existing GM manufacturing facility located in Anderson, Indiana." An entry on the Guide Lamp plant was included in the November 15, 2006, edition of *Plant Closing News* ("52 Companies Closing 57 Plants + 14 Bankruptcies"):

Guide Corp Closing Two Auto Light Plants
Guide Corp. will close its headlight plant in Monroe, Louisiana on June 1, 2007 . . . A similar scheduled closure will be followed at Guide's tail lamp plant in Anderson, Ind.

The history of the Guide Lamp plant in Anderson paralleled that of Budd Detroit. Its closing was announced five months after Budd's, and it closed about five weeks after. Begun in Cleveland in 1906, Guide opened in Anderson in 1928, was unionized in fits and starts over the next decade, made munitions during World War II, hit its peak in the 1950s and 1960s, and employed as many as sixty-five hundred. It, too, underwent numerous name changes—Guide Motor Lamp Manufacturing Company, Fisher Guide, Inland Fisher Guide.

Of Guide Lamp's 2006 closing, Anderson's *Herald Bulletin* bluntly wrote: "The announcement effectively signals the end of the automotive industry in Anderson." When the auto industry moved out, the scrap rats moved in. Like so many small towns that appeared in *Plant Closing News,* Anderson was a single-employer town that had lost its single employer.

THE TRUCKS

What follows—forgive me, Father—is a partial list of what I took out of the Budd plant over the months: a framed picture of Mr. Edward G. Budd, company founder; the poster with the aerial picture of the plant from March 18, 1940; a map of the plant, produced by the Employee Involvement Group, titled "Budd, Sweat, and Tears"; a map of the plant, five feet tall and framed, produced by ThyssenKrupp; a framed picture of a 1992 Ford F-150 Flareside, to commemorate the completion of the plant's first stamping job for the truck on November 18, 1991; a bumper sticker, featuring a bulldog and bearing the message "Budd Gary Plant Builds the Safest Automobiles," that I unpeeled from a pillar in the plant; a plaque, dated June 1, 1988, and signed by members of UAW Local 306 and the Detroit plant staff, titled "Detroit Plant Commitment to Quality"; and a plaque, dated 1991 and presented to the Budd Company Stamping and Frame Division from the Ford Motor Company, conferring on Budd Ford's Q1 Preferred Quality Award.

I took pamphlets printed for employees. On the second floor of Independence Hall's west side was the Jobs Center. "Please note," a yellow sign that I nabbed said, "the JOB CENTER will close for good 12/1/06. *No computers will be available after that to create resumes or conduct job searches.*" Employment leads, no doubt as dead as the Budd plant by that point, remained tacked to the wall:

7/31/06

Electrician/Electrical Maintenance

Old Milford Fabricating

Detroit, MI

8/21/06

Production Supervisors

Form Tech Industries

Detroit Plant

I put the notices in my pocket. Should such leads lead nowhere, there were other materials in the Jobs Center, samples of which came with me. The UAW provided a pamphlet titled "Can Food Stamps Help You?" It had questions and answers: "What Are Food Stamps?" (Coupons used like money to buy food.) "Who Can Get Food Stamps?" (Those who work for low wages, are unemployed, and so on.) The United Way provided a packet, "Surviving Unemployment: A Guide to Finding the Help You Need." From the introduction: "A lay-off is generally not the result of poor performance on the part of an individual employee. Rather, it is an outcome of economic concerns that may be well outside of your control." A flyer from the AFL-CIO, "When the Paycheck Stops," contained a financial action plan. The plan's steps started at a gentle slope ("Step 1: Prepare a Complete Household Budget") and got increasingly steep. Step 5: Notify Your Creditors *Before* You Get Behind. Step 10: Sell What You Don't Need. Step 11: Check into Other Financial Resources. ("Life Insurance—Talk to your insurance agent to see whether you can borrow against your policy.") The image on the cover of the UAW pamphlet was a grocery bag overflowing with food. I took it home and read it all over.

I looked for union stuff to take. One day, on a tour with Eddie and Guy, I took a narrow stairwell past the old teletype room and up to Independence Hall's attic, where it had been Eddie's job to raise the flag that flew above the cupola when the plant was open and stamping parts and its employees were represented by United Auto Workers Local 306. "That was part of security," Eddie said. "Raising flags, lowering them to half-mast." Scattered about the building's attic were stacks of union grievances. I took what I could cradle under an arm. The oldest, Grievance No. 0555, was handwritten and dated March 4, 1965:

Budd Automotive
Detroit Plant
Grievance Report—Salaried
COMPLETE DETAILS OF GRIEVANCE
The Technical Unit Protests the action of the Company in docking members for absence on Thursday and/or Friday, February 25 and 26, 1965, due to the unusually severe weather conditions. The Union demands full payment for the (2) days for the members that were docked.

Management's typewritten decision came down a month later:

On 4-2-65 the Union was informed that it is a Company decision that those employees who did not receive any payment for February 25th and 26th due to absence because of the emergency snow storm would receive payment for those days. This payment is made on the basis that it does not establish any precedent.

There were hundreds more. They all began, "The Union charges," "The Union objects," or "The Union protests." One began, "The union objects to the rationality being used." Grievance No. 1998, dated November 23, 1983, elicited this management decision one week later:

Subsequent to investigation, determination is made [that] above employee was subject to a Reduction In Force Layoff due to economic conditions of the company effective 11/30/83. No violation—request denied.

An initialed note in the margin—"To Step V 12-7-83"—implied a further appeal, but I couldn't find the paperwork.

From a supply cabinet, I took a copy of the final union contract between

The Budd Company

A ThyssenKrupp Automotive Company

and

THE

INTERNATIONAL UNION

UAW

and its

LOCALS 306, 813 and 757

February 26, 2001–October 28, 2005

Locals 813 and 757 were from the Budd Philadelphia plant, which closed a year after its last UAW contract kicked in.

I told myself that it was all stuff that would help me to do my job. Likewise, workers on the rigging crew had to look for stuff that would help them do theirs. One day, a bit before lunch, Eddie and I were sitting on his fire cart in a dark, unlit area south of the press shop when we saw the two workers walking north, arms full.

"You're busted for stealing company property!" Eddie said.

They laughed. Eddie offered a hand. "Whaddya got? Put

some on the cart, I'll take it over there." "There" was the pit beneath 8-line where they were working.

"We were looking for cardboard so we can lay in that oil," one of the pit workers explained.

They carried strips of cardboard, along with plastic cover-ups. Oil still floated in the pits, and they needed a way to work without taking a swim. "I'm still looking for Jimmy Hoffa," one of them said of his search in the pits.

This fellow was wearing what Eddie called "security pants"—navy blue work pants with black stripes down the sides—that Eddie himself had worn when the plant was still open. The crew member said that he'd taken several pairs from lockers on the second floor of the central maintenance building. He'd also found a black, white, and gold patch that he gave to Eddie and that Eddie, later, gave to me. It said: "Local 306. 50 Years of the UAW. 1937–1987."

Eddie was moved. "Seventy years this place was a union shop. Not bad, eh?"

■

Not everyone agreed that this wasn't bad. There were some in the plant, even after Duane's departure, who thought that a union shop was—if not bad—not *not* bad, either.

The first Saturday in February, a thirty-degree morning, I pulled in to the plant just as Eddie, in his truck, was pulling out to get coffee. There'd been a few inches of precipitation the day before, but Guy had assured me that the crew would be in, "snow or shine." Eddie rolled down his window and wiped his nose with a Kleenex. "My nose is cold," he said. "Cold noses is only for dogs." Eddie was now the sole seasoned security guard at Budd; Dave was out of town, securing Maytag. I noted that Eddie was wearing a new pair of gloves—gone was the pair with the duct tape at the fingertip. "Dave took my duct tape to Iowa," Eddie explained.

I spent much of February talking to truckers from Texas and a translator from Brazil. The truckers were from Fitzley Inc., the same hauler that the previous summer and fall had taken 16-line down to the Mexican border. The translator, Marcelo, was from Delga, the Brazilian auto supplier that had purchased 2-line and was having it hauled by Fitzley to Houston. It was being crated and stored at a Houston cartage company before the entire line would be loaded onto a single ship bound for Santos port in Brazil. It took seventy-eight trips to move the more than two thousand tons of machinery in 2-line from Detroit to the Port of Houston, and it took more than two months, from January to mid-March.

The Fitzley truckers made repeated round-trips between Detroit and Texas during the worst of winter, getting down and back in some cases in little more than a week. They hauled crowns, columns, bolsters, rams, rods, robots, nuts, bolts, conveyors, cushions, eccentrics, control panels, electric panels, all tagged in Portuguese and laminated against the elements— *cabeçote, coluna, mesa, martelo, estirante, robô, porcas, parafusos, esteiras, almofadas, bielas, painel de controle, painel elétrico.* The tags would help with the sorting and crating at the Houston docks and, after the long boat ride, with Brazilian customs. Paper scraps scattered about the plant were pressed into service and scribbled on in Portuguese. On the back of a tag marked "BIELA

CABECOTE 01 F. D. LADO INT.," for instance, was a Budd Company card—"Paid Absence Allowance Authorization"—that there was no longer much call for. There were a bunch of these about: "Request for Shift Change," "Job Opening," "Application for Supplemental Unemployment Benefits."

Until they crashed it, the Brazilians rode into the plant in a Toyota Corolla with Illinois plates. It was replaced by a Chevy Equinox, also from the Land of Lincoln. "They were trying to do donuts again today," Eddie said on Super Bowl Sunday. "That is so amazing."

The Delga translator, Marcelo Nakayama Dias, spoke Portuguese, English, Spanish, and Japanese. He was half Japanese and had lived for five years in Japan, where he worked at a cell phone factory, and for seven years in New Zealand, where he had an ex-wife. He had some strands of gray in his thick black hair but was otherwise youthful in appearance and ironic in speech and action. Detroit, where he had spent six months of mostly winter, he found lacking in comparison to, say, Auckland. He often promised that on his last day in the Budd plant, he'd throw his clothes in the flames of the fire basket.

Marcelo carried a sixteen-gig iPhone; the white buds in his ears blasted Slayer, Megadeth, and Metallica. "I like heavy metal," he said. He smoked and seemed to believe, as did others, that cigarette smoke was the cleanest air in the plant. He showed me pictures that his second wife, pregnant, had sent to his iPhone from Brazil; the pictures detailed the progress of her bump. A former ballet dancer, she was due in August. I asked Marcelo how the bump happened, given the many months he'd been in Detroit. "I spent the whole of December there," he reminded me.

His partner, Julio, the Delga engineer who'd crashed the Corolla, wore glasses and looked scholarly. He often carried a can of spray paint or a small tube of red paint, stored near the flames to keep from freezing. He used the paint to mark the loads. Julio was forty-five and knew little English, which is why Marcelo was around.

The morning of Eddie's cold nose, two of the Fitzley truckers, Danny and RJ—no relation to the scrap company— were standing around the basket fire, warming themselves and waiting for their loads. They were both white, middle-aged, whiskered, bellied, bespectacled. RJ, a bit shorter and rounder, wore a Peterbilt hat. Danny's hat said "Caution: Does Not Play Well with Others." It was Danny who'd remarked that the plant was so cold you needed a pill to piss.

I was nearly asleep from the warmth of the fire when some asshole threw an aerosol can in the basket. It exploded, scaring the shit out of the pigeons in the plant, among others.

"You need to write a book about oversized loads," Danny said when I came to.

Both Danny and RJ were waiting on bases. The bases were oversized, which meant that they needed to be escorted. I'd seen an escort truck days before, a royal blue Dodge Ram 1500 waiting to accompany a Fitzley truck. It was from Rocking J's Pilot Car Service of Center, Texas—"You Drag It, We Flag It!"

"Not anybody can do them," Danny said of oversized loads.

"Takes a lot of common sense," RJ agreed.

"It just so happens, in Michigan, you cannot move whenever the roads are iced up or there's less than five hundred feet of visibility," Danny said. "Yesterday, we couldn't move because of the heavy snow and so many roads being iced up. So they're not in a hurry"—the rigging guys weren't—"because now we can't move until Monday."

This was RJ's second trip out of Budd. The first one "was a ram. What they call a slide. It goes up and down inside the press." It was Danny's third trip out of Budd. "I took a crown out," he said. "I was scaling 238,000 pounds." That was three weeks before. "See that piece that's sitting right there?" he asked, pointing to the crown of 2-1. "I hauled one of those. It was on one of them smaller presses. It was 135 feet long, 14 foot wide, 14 foot tall."

Based on what I saw in Budd, truckers spent the time they didn't spend trucking waiting. I said it seemed that they had some time to kill. "Little bit," RJ said, laughing. "As soon as we get through loading this one, we're going to a truck stop. Half the truck stops offer what's called the idle area. We're going to hook up to the idle area—that way we quit wasting fuel." The truck stop he preferred was in Dexter, west of Ann Arbor. "We'll be back over here Monday morning—hooked up and ready to go when our escorts get here." Their loads, once secured and measured and weighed, would remain at Budd over the weekend. "Bobtailing," RJ called the drive over to Dexter. "We're leaving the tail of the truck here.

"I've been hauling stuff out of plants that have been shut down by the automotive industry," he went on. "Not just out of Dee-troit, but out of Canada. And everything's going south, to the other countries. And I really feel for these people. This is where it all started. Right here in Dee-troit, Michigan. And if they can't keep these people going, and these plants . . ." He mentioned, though, that car prices were "*outrageously* high for a tin can."

"Part of it they brought on themselves," Danny said, "because of the unions."

"A union'll bring a company down real quick," RJ agreed. "I will never be in a union. They ain't worth a . . . flip."

"Our boss started this company eight years ago," Danny said. "Right now, he's working on a program to get us retirement benefits, insurance. But we're not union, and he won't have a driver that is union. Never happen. He'll tell you that a union will break a company in a heartbeat."

I'd heard that the crown of 16-1, which had come down six months before and had left the plant nearly a month before, hadn't gotten far. Playing a hunch, I asked Danny if he knew of its whereabouts. "They're down in Indiana and can't get a permit," he said, adding that it wasn't the only stranded heavy haul in the area. "Just outside of Toledo, Ohio, at the scales, there's a Turner nineteen-axle sitting down there, with a big load on it, and they say it's been sitting there two and a half months," Danny said. "Can't get a permit to come into Michigan. It's going into Canada."

■

I pulled in to the plant the next Saturday around 8:30, a mix of snow and rain coming down. There was no sign of Eddie, but I saw another cold nose. A Peterbilt with Texas plates sat on the scale outside Eddie's shack, getting set to haul thirty-nine thousand pounds of counterbalances and motors. The truck and trailer weighed about thirty-four thousand pounds, about thirty pounds of which belonged to a black-and-white border collie in the passenger seat. The driver said that the dog had been traveling in the truck with him for thirteen years.

Marcelo and Julio, the Delga translator and engineer, were out in the rain and snow, keeping tabs on the trucks. Nedzad was running the scale in Eddie's absence. A second Fitzley truck at the scale was being driven by an older black man hauling a couple of cushions—*almofadas*. The load was light, so he backed up into the plant for more equipment. While the rigging crew put a third cushion on the rear of his truck, Dayton Williams and I talked.

"I'm not going to haul an animal in my truck," he said about the border collie.

Dayton was six feet tall. He wore glasses, had a salt-and-pepper beard, and was missing one of his middle teeth along the bottom and most of them on top. He had been driving a truck for thirty-three years and, on this morning, was eating a McDonald's biscuit while he waited for the crew to load more equipment. His talk was mathematical, precise. He used decimal points where others approximated, and he worried about weight like a boxer.

"They try to keep the weight of the truck and the trailer, with all of the equipment, at thirty-five thousand pounds," he explained of his 379 Peterbilt, "which allows you forty-five thousand pounds to haul, because eighty thousand is the gross." Fuel weight, he said, is eight pounds to a gallon, and he could carry 250 gallons. Though he could carry two thousand pounds of fuel, he drove with less than a full tank with loads that took him close to the eighty-thousand-pound limit. "Sometimes you run low on fuel to compensate," he said.

Dayton didn't like jobs such as Budd, which meant hauling "used machinery. It's dirty, it's greasy. You gotta tarp it." I asked who told him that he had to cover the load with a tarp. Dayton pointed to Marcelo. "The directive came from thither," he said.

After the third cushion was loaded onto his trailer, Dayton asked for a broom to clean it off, getting a big laugh.

"We don't keep house around here," Guy said.

Where did Dayton come to Detroit from? "I just came from Indianapolis, Indiana," he said. "I picked up a C-315 Cat excavator. I picked it up at Fayetteville, North Carolina." He deadheaded to Detroit from Indianapolis "to pick this up and take this to Houston." He was worried about the weather—rain, sleet, ice. "You saw I put that first piece way up on the front? That's to give me traction on my drive axle, so I don't do a lot of slippin'. This is a three-axle tractor. And this is what they call a spread tandem trailer—because, if you'll notice, the axles are spread apart. They're not grouped together. And that allows you to put more weight.

"I enjoy what I do," Dayton said. "I have a great passion for transportation. I always wanted to be associated with transportation. But I'm getting tired of being gone from home." Home was Abilene, Texas; Fitzley, his employer, was in

Laredo. "I live 397 miles from my terminal," he said. "I was born and raised in Texas. I've never spent much time in Texas. I was born and raised in a little town of 951 people. And I got to get out, and I went to the military, and I wanted to be a truck driver, and my brother's a truck driver, I have a son, Charles, he's a trucker driver, I have a brother, Marcellus, he drives truck, my brother Mark, he drives truck."

Dayton had been to Budd before. "I was up here three years ago," he said, "and I hauled some stamping dies out of here. But the plant was up and running." The dies, he said, "went down to Laredo, to cross into Mexico." His voice turned serious, full of weather worry. "I hope we can get this loaded, and I can get it covered, and get out of here, before the weather gets bad again." Unlike Danny and RJ, Dayton was not a heavy hauler, and so was allowed, weather permitting, to drive on weekends.

Dayton got called away by the rigging crew to check on the load. When he came back, I was talking to Marcelo. "I have no idea," Marcelo said, in response to one of my questions.

"He doesn't speak English," I said to Dayton.

"He speaks English and smokes American cigarettes," Dayton said.

Dayton looked at the filth on the floor of the plant. "These shoes? I can forget it.

"I'll be there Monday morning," he went on, meaning Houston. "From here to Cincinnati, to the line, is 269 miles— the Kentucky line. That's five hours. That leaves me six more driving hours. To cross the state of Kentucky is three and three-quarter hours. Then I'll run two and a quarter hours across Tennessee—that's where I go to bed at tonight."

Would he really get that far tonight? "It all depends," he said. "I need to hurry up and get out of here. What time you got, boss?" he asked Marcelo.

"Ten o'clock," Marcelo said.

"Too long. Been here too long. Two hours too long. You'd like to just set it on there and just go on," he said of the press pieces, "but you can't. So, in order to, we'll just say, *appease him*"—that is, Marcelo—"we set it on there gently, then we have to tarp it. He's going to help me tarp."

"I'm not allowed to do any work," Marcelo said.

■

I saw the trucker RJ again weeks later. This time, he was taking a bolster off of 2-line. He said that the trip down to Texas three weeks before was easy. "Once I left him," he said, pointing in Marcelo's direction.

I'd spend most of that Saturday with Rafael, another Fitzley trucker. Rafael was forty-three and looked younger. He wore camouflage pants and an American flag shirt. I asked him what he was driving. "I just got me a three-axle Kenworth W900," he said. "They call me Ghost Rider on the radio when they ain't mad at me. When I first started driving, back in '85, I was hauling livestock. Had about seven or eight different loads, back-to-back, that were basically cows trying to kill me. They try to run over you. You get a couple good-sized bulls, they try to literally run over ya.

"I'd been driving maybe about a month or two, and one of my buddies saw the trouble I was having. He was listening to Johnny Cash—'Ghost Riders in the Sky.' All the guys that heard the song, they just kind of looked at me—'That's it. There's your handle.' " His buddy who was listening to Johnny Cash was named "Crazy Horse—a boy named Chris out of Pueblo, Colorado. One-legged cow hauler. Lost his left leg just below the knee in a loading chute."

I asked if Crazy Horse was Native American.

"I think he got a little Indian in him," Rafael said. "He knows I am. I'm three-quarters American Indian. I'm half Lakota Sioux and one-quarter Choctaw." I asked after the other quarter. "Irish," Rafael said. "So it dudn't matter what I do. If I drink whiskey, I'm in trouble."

This was Rafael's third time in the plant. He'd been up at Budd eight days before. "Loaded up here Friday," he said. "Went from here to Houston. Unloaded in Houston. Dead-headed to San Antonio. Picked up a coil. Went from there down to Laredo. Dropped the trailer in the yard. Grabbed a train motor. Took it to Charleston, South Carolina. Put it on a boat going to South Africa. Picked up a coil in Charleston. Took it to Valley City, Ohio. Dropped it yesterday afternoon. Came up here."

I asked what he was taking out of Budd Detroit today.

"I'm taking those two big gears with the crankshaft," he said. "I'm gonna put it in wind, brother. I'm gonna be in Houston Monday." Like Dayton, Rafael was not a heavy hauler and could drive on the weekend. I asked if he'd have to tarp this load. "I hope not," Rafael said. I asked who determined if a load needed to be covered or not. "Normally, the guy with the cleanest clothes"—he indicated Marcelo—"he's the one that'll tell you whether or not you're tarping."

Marcelo laughed.

"I hope I don't have to," Rafael went on. "I hate draggin' the rag. It's a pain in the butt. Plus, if you tear it up, you gotta get it repaired." It was just a "junk load," Rafael said, employing his term for equipment hauled "when they're emptying out a plant."

He contemplated the Kenworth with which he'd be hauling his junk load. "It's the first truck I've ever driven in twenty-two years that wasn't a Peterbilt," he said. "Ain't no feelin' like Peter-mobilin'. There's a lot of brand loyalty with drivers." He disliked Freightliners. "They call 'em Freightshakers for a reason. They'll rattle you out of the damn truck."

Though he'd once owned his own truck, he now just drove for Fitzley. "I wanna buy another one, but with fuel prices—I paid $3.53 yesterday for fuel. I paid $4.00 in California before. They gotta do something, man. Nobody'll listen to me, 'cuz I'm just a stupid truck driver. But if politicians ever'd pay attention . . .

"Sorry," he said, "I get political sometimes. I hear people talking all the time about how we need to get out of Iraq. Talk to the people that have been there. I live in a military town. I live right outside of Fort Hood, which is the largest military base in the U.S. My dad's retired military. I'm prior military. My son's a Marine, my ex-son-in-law was in the Fourth Infantry Division. My best friend was Fourth Infantry. Every one of them's been there. My dad did two tours in Vietnam." Rafael was in Grenada in 1983. "I was Air Force combat controller," he said.

Like RJ, Rafael said he'd been in closed or closing plants before. "The worst part," Rafael said, "is the guys that are working when we come in to take the equipment out look at us as being the bad guys. The union guys look at us as the bad guy. And we're just like them. We're just trying to make a living. Trying to take care of our family. I feel bad for them, but the union really priced them out of a job. I don't mean to sound cold when I say that.

"I want nothing to do with a union," he went on. "I don't want somebody regulating my life. My family relies on my paycheck entirely too much. I delivered a load one time up to General Motors, up in Ontario. Backed onto the door, sat on the door for four hours watching the forklift operator collect his paycheck—sitting there for four hours—because he was not allowed by union rules to put the dock plate in place. Now, a nonunion shop, he'd a put the dock plate in there, unloaded the truck, I'd a been out of there in half an hour. It's ridiculous."

Rafael knew the 2-line equipment from Budd Detroit was going to Brazil. "The only reason I know that is because I saw these guys"—the Brazilians—"the last time I was here. First time I was here, it was a Saturday when they loaded me. They loaded me heavy. I didn't know it, so I took off. Had to come back and have a piece taken off. Last week when I was here, they loaded a legal load. We got down to Houston, there was four of us running together"—that is, four Fitzley trucks with equipment from Detroit. "Before we got to check in, at 7:15, there was, I think, twelve Fitzley trucks there. From here.

"That's me," he said, pointing to his load.

I asked him again what it was.

"Probably a pain in my butt," he said, "because I bet you it's going to have to be tarped."

Marcelo, the guy in the cleanest clothes, laughed.

"He just laughs," Rafael said. "He ain't saying no and he ain't saying yes."

Rafael showed me his tattoos. He had an "American eagle, because of my belief in my country and my love for America and my willingness to fight and die for it." In honor of his deceased grandmother, he had a tattoo of a phoenix. "The white man calls it the fire bird," he said. "Fire, for the hell she had been through, and bird, for the freedom her spirit now has." He planned a tattoo on his back that would tell his life story. "That's gonna run into the thousands," he said. "Then, of course, my sense of humor's gotta take over. Right below my left knee, I'm gonna have a gallows, and have a rooster hung from the gallows. That way I can honestly say I've got a cock hung below my knee."

When his truck was loaded, Rafael drove it outside to the scales, where Eddie filled out the bill of lading—or, as another Fitzley trucker once called it, "something to show we ain't stolen it." Eddie figured that the gear weighed 25,000 pounds and that the four "crank rods," as Eddie called them, weighed 3,000 pounds apiece. Including truck and trailer, the total came to 68,500 pounds. It was to be shipped to Morris Export Services of Houston, Texas ("We Pack the World"), where it would be crated and stored before being shipped.

"How well does this need to be tarped?" Rafael asked Marcelo, climbing on the back of his Kenworth. The question was rhetorical. Rafael had two tarps, a black and a red one, and used both. The black tarp was covered in ice from his having unloaded in Ohio, where there was an ice storm the night before. The ice crunched as Rafael unfurled the tarp. "This is the worst part of the whole fucking deal," Rafael said. "It won't rain the whole way down to Texas now. Because I tarped it. It's going to get wetter *from* the tarp."

I shook Rafael's hand and told him I hoped to see him up here in another eight days. He said he hoped not. I asked what he had against Detroit. "It's cold, it's miserable. I want to go home and ride my motorcycle and my old lady," he said.

He thought about when he might want to return to Detroit. "Make it twelve days," he said.

IMPORT-EXPORT

It was Alex Kumai, the man in charge of Degla's Import-Export Division, who had hired Fitzlcy to truck 2-line to Houston. Alex would arrive in Detroit in early March, days after Marcelo's departure. He was handsome, slight, and delicately featured. He spoke English, Portuguese, and Spanish. His clothes were crisp and cosmopolitan; his black scarf offered small protection against the plant's cold but was worn with panache. We stood talking near the fire basket north of the press shop, but it's hard to say that we stood side by side. Though Alex was in the same plant as everyone else, he seemed to occupy a separate plane of existence.

"A crazy Japanese guy," Alex said fondly, recalling Marcelo and emphasizing the half of Marcelo's inheritance that Alex himself shared. "My great-grandparents were Japanese," he said. "I'm fourth generation in Brazil."

The 2-line presses from Budd Detroit were to be installed in a new Delga plant "under construction one hundred kilometers from São Paulo." The press pits, Alex said, had already been built. He anticipated that there'd be four press lines in the new plant; for the other three, "we may bring some new press lines from China." The four lines in the plant in progress would be stamping "a diversity of parts," Alex said. "We supply to 80 percent of the automakers that are in Brazil: Volkswagen, General Motors, Ford, Fiat, Toyota, Honda. The strongest one is Volkswagen. And Fiat. They are the leading companies."

I asked what was attractive to Delga about Budd Detroit's 2-line.

"The lead time for a new press line is about two years," Alex explained. "This line was completely ready. It had some big presses. There are not many press lines this big available for purchase" in Brazil. The presses were all Danlys, and "the price was relatively good. Around 1.5 million. The whole line, including robots, all the electronics, everything. Originally, we came here to buy a press line from another company. It was an old General Motors press line. But it was disassembled for ten or fifteen years."

Budd's 2-line, by contrast, had been stamping as recently as eighteen months before. Alex said that the line "was renewed—it was totally refurbished, the electrical parts—in 2001. They spent a lot of money doing that. Five years later, the factory shuts down. What kind of planning they had? Spent over a million dollars to refurbish those presses." The total cost to Delga, "including all the costs for logistics, for service to take it all apart, it's up to five million dollars, the whole operation.

"It's not our first press line from the U.S.," Alex went on. "Last year, we bought a press line from Eaton, in Fort Wayne, Indiana." It had stamped "clutch brackets for trucks—big clutch brackets. We bought a seven-press line from them last year. It was the same procedure, but they were smaller presses. So we didn't have to take it all apart. Just remove the motor, lay it down, put it on a skid, send it to Brazil."

The Eaton plant, unlike Budd Detroit, was not closing. "They were outsourcing that part of production," Alex said. "They didn't want to do it themselves anymore. When we moved that line from Eaton, those guys didn't like it. We were taking those presses away from the plant. The guys who were working for us said that one of the employees was fighting with them. They say, 'I'm just being paid to take it all apart. I didn't fire you.' "

Alex understood the frustrations of the Eaton workers. "They have to find someone to blame," he said. "It's man's nature." The clutch brackets that Delga was making with the press line from the Eaton plant were being exported from Brazil back to the Eaton plant, in free-trade circularity.

Alex looked around the emptying Budd plant. "It's very weird," he said. "Did you go upstairs? The office on the second floor? It looks like there was a tornado warning. Everybody stood up and ran away from the plant to protect themselves. Everything is still up there. It's like nobody moved from that place. They just abandoned the place."

The second-floor offices Alex referred to were not in Independence Hall but alongside the press shop, to its east. A large office window provided a clear view of much of the plant floor from a story above. It was the spot in the movie from which the pensive company executive would survey the activity on the floor of his struggling factory. Orders were down, profits plummeting, cash reserves kaput. The projections from the accountants—he holds their spreadsheets in his hand—are even worse. He looks down at the people, his workers, whose fates he controls. They're unsuspecting, hopeful. How can he abandon them? A scion of a once-prominent but now-declining family, he has something at stake in the plant that goes beyond the monetary: he needs to show he can make his own way in the world. He clenches his jaw and says to his secretary, "We can turn it around."

At Budd Detroit, as at Budd Gary and Budd Philadelphia, the message had been "Shut it down," or some idiomatic German equivalent. People left, and they left a lot behind, as if workers couldn't get out of the place fast enough. It was the impression produced by much of Detroit—a citywide tornado warning, with no one bothering to return at the all clear. The offices were such a mess that it appeared, moreover, as if the tornado had touched down in this very spot. Windows were broken. Partitions were tipped over. Paperwork and binders were everywhere. "Now, theoretically, all the paperwork was supposed to be put in Dumpsters," Tim Hogan, the old plant engineering manager, had told me. "I know that, at some point, an awful lot of it did end up in Dumpsters, but it also overfilled the Dumpsters and rained all over onto the ground and they threw it out of the upper-floor windows."

It was in this same suite of offices where the Mexicans from Gestamp, Salvador and David, had secured a work space the year before. The sign taped to the window of their locked office door read:

Müller/Gestamp
Restricted Area
6/19/07

After the Mexicans had left, I wanted into this office, to see what I could find. In particular, a dry-erase board with a time-line—apparently detailing the progress of parts to Aguas-calientes—had caught my eye through the glass. But the locked door was a deterrent. Eddie, surprised I was so easily discouraged, told me to break out the goddamned glass. If I didn't want to punch through it, he said, there were plenty of things I could throw through it.

I couldn't bring myself to do it. I cursed my upbringing. What if the plant came back to productive life? It could happen. What if someone bought the place, turned the power back on, turned the water back on, got a boiler going, got some presses going, and started to stamp out parts? I would have been the party responsible for breaking out a perfectly good window in a perfectly good door.

Occasionally, I read through the equipment manuals that I found in these offices. A manual for press 8-4, a Clearing, had sections titled "Bolster Conversion & Track Layout," "Bolster Piping," "Moving Bolster," "Bolster Data Tag." I read some of this, set it aside. A manual for press 3-1, another Clearing, contained a list of parts for the press's clutch assembly. The list was dated "5-29-68." Included were twenty-two gaskets, twenty-two springs, twenty-two spring retainers, sixteen friction discs, ten thrust washers, eight drive bolts, five planet gears, five planet pins, four dowels, and a flywheel, among much else. Included in this same binder was an invoice for a clutch change that had been completed, by an outside company, on March 18, 2005. Total cost: thirty-five thousand dollars. March 18, 2005—a year and change before the closing announcement. What kind of planning did they have? I read on, trying to make some sense of the workings of the press equipment, most of which had long since departed the plant. I was forever playing pointless, belated catch-up.

There were shelves of such manuals and binders, some of which had slipped or been swept to the floor. I took a few home. Others I read through during slow days in the plant. On several such binders, I removed the title tags from the sides, most of which bore a sequence of letters and numbers that identified different stampings for different makes and models. After so many months in the plant, I could now identify some. It was akin to recognizing a license plate number. U-222, off of 9-line, was the Ford Expedition roof. UN-93, off of 16-line, was a Ford Expedition body side. M-205, off of 2-line, referred to body stampings for the Thunderbird, which Ford had brought back in 2002. I liked knowing that the roof for the Ford Econoline van had come off of 1-line and that a stamping for its door had come off of 4-line. I was sure that at some point there'd be a quiz. Which line had stamped the Ford Ranger roof? (Answer: 9-line.) It was like remembering the date of the signing of the Magna Carta—useless information, of no interest whatsoever, and yet for some reason I cherished my ability to remember it. I saw Ford Thunderbirds, Ford Expeditions, Ford Rangers, and Ford Econoline vans on the roads daily, and being able to identify which parts came from which press lines in the Budd plant made me feel as if I understood some small part of the planet's workings. That the plant had closed didn't undercut such knowledge; there was a lesson in that, too.

"Do you know what they're going to build here?" Alex asked me as we stood near the fire basket.

I told him, as far as I knew, nothing. The plant's production days were behind it, which was why he was here.

"What a waste," Alex said. "You know something that I feel about the U.S.? The U.S. is becoming a licensing country. You're not producing anything. You're just importing and licensing. That's why all the plants are shutting down, people are getting fired. It's like a service country. It's not a production society anymore. For example, Chrysler was outsourcing their production. One of the market studies they were doing was in Brazil. The other one was in Mexico. Because they would like to outsource a lot of parts from here to those low-cost countries. Everybody's doing that." He said that the guys from the rigging company "told me that all the press lines they sold, none of them was to an American company."

This was true, and not Alex's problem. Rather, it was the proximate cause of his employment. "I hired a freight forwarder to take it from Houston to Santos port in Brazil," Alex explained. He was headed to Houston in the coming days to visit the crating company. "There are some identification labels that were in Portuguese, so I have to go down there and translate that into English," he said.

The ship would take thirty days to get from Houston to Brazil. Then, he said, a "couple weeks for customs clearance in Brazil, and a few more times to truck it to our plant for storage. It's such a long process."

A dirty one, too. Alex said that Marcelo, as promised, had made a bonfire of his clothes before leaving the Budd plant on his last day. As Alex said this, he looked down.

"I have to throw away these boots," he said.

CHAPTER 5

. . .

Picking
the Carcass

THE BUDD JOB's final phase—with the Delga guys back in Brazil and the Fitzley truckers back home in the heart of Texas—was essentially a salvage operation. The final five weeks went by in a blur. By this point, there wasn't much left for me to learn about the process of an auto plant closing down and coming apart. What I didn't yet know—a considerable category—I never would.

What sent me back to Budd, again and again, was a wish to live deliberately. This sounds absurd—a cabin in Concord Budd was not. But I'm a product of my environment, and a Detroit auto plant would be my Walden Pond. Of course, I wasn't alone there. Though there weren't the thousands in the plant that there'd been at its peak, there were still days when a dozen, two dozen, a half-dozen guys were still around. But Budd was time away from the day-to-day. I don't own a cell phone. I carried no computer. There was no cable, no Internet. Outside of Eddie's shack, there was no television. The sight of the day's newspaper in the plant—a rare occurrence—seemed a gross technological intrusion. There was nothing to focus on except for what was in front of me, which was the city of my birth in microcosm: a lot of space, inhabited by a scattering of people who were, in a sense, the last of their kind.

What follows is some of what I heard and saw during some of those final days.

By the first full day of spring—Good Friday—there were five weeks of rigging work to go. The winter the crew had worked through had been among the coldest on record and, no matter what the calendar said, it wasn't quite done. It was thirty degrees outside, which converted to low teens in the plant. When I pulled in, a quiet kid on the crew who wore glasses and drove a rusted Dodge Ram was at the leaking fire hydrant along Charlevoix, filling extinguishers.

I entered the plant and stood by Nedzad, whose task that day was to take apart a Clearing tryout press. He stared at a toolbox in disgust.

"People take, they no bring back," he said. "No sockets. Sockets lost."

"Did you do this kind of work in Bosnia?" I asked.

"Maybe. Maybe not. I'm here."

I pointed to the two presses, 1-1 and 1-2, that were still standing in 1-line.

"Canadian guys?" Nedzad shrugged—his opinion of their performance.

The newest additions to the closed plant's cast of characters, the Canadians, as everyone called them, were presumably Americans, in the employ of a Detroit-area machine moving company. The Canadians were taking out 1-1 and 1-2, the two biggest presses in the plant—and, as Ray Dishman had told me sixteen months before, two of the biggest presses in the state. The Canadians had added their Ford F-250 to the collection of trucks parked outside the press shop bay door. Eddie had said that the rigging crew needed to be out by April 15 and that the boss was bringing in reinforcements. He also said the Canadians were making his life difficult.

"They wander," Eddie said. "There's no reason for them to leave 1-line."

I asked Guy if they were any good.

"They're slow as shit," Guy said. "I think they're union."

Nedzad, still at the toolbox, was waiting for the lift. The crown of 9-1 was on stands north of the line; the crane couldn't budge it. Nedzad told me that he needed the lift to get on top of the Clearing tryout press. His job was to "take out pump, motor, pipes—everythings."

We watched as a big pile of wood chips was dumped into a pool of grease and ice above 8-line, to provide the forklifts and floor cranes traction. "Is nice," Nedzad said of the wood chips. "No grease." Never had "no grease" looked more like the beaches of Alaska after a spill.

When the lift at last came free, Nedzad and I went up in its basket to the top of the Clearing. While we were a couple stories above the shop floor, he discussed his status. "I am legal," he said. He had a green card, but was still not a full citizen. His daughter was sixteen months old when they came over. The family lived in Sterling Heights, making Nedzad an East Sider on a crew composed mostly of West Side and Downriver guys. I asked him if they'd lived anywhere else in Detroit.

It was as if I'd asked the question on behalf of Immigration and Customs Enforcement. "I stay," he said. What he meant by this—stay in the plant? the state? the country?—I couldn't be sure.

When I returned to earth, I talked to Uli, the German from Müller Weingarten. Sergeant Schultz was taking pictures of the crown of 9-1, still on the stands and refusing to budge. Uli said that he was going back to his home outside Mexico City. "I make my pictures," he said. "My reports. There is nothing for me here." We shook hands and said so long.

Uli wasn't the only one leaving Detroit. I went to warm myself by the fire basket and sat next to a crew member about to depart for Iowa and Maytag. "I'll be glad to get out of this place," he said. "Breathing in all that smoke and shit."

I put my feet on the basket to warm my toes and in no time had roasted the rubber bottoms of my boots. They bubbled and smoked before I noticed. When I stood to walk, it felt as if I were walking on marshmallows.

Guy came over. "See that guy in the yellow hard hat?" he said, pointing to a new crew member helping Nedzad with the Clearing press. Guy said that the fellow was working for free, since Guy couldn't hire him without talking to the boss. The man had licenses for lift, gantry, hazardous materials, overhead crane, and confined space, Guy said. He was willing to go to Iowa tomorrow and wasn't worried about Easter. He'd been out of work for six months and was desperate. "I told him this morning he might as well sit," Guy said, "because I might not have a job for him. He said he'd rather work."

Eddie, who sat on his fire truck, felt low. His new house had been robbed. "They got cameras, some cologne, my wife's jewelry," he said. "I had ten thousand dollars' worth of guitars they didn't touch. Probably have twenty thousand dollars of musical equipment, all in all." He paused. "I'm gonna get a burger at Joseph's," he said. "They got good burgers."

■

We ate in Eddie's shack with the TV on. The local news at noon—local news anytime—depresses me profoundly. Investigators say that the four-year-old boy's ear was mangled by the family pit bull . . . According to Detroit police, a six-year-old girl found her mother's boyfriend's handgun . . . The fire chief says that the family was using the burners on their stove for wintertime heat . . .

I resented even the scant good news from outside when I was at Budd. I'd sometimes forget what day it was, even what I was doing there. I was simply hanging out at an empty, two-million-square-foot auto plant that sat on eighty-six empty acres in the center of the city of Detroit—how better to pass the time?

Guy joined us to eat his Coney Dog. Eddie told him that on his way back from Joseph's, he'd driven behind a Dodge Ram with a bumper sticker that said "This Ram Eats Chevys and Shits Fords."

"It should have said, 'Eats Nissans and Shits Toyotas,' " Guy said.

"Exactly," Eddie said. "Why shit on your union brothers?"

Eddie turned on a soap opera.

"Come *on*," I said.

"I like looking at the pretty women."

That he did. Months before, he'd paused at a noontime

news segment on a Miss Michigan from Farmington Hills in the running for Miss America. "Maybe she'll want to go out with me," Eddie said. "I'm working security at Budd, making decent money."

Eddie pulled out his binoculars and spied crew members coming back from lunch. When he put the binoculars back down, he returned to the robbery. "Five thousand dollars' worth of stuff," he said. He'd recover half of that, he said, from State Farm. "I get a new door on Monday. Contractor's coming out. You work your whole life, dream of building a new house, and then this. I stare at the footprints of him coming through the field, and I think about it. I think what could cause someone to do that."

A scrap truck came by, the first in a while. Most recent trucks had been hauling press pieces, not scrap loads. This load was odds and ends, nothing you'd notice if it were sitting on the floor of the shop. It weighed seventy-three thousand pounds. "Going to the yard in Battle Creek," the big-bellied driver told Eddie as Eddie did the bill of lading.

Eddie watched the truck pull away through the shack window. "Boy, that's one ugly load," he said.

■

There was six new inches of snow on Holy Saturday. I got to the plant at 9:00. Eddie was sleeping in the shack with the *Today* show on. Only Nedzad, the Canadians, and a couple of the Arkansas Boys were in the plant. The local weatherman, on TV, said that this was the fifth-snowiest Detroit winter on record. Cities and municipalities were running out of road salt. As I was driving down Charlevoix on my way into the plant, a salt truck going the opposite direction—which is to say, the wrong way, since Charlevoix is a one-way street—dumped a bluish concoction that looked like frozen pellets of windshield-wiper fluid onto the road and my car.

It was the Easter weekend, perhaps, that turned Eddie's thoughts heavenward when he awoke. "God loves all souls the same," he said sleepily. "Your kids, my kids, the lowliest bum on Charlevoix Avenue." He smiled at the mystery. "That's hard for the carnal mind to understand."

We left the shack, and Eddie got in his fire truck. "Get in my Cadillac," he said. I climbed in. "Got my thermals on today," he said with a smile. "It's a good day."

We toured the plant, eventually stopping next to Jerry, a black guy from MCM Management, the demolition company taking down Tiger Stadium and several auto plants in the state. Jerry had been hanging out at the Budd plant, for reasons obscure to me, since the fire in December. We had a balanced relationship: he hadn't much of a clue why I was in the plant, either. "So, you're working on a book?" he said one day, after several months of seeing me take notes. He was warming himself at the fire basket between 8- and 9-lines, and I asked after the Arkansas Boys.

"Mark that I'm an Arkansas Boy, too," Jerry said. "From Stamps, Arkansas. I grew up next to Maya Angelou's grand-dad. You see that movie, *I Know Why the Caged Bird Sings*? That was filmed in my county—Lafayette County, Arkansas." He smoked what I thought were expensive cigarettes but were, instead, small cigars—Black & Milds. "Made out of pipe tobacco," he said. "Ain't but fifty cent."

"How long have you been in Detroit?" I asked.

"Thirty years, but my friends up here still call me Country."

Days later, I asked him where he was going after Budd. "Don't know," he said. "Want to knock this place down. They say GM was in here the other day, looking at the place."

I asked why GM would be interested.

"Especially when you got Chrysler there" (he pointed to the Jefferson North Assembly Plant) "and there" (he pointed to Mack Avenue Engine).

"GM's cutting shifts and closing plants," I said.

"We're knocking down two GM plants," Jerry said, "in Lansing and Grand Blanc."

I said that the story I'd heard was that the property owner wanted the land to store shipping containers.

"You know how that shit goes," Jerry said. "That's one day. Next day, it's a missile site."

■

The days blended together. I talked to anyone and everyone, wrote page after page in my notebooks, and came up with no observation close to "As if you could kill time without injuring eternity."

It snowed three or four more inches on March 27. Such springtime precipitation felt like a betrayal, given the length of the winter just endured. Transportation around the plant was becoming a problem. The driveway into the plant had become brutal, pocked with potholes. You couldn't see them, covered as they were with ice and snow, so you weaved this way and that, following intuition and failing memory, hoping to avoid a land mine.

Eddie had blown a rim on the driver's side rear of the fire truck. The Gator had been up on three wheels in front of the shack. The golf cart wasn't holding its charge. All of which put Eddie in a bad mood. When I asked after some kittens he'd seen in the plant, Eddie said, "They're hanging up outside the shack." When I asked him what was going to happen to his shack when the job was done, he said, "I'm going to shoot it. I'm going to shoot it up."

I walked into the plant and met up with Guy at the fire basket, from which perch he scanned the press shop floor. "Now it's all open," Guy said. This was true: presses had disappeared, providing clear views. "Now I can see who's working, and who ain't. Before, I had to walk around."

Eddie joined us on the Gator, which he'd got going. "This place gave me a good living," he said, looking around.

"Ford let me buy a brand-new truck every year," Guy said.

Eddie and I took the Gator out to the hole in the fence underneath the Mack Avenue bridge. Eddie, as part of his security work, occasionally covered the hole with scrap to deter trespassers and thieves. When we arrived, we saw that the scrap was gone.

"They did us a favor," Eddie said. There wasn't much time left, so what was the difference? "They cleaned up a lot of that scrap metal."

Even better, the crooks had left behind a ladder, which Eddie took for his new house. He put it in the back of the Gator, and then in the back of his truck, thanking the men who had left it as he did.

He got on the phone to Dave Scarlin. "Did you notice that the fence is gone? Back there at Conner Lane? Them dagos had a helluva time loading up all of that scrap steel."

Eddie said this with a wink. The area's demographics argued strongly against the crooks' being Italian. He was out to get Dave's goat.

By 11:00, we were back at the shack, our morning security tour done. Eddie was tired. "Damn," he said. "I've done too much work today. Now I got to decide what to do with that fence."

I asked when Dave was coming in. Eddie called him up again to find out.

"He says he doesn't know," Eddie said to me, Dave on the other end of the line. "How's that for a retirement mentality? I got a breach in security, and my ace guard, who I've known for thirty-one years, tells me he doesn't know. Can't have that shit"—fence cutting along Conner Lane—"on second shift. Them dagos, they worked they butts off. They'll come in further next time."

■

"I needed someone with common sense," Guy said a week later, explaining the hire of his brother, Eddie Yee, who was working a hi-lo his first day on the crew. The original date of the crew's departure—April 15—was closing in. "I got a court date next week," Guy said. "Code violation on the house. Need someone here I can trust."

Eddie Yee was actually Guy's stepbrother, half Chinese and half Cherokee, though they resembled each other despite not sharing a blood bond. He'd been laid off from his trucking job at Hare Freight. "Our biggest jobs were American Axle, General Motors, and Delphi," Eddie Yee said. American Axle was on strike at the moment. GM, as a result of said strike, had dozens of plants with production problems. And Delphi had been in bankruptcy for years. "Five more GM plants want to strike," Eddie Yee said. "They fucking nuts?" He looked around the Budd plant. "I used to deliver milk here for the cafeteria," he said. "Borden's. The place was filled with people then. That was twelve years ago now."

More and more of the plant was in darkness, as fewer floodlights were needed for fewer workers taking apart fewer presses. Only two fire baskets were going, as the areas where workers worked dwindled. Pipes continued to burst. Paint flakes the size of construction paper floated down from above. The pits, when not pumped out, looked full of oil, though this was largely an illusion. Since oil floats, the pits were mostly water, with an oily film on top.

Eddie and Dave arrived at the plant at 9:00, about ten minutes after me. Dave, who'd been away in Iowa, said that he'd been forced to fire on a guy his first day back.

"I could have killed him," Dave said.

"I bounced a BB off his ass," Eddie said.

■

The next day, a sunny Saturday, temperatures would hit the fifties. I arrived in the morning to find Eddie at the scale weighing a truck taking the eccentric gears from the crown of 9-1. "Ain't it nice?" Eddie said of the warming weather. "You can leave the shack door open, get a breeze coming in, take a piss without freezin' your little wanger. Shit, it's just gorgeous. I haven't been in the plant in a while. I've been out here, milking the cow." He pointed to the mess on the floor of the shack. "Afternoon shift, it's like the broom don't fit their hand. Pop bottles. Candy wrappers. Things is gotta change around here."

We took the fire truck into the plant. There were Dumpsters about, and Eddie said that the boss wanted them filled. "Scrap's high! Scrap's high!" Eddie said, quoting the boss. He himself needed no reminders. "Tell me about it," he said. "They're stealing it out back." Two robots bought at the auction ten months before and never picked up were upended in one of the Dumpsters.

We drove alongside Dave as he walked out of the press shop. Eddie said that he had used a 9-millimeter to shoot at the guys yesterday afternoon. "Damn dagos," he said.

"That truck had Tennessee plates," Dave said, attempting, in turn, to insult the Southerner in Eddie. Returning to the actuality of what happened, he said, seriously, "Can you imagine shooting one on MLK day?" The day before had marked the fortieth anniversary of the assassination of the Reverend Dr. Martin Luther King Jr.

"All them wreaths," Eddie said. "I need to get back to church. I been bad. Yesterday, I wanted to kill someone."

∎

I left the plant not long thereafter, returning in the late afternoon to watch the gantry lift of the crown of press 1-2. The Arkansas Boys, with Arkansas Dave controlling the gantry from north of the press, were leading the crew, as the Canadians had left over some disagreement. Eddie, Dave, and Guy were observing from the south, by Dock #5, where I joined them.

It was eight months to the day—August 5 to April 5—that I had watched the crown of 16-1, the first disassembled Budd press, be lowered by Jeff Jinerson and Matt Sanders. "Look how fast the Arkansas Boys got this gantry set up," Eddie said. "They had to re-level everything today, right from scratch, and they got that crown up." He was drawing a distinction between the Razorbacks' speed and the Canadians' slowness. Eddie said the crown weighed about 250,000 pounds.

It had taken about five hours to set up the gantry and to measure. It took a few minutes to lift up the crown; a minute or two more to slide the crown out on the rails, so that it was clear of the columns; and a few more minutes to slowly lower it onto blocks.

"That's coming down straight as an arrow," Eddie said.

∎

I took a few days off from the plant, prompting this message on my machine: "Hi, Paul. This is Eddie at the plant. I just wanted to let you know things are really kind of picking up and we got a crew, they're cleaning it. Looks like it's getting close. We gotta try to be here 24/7, so if you wanna take some captures of what's going on here, we'll see you when you come down. All right. And that big press may be coming down tomorrow, or the next day. Just wanted to let you know. All right, buddy. Take care. Bye."

I called him back a couple of hours later. Eddie told me that I was "missing all the fun," and said that they were guarding the plant around the clock now. They'd gotten three guys the other night.

"We ran 'em off," Eddie said.

■

The next day, I arrived at the plant at 1:00 and parked next to Eddie's truck. A group of guys I'd never seen before— the cleanup crew Eddie had referred to on the phone—was eating lunch outside.

Eddie told me that the rigging crew had a week's extension, to April 22. "That's April 22, 2009!" he said, wishing. He'd received this bit of news from the boss, who'd been by in the morning. "Our butts are sore," Eddie said of the visit. "He walked us all over the plant. Walked, kicked. Kicked, walked."

A new addition to the press shop floor was an enormous red Laramie floor crane, rented by the rigging company— "costs a hundred dollars an hour," Guy said—to help get down the overhead cranes in the bays above the press lines. It was held in place by four braces that popped out onto the floor.

It was then that I heard the story that Eddie had alluded to on the phone. Two days before, Dave and Eddie caught three guys trying to steal racks from under the Mack Avenue over-pass. The attempted scrap thieves had a truck—a Ford Ranger, Dave said, with a fifteen-day plate in the back window—along with a landscaping trailer to haul the racks away in. Dave and Eddie got them down on their knees with their hands behind their heads. Two of the guys had gotten inside the gate when they caught them; one was still just outside. One of the guys had an arrest warrant, Dave said, and pleaded with them not to call the cops.

"They were shitting their pants," Guy said. "One guy asked me for a job. Said, 'Hey, you guys hiring?' I told him to write down his info. He did! We got his name, phone number, where he lives." Guy also got the trailer, for the reasonable sum of not calling the cops, plus $150 cash.

■

A month earlier, Eddie hadn't been feeling well and had taken "a big capful" of cold medicine before coming into the plant. The medication had made him drowsy. As we sat in the shack, he closed his eyes and told me to keep watch. A minute or two later, I informed Eddie that a guy in a red truck was pulling in to the plant. I'd seen the truck before, but was unsure whom it belonged to. "That's just Smitty," Eddie said, eyes still closed. Smitty, he told me, had bought a boring mill at the auction, back in June, and still didn't have it out, nine months later.

"He never wants any help," Eddie said, "but he's gonna need a hi-lo."

Smitty was sixty-six and handsome, with a shock of white hair. When we first spoke, a month later, he wore a plaid flannel shirt, blue jeans, steel-toed boots with the steel showing through, and three layers of sweater—one gray, one brown, and one light green. He was standing over the base of the Giddings & Lewis boring mill he'd bought at the auction for fifteen thousand dollars. Though the boring mill was now gone, its base still hadn't budged. Smitty's red Ford Ranger XLT was parked nearby, a couple of toolboxes in the back.

"Ten months?" I asked, referencing the glacial pace of removal since the auction.

"How hard you see me work today?"

Smitty owned a machine shop in Livonia named ESK, which he said stood for Earl Smith Kellering. "We machine dies for the tool-and-die trade of North America," he said. It had been his dad's shop, started by his father in 1949 or 1950. "I grew up in a shop," he said. "The computer killed old-style machining. It's the evolution of production."

A couple of RJ torch men were half a football field away in the darkness, cutting up an overhead crane that still remained intact. The sparks from the torches made it look like the night of the Fourth of July. Smitty told me that RJ Torching was cutting up the GM Guide Lamp plant in Anderson, Indiana, too. He knew this because his son, Daniel, was down in Indiana, doing the cutting. He pointed to the left rear taillight of his Ford Ranger as an example of the kind of thing that the plant had made. "We're being killed by free trade," he said. "It can go to China. How many of these things can you put in a shipping container?" He ran his hand over his brake light.

One of the RJ torch men walked over and asked us what we were up to.

Smitty stared down at the boring mill's base, secure in the floor. "We're waiting for it to levitate," he said.

In the dark, with flames nearby, it felt as if we were around a campfire. "One of my son's wife's girlfriends, her and her husband worked at Dana, outside of Reading, Pennsylvania," Smitty said. "The plant stamped truck frames. They got laid off five years ago." He said his son's brother-in-law worked at a Chevy truck plant in Flint. "At the Christmas party," Smitty said, "they told him the plant would be shut down in six months." He contemplated this. "How are twelve- to fourteen-dollar-an-hour workers going to afford the forty-thousand-dollar trucks they build? They'll buy a Kia instead."

"There was an auction in Northville a couple of months ago," Smitty went on. "A guy from India bought two Japanese boring mills. He was crating it up and shipping it to India."

I was wearing shoes, not boots, and my feet were beginning to freeze from the cold coming up from the plant floor. Smitty grabbed a piece of cardboard and told me to stand on it. "All new machinery is manufactured with used machinery," he said. "Think about that. This"—he pointed to the boring mill's base—"is the last machine tool in this shop." He looked around the nearly empty plant. "Hundreds, thousands of industrial buildings are for sale in metro Detroit," he said. "What does that tell you about the future of the middle class?"

To whom was he going to leave the shop that his father had left to him? Smitty looked over at the sparks, where RJ was cutting scrap in the dark, and nodded.

Later, when I'd flip through old copies of *The Directory of*

Michigan Manufacturers at the Detroit Public Library, I'd find Smitty's shop. "Location: W. 8 Mile Rd. Est.: 1942. Square Ft.: 1,500. Annual Sales (as of 1995): $1,100,000. Machinery & Eqpt., Ind'l., Comm'l." Though its birth and existence were tracked in *The Directory of Michigan Manufacturers*—the 1961 directory listed it as Smith, Earl, Kellering—its obituary would never appear in *Plant Closing News*. The employer of under a dozen and the size of a small house, it would fly below Jon Clark's closing radar. And yet it was shops such as Smitty's that formed Detroit's middle-class foundation. When I was growing up, it seemed that all of my father's friends had a shop, places where he sometimes worked, with these little shops dependent on the bigger shops, and the bigger shops dependent on suppliers like Budd, and suppliers like Budd dependent on the big carmakers. If you ever want to see this relationship distilled to its essence, drive up Mound Road into Macomb County. Surrounding the GM and Chrysler plants, like satellite fish, are countless machine shops, tool-and-die shops, and union halls. The sight stretches on for mile after mile, a working-class wonderland with an uncertain future.

Smitty seemed more certain of what the future held. "After we ship the equipment to the scrap yard," he said, "and use the money to buy beer, and drink the beer and return the bottle, we'll see what we've got left."

■

Eddie was drinking gas station coffee from a Citgo cup when I arrived at 10:00 three days later. He grimaced, saying he was injured.

"Pulled an ass muscle," he said. "Here. Feel."

Nedzad was on a Yale hi-lo, loading an Ingersoll Rand compressor and some crates onto a truck. Eddie, speaking to Arkansas Dave, pointed to the plant's largest press, the first in 1-line, which was the last still standing. All of the other presses had either been scrapped, trucked, crated, stored, shipped, or some combination of the above. They were, or would be, in India, Mexico, Brazil.

"If you guys had been taking it down," Eddie said of the press, "it'd be down already."

"I don't give a fuck who takes it down," Arkansas Dave said, "as long as it comes down."

The Clearing presses in 8-line, Guy told me, were China-bound from the Camden port. One of the truckers from Huff Contractors Inc., the firm hauling the 8-line presses, said he was headed to Philadelphia. It was a small distinction: the two ports sit on opposite sides of the Delaware River. I could never verify this sale to China, beyond what Guy and the trucker told me—people in the plant-closing business are tight-lipped—but I noticed, going through my pictures long after, that a Clearing 8-line press was spray painted "JD." Wondering what "JD" might stand for, I came upon an entry in the May 1, 2007, *Plant Closing News:* "Changes in the manufacturing industry have driven a Muncie, Indiana tool and die business to close its doors. City Machine Tool & Die, founded in 1935, closed in mid April. Much of the company's work for farm equipment giant John Deere was lost to a plant in China."

At lunch, I drove a mile and went by the building that had housed the old Budd local, UAW Local 306. Though Ray

Dishman's Crown Vic had been gone for over a year, cars still filled its parking lot. People were going in and out, and a barbecue was set up out front in a fifty-five-gallon drum. A cook made preparations. Buns, hot dogs, and bratwurst had been set out in anticipation of a lunch crowd.

I parked, walked up, and asked an older woman, who seemed authoritative, if she was the owner. She said no. Just then, the husband and wife who owned the place walked out.

The woman, who had a kind face, gave me a smile. I explained myself as best I could, and said that I'd been told that the old union local had become a tax service. As it was April, I thought that the service might be busy and open on weekends. The man, who introduced himself as Mr. Hill, said that the building had indeed housed a tax service, but only briefly. He was wearing a gold EEOC pin. He said that he bought the building from the previous owners, a Budd couple who'd bought it from the local to set up their business. Mr. Hill said that he was working to empower people "like this gentleman here"—he meant the cook. A "BBQ" sign leaned up against the building's wall.

I realized that the man before me was Mr. Hill of Hill's EEOC next door. I asked if he was moving into the old Budd local. "No," he said. "Expanding. I'll buy the whole block. Come back later and I'll give you a tour." I told him I would.

I got back to Budd a bit after noon and told Eddie where I'd gone. He said that he went back a ways with Bob and Mary Turner, the black couple who'd bought the Local 306 building and turned it into their tax service. "His dad, Jesse Turner, was supervisor in Department 306. My dad was an hourly worker in 306, and me and Bob called each other 'cuz.' He won a lawsuit against ThyssenKrupp for discrimination. They sent him from purchasing down to 306 and put a young white lady in his place." Eddie said that he once sent a guy to see his "cousin" in purchasing. The guy wandered around for half an hour, expecting to see a white man.

I asked Eddie if he wanted to go to Local 306 for lunch and get some barbecue.

"You have no idea what kinds of chemicals were in there," Eddie said, meaning the fifty-five-gallon cooking drum, "nor how well they cleaned it." This seemed a minor concern, coming from a man who'd just spent a winter in a plant where oil drums burned noxious wood around the clock, but I said nothing.

I left at 1:30, just as Smitty walked in. That morning, I'd walked over into the dark to the west of the press shop to inspect the base of his boring mill. It was still there, but it had chains around it, in preparation for its being pulled up.

"We're looking at the end of something," Smitty said, looking around.

■

It was snowing again the next day, a Sunday, with temperatures back down in the thirties. The yard outside was filling up with scrap from the plant. Inside, it was January again.

Arkansas Dave, sitting around the basket fire, wanted to go home. He yelled encouragements to the Canadians, who were lifting the crown of 1-1. "Get 'er down! Milk that motherfucker!" The Canadians, like Jeff and Matt eight months before, used tape measures when doing gantry work. The crown, Dave told me, weighed between 380,000 and 400,000 pounds; the press as a whole weighed about a million.

Arkansas Terry joined Arkansas Dave and me around the fire. He said they'd have the crane above 16-line down by lunch. "Hope so," he said. "Gotta go warsh clothes. When I'm done here, I'll throw them in the fire, but till then I gotta warsh 'em." There was a ripped flap dangling from the back of his Machines International jacket. "Is it still snowin'?" Terry senior asked. He took a look outside. "Sheeyit. Arkansas, it's seventy." He went back to help the boys among the Arkansas Boys with the crane in the bay above 16-line.

Dave was sick of it all. He had memorized what he called "a little praise I picked up," which for him summed up the plight of the itinerant rigger: "We the willing, led by the unknowing, are doing the impossible for the ungrateful. We have done so much with so little for so long, we are now qualified to do anything with nothing." Dave sought poetic comfort when faced with malfunctioning cranes, fuel shortages, generalized incompetence, and Germans. He quoted, word perfect, Hamlet's fourth soliloquy. At present, Dave seemed to prefer not to be. He had made a fifty-dollar bet that the Canadians wouldn't get the crown down today. "I'm surprised they got it down this morning," he said. "I figured it'd be next Wednesday at the rate they were going."

Terry senior walked back to the basket to warm himself. "Gonna have that sumbitch down?" Dave asked him. He was talking of the overhead crane.

"Yeah, maybe," Terry senior said.

"Tie the sumbitch *on!*" Dave yelled up to Josh, who was working on the crane from the basket of the lift. "You look like the goddamned Canadians!"

■

Eddie was behind the wheel of his white Pontiac Vibe when I arrived a couple days later. The car idled in the sun by the plant's old powerhouse, a football field away from where Eddie usually parked, near his shack.

"Don't want to drive back there," Eddie said, motioning to the press shop, and the shack, and the scale—the spots where he'd spent the last year of his life. "Too much metal."

There were sharp bits of this and that everywhere, as the cleanup crew continued to drag junk from inside the plant outside it. I drove through it and parked where I always did. I walked down to Eddie's car and said that the metal had been cleared. He drove back, warily, and parked his Vibe on the scale alongside his shack. When he got out, he saw two screws nearby.

"See, that's why I don't want to come in here no more!" he said. "Four hundred dollars' worth of tires I just put on that car!"

Eddie and I went into his shack. "I don't want to go in the plant and breathe all that smoke," he said. There was more smoke than usual, from all the cutting going on. Eddie's not wanting to do anything he'd done every day for the last twelve months gave things an end-of-the-school-year feel. "It's better than that," Eddie said. "At the end of the school year, you know you're coming back. Here, we know we're not."

For reasons I couldn't fully have explained at the time, I was hurt to hear Eddie say this. He didn't want to come in to the Budd plant anymore? Why not? Not long before, he'd joked—had half-hoped—that the extension the rigging crew received was for another year. Why the change of heart? I'd gotten so used to seeing Eddie, and Guy, and Dave, and Nedzad, and the Arkansas Boys, and the old Budd plant itself, that I'd begun to miss it all before it was even over.

It occurred to me later, as I started to sort through the notes I'd compiled—as I read, over and over, my journal of that plague year—that I didn't want to write this book at all. What I wanted to do was to "research" it for as long as my entry pass would allow. It pleased me in a way I felt in my bones to be able to say, "I gotta go to the plant." I had work to do there, even if it was just to observe the work that others were doing, work that needed doing since the plant's productive work had ceased. People expected me at the plant; they called my house when something important happened, or when I stayed away for more than a couple days. The plant was real to me, and, apparently, I was real to the people in it. Not to go to it anymore meant that one of my connections to actuality was being cut.

Still, I understood why Eddie was sick of it. As we sat in the shack, he told me that with the weather getting warmer, gunshots had become much more common. "They've been firing like crazy around here," he said. He told me that Dave, who'd worked the midnight shift, "thought they were firing *at* him. They might have been." The summer before, Eddie said that he'd been "pinned down," and had taken cover behind the skimmer pit. He opened the desk drawer and pulled out a bullet.

"Picked that up from the driveway," he said, admiring the bullet. "If that'd hit ya, that'd hurt ya."

I went into the plant and saw Smitty standing by the basket fire. It was still cold inside, despite the sixty-degree temperature outside. Smitty had gotten the base of his boring mill out a couple days before with the help of Guy's son-in-law, who used the red Hyster to complete a job ten months in the making. Smitty and I stood and watched the crew members cutting down power lines. It was difficult, in spots, to see through all the smoke.

"The vultures are picking the carcass," Smitty said. "Do you know scrap merchants are the only ones working overtime in industrial America? Think about that."

■

It was a Friday, the final payday, when I saw Eddie for the last time. "These guys have been rough on me the last year," he said. "I feel like I've worked another thirty years."

We'd left the press shop's smoke and noise and walked out to his shack, where it was even louder. An orange Hitachi backhoe on steel runners was dumping scrap steel into a container.

"See," Eddie said, "I wish they'd cut that shit out. I try to nap on my break."

Eddie said that Nedzad and the Arkansas Boys had worked on the ram of 1-1, which was going out on a truck. "Tomorrow," he said, "they'll ship the base and columns."

Guy walked into the shack. He was wearing a black bandanna covered in jalapeño peppers. "Mama wants a vacation," he said of his wife. "Vegas." Guy looked as if he needed a shower, shave, and sixteen consecutive hours of sleep. A beard was filling in around his Fu Manchu.

"Vacation here," Eddie said. "We got a TV, a shack, sunshine, a nice big plant to wander around in. A map of it on the wall, so you know where you're going."

By 3:00, guys had begun to head home. Before leaving, they dropped off tools at the shack to be locked up overnight. An older worker brought out an orange circular saw for safekeeping. With so many new workers around, there was a concern about tools walking. He had been using the saw to cut copper lines. There was talk, too, of precious metals disappearing.

"You need to walk through a metal detector," Guy said.

"I know," he said. "I might have some copper chips on me. A bit of dust."

"You need to work harder tomorrow," Guy said. "I saw you with that saw on half speed."

"If bullshit were gold, you'd be a rich man."

Nedzad brought back a couple of torches, carrying them to the shack over his shoulder like golf clubs. I told Nedzad it might be my last day; we shook hands. Guy told Nedzad not to listen, that I'd be in again—what with guys quitting, he needed me to work on the columns of 1-1.

By a quarter after three Guy and Eddie had started to fall asleep, leaning back in the shack's busted chairs.

"Paul, you're in charge," Eddie said, shutting his eyes.

As they snored, I watched through the shack's open door as the backhoe continued its work. It scooped into its basket carts, containers, lockers, racks, piping, shelving units, and a section of conveyor from beneath a press, dumping all of it in the large scrap container. Somewhere in that pile was a Ford Explorer door that Eddie and I had seen the day before.

Despite the skill of the operator, there were awkward pieces he couldn't pick up off the concrete. Such pieces he smashed, in the hope of making their shapes manageable. Once a sufficient amount of junk was in the container, the operator closed the backhoe basket and punched the junk down, making room for more. When it was full, the container was loaded onto an Upco Waste Service truck and driven away.

Fifteen minutes after he fell asleep, Guy's phone rang. He didn't stir. Five minutes later, it rang again. Neither he nor Eddie moved.

■

The crew's last full day was April 24. I arrived a bit before one o'clock and parked next to Nedzad's Chevy Caprice, as I'd done several days consecutive. The scale was no longer sitting beside Eddie's shack. It now sat in three large sections on a running semi, set to be hauled away. Outside, it was sunny and in the high sixties. Inside the plant, where it was still cool, the fire basket still smoldered, though it was soon to be out for good. The Porta-Johns that had been north of the press shop were now outside, waiting to be picked up.

Guy walked in. I asked him how long they'd be in today. "Till midnight to clean up, if that's what it takes," he said. Guy was a bit banged up. Days before, I'd noticed a large bandage on his forehead, and had asked Arkansas Dave what happened.

"He fell in a goddamned pit," Dave explained.

I hoped, for Guy's sake, that he'd taken anesthetic beforehand.

When next I saw him, I asked Guy how he felt. "Sore," he said.

How'd it happen?

"Dark."

Despite how bad the bandaging had looked, Guy hadn't required any stitches. Apart from Guy and me, the plant looked absolutely empty. It was the end of the lunch hour, and Guy said that crew members had better come back; if not, there'd be no bonus, and they'd be out of a job.

I wasn't quite sure what this meant. My sense was that quite a few of the guys were out of a job on the crew anyway, at least until the next big plant-closing job came along—at which point, perhaps, they'd get another temporary gig, on this crew or one like it, working in a place where tens of thousands had worked before them. The odds would favor it, in fact. With a couple hundred thousand auto-related jobs lost in Michigan over the course of the decade, it was simple statistics.

I did another quick scan of the plant, to secure a last mental snapshot, and noticed Nedzad working alone along 1-line.

I wanted to close my eyes, so as not to contaminate this closing image, which seemed perfectly apt. I didn't close them, of course—I was afraid I'd fall in a goddamned pit if I did—but managed to keep the snapshot of Nedzad unsmudged nonetheless.

It had been a few weeks shy of two years since I'd seen the headlines in the papers: "Detroit Parts Plant Closing." "Landmark Plant Shuts as Sales of SUVs Fall." "ThyssenKrupp to Shut Down Detroit Plant." It seemed to me now that in addition to the immediate, ground-level pain and dislocation they caused, plant closings provided an unwelcome glimpse into something astral: they proved life's impermanence. Things change, stories end—we understand this. But how can a plant *stop*? How can all its stuff, weighing uncountable tons, be cut up and trucked away? How can all the equipment that once made such a racket be quieted so completely? How can two million square feet that once made so much now make nothing? Permanence, to a degree almost onomatopoetic, is part of the word—"plant." The very sound of it implies rootedness that stretches into centuries. Anything that could cease tomorrow and see its insides disappear within a year should really be called something else.

As I walked out of the Budd plant a final time, I asked Guy about the crown of 1-1. He said that it had been trucked out of the press shop door the day before, an inch to spare on each side.

"It scraped the walls as it swayed," he said.

■

After I left, I drove north on Conner Avenue. Alongside the plant property, up near the intersection at Mack, a middle-aged black man sat in a wheelchair facing the plant's fencing, which was twice as tall as he was, with razor wire atop. The man, looking up from his wheelchair, appeared to be reading a sign posted to the fencing. In black letters on a white board, it said:

NO TRESPASSING.
VIOLATORS WILL BE PROSECUTED.

We'll see about that, I thought. Once the crew departed, only the Pinkertons would be left to guard the place. There were similar signs posted on the property of closed plants all over the city, and the urban spelunkers still got inside and snapped their pictures. The artistes were sure to come around to the corner of Charlevoix and Conner avenues as well, armed with telephoto lenses, French theory, and poetic notions. Another ruin to roam and photograph, Budd would be their plant soon enough.

Absent from their accounts and pictures would be people, and presses, and the interplay between them. Their pictures would depict a corpse; I felt as if I'd witnessed an execution. I watched the process of dismantling a press many times, and never found the sight any less awesome, or any less saddening. At Budd, all of the skill of the Arkansas Boys—and of Jeff, Matt, Guy, and Nedzad—was in the service not of making things but of taking apart the things that had made things. It seemed a waste of such talents, a wound somehow self-

PAUL CLEMENS

inflicted—an act of violence against the prospects of blue-collar Americans by blue-collar Americans, who had no other choice. When Duane, the former electrician on the crew, had seen his job on the line at Ford usurped by a machine, he'd said, "Now I gotta learn how to build machines." An American worker motivated to improve his skills still had one more move to make. But when the machines themselves are shipped abroad, the worker is checkmated, and the statement can only be phrased as a negative: "Now I gotta learn how to unbuild machines."

EPILOGUE

■ ■ ■

You from
Detroit?

■ ■ ■

THOUGH MY FLIGHT, Houston to Aguascalientes, was two hours late, Salvador Sierra Bernal, *jefe de mantenimiento* at Gestamp Mexico, waited for me at the airport, welcomed me without complaint, and drove me the twenty-five miles to my hotel. It was good to see him—it'd been a year—and terrific to be on land. There were storms around Houston, and terrible turbulence; even the drinkers, after a few jokes, paid solemn heed to our plane's bumps and bangs. The stewardess, no rookie, said it was the second-worst turbulence she'd ever experienced. During our uneventful approach to Aguascalientes, she passed out the customs forms. Though the storm was an hour back, it still struck me as an act of overwhelming optimism. Before takeoff, as she announced the flight, she tried, and failed, to pronounce "Agua-Aqua- . . ." "Central Mexico," a seasoned traveler said, assisting.

The stress of the flight, following my four-hour talk with Jon Clark of *Plant Closing News*, had left me close to collapse. It was nearly 11:00 p.m., local time, as the maintenance chief drove us through the dark along Highway 45 into Aguascalientes. A banner draped across the top of Nissan's massive Sentra assembly plant, to the right of the road, congratulated workers on the production of the plant's six millionth Sentra. Though the banner was large, I had to translate quickly. Salvador's Ibiza, passing everything in sight, settled in at a bit above 140 kilometers per hour. "About 70 miles an hour," he said, miscalculating. Standing in the median of a busy intersection was an enormous white-on-black painting of a human skull. The week before, there had been celebrations of the Day of the Dead.

In English better than he believed it to be, Salvador talked of the Detroit Pistons, who had just traded the dependable point guard Chauncey Billups to the Denver Nuggets for the turbulent talent Allen Iverson. Neither of us liked the trade. Recalling his great memory of Detroit, Salvador said, "LeBron James," and reminisced about James's performance to beat the Pistons, almost single-handedly, in Game 5 of the previous year's Eastern Conference Finals. If there was one sporting event to have seen in his time in Detroit, Salvador saw it: the game that solidified James's greatness—he scored forty-eight points, including Cleveland's final twenty-five—and effectively ended a Detroit mini-dynasty. Salvador's fondest memory of Detroit, fittingly, was a Detroit loss.

It was nearly a year to the day that Salvador had returned to central Mexico from Detroit, where from late April until mid-November 2007 he had documented the disassembly of Budd Detroit's 16-line. Between July and November, Fitzley, the job's main hauler, took sixty-five shipments, totaling some seventeen hundred tons, down to Laredo. Fitzley's Mexican partner, Trak Transportaciones, took the machinery over the U.S.-Mexican border and on down to Aguascalientes.

As he drove, Salvador told me that the crown of 16-1—which I'd watched come down fifteen months before—hadn't been hauled to Mexico by Fitzley. Three months after the gantry lift that had lowered it, when Salvador left Detroit for good, the crown was still sitting on blocks in the Budd plant. It sat around the plant for another two months, finally leaving Budd in early January 2008. It arrived in Aguascalientes two months after that, in the first week of March. Its two-month trip from Detroit to Mexico remained, to Salvador, a mystery. "We lost a lot of money with this problem," he said. He told me that the line was now stamping parts for the Dodge Journey.

I smiled to myself in the Mexican dark. The largest press line in a closed Detroit parts plant—a plant that had sat sandwiched between Chrysler's Mack Avenue Engine plants and its Jefferson North Assembly Plant—16-line had been moved two thousand miles south to stamp parts for Chrysler.

■

Now thirty-seven, Salvador had strands of gray hair, a bit of a belly, and a boyish face that lit up when amused. The father of two, he projected dependability devoid of dullness. He'd missed his wife and daughters terribly while in Detroit, but what can you do? "It's very important to take on the big project," he said. He met me at my hotel the next morning, and we continued on in the same direction as the night before, taking Highway 45 toward the village of San Francisco de los Romo. When we stopped for gas, I nodded toward the men who stood sentry by the pumps. "Jobs," Salvador said. "No work. Make work." In intersections, men and boys sold bags of oranges.

The approach along Highway 45 to Gestamp's Aguascalientes plant was less bleak by a long shot than the approach along Charlevoix Avenue to Budd Detroit. The Gestamp plant's relative isolation was by design rather than the result of decades of depopulation. As with Budd, the Gestamp Mexico plant sat between two other plants. To one side was Unipres, a Japanese auto supplier; to the other, Hexpol, a Swedish compounding company. Down the road a stretch was Yorozu Mexicana, a Japanese transmission plant. In the distance were the Sierra Fría.

The plant was small, despite having had its size doubled to accommodate the press line. There was something barnlike about its exterior, painted royal blue with white stripes. Salvador stopped at the entrance gates, and a dapper, uniformed security guard emerged from his guardhouse. He pulled open the half of the double gate nearest his guardhouse. Salvador drove slowly inside, stopped, and popped his trunk so that the guard—far more professional and comprehensive than the Pinkertons in Detroit—could conduct his search. Like all the Gestamp guards, this one wore brownish green khakis with a white shirt and a brownish green hat. After the guard slammed shut the trunk, Salvador pulled forward and parked, backing into his space. Most of the other cars in the lot had done the same. Salvador explained to me that this was for fast exit, in case of emergency. I didn't ask what the emergency might be, but had no trouble comprehending a cultural mindset geared for calamity. My old Detroit neighborhood, too, had once been a Catholic country.

In an alcove above the entryway to the plant's shop floor was a statue of the Blessed Mother. She stood on a blue pedestal, surrounded by red roses, framed by Christmas lights, a golden sunburst behind her. "December 12 is the Day of the

Virgin," Lorena Rios Camacho, the plant's *compras generales*, told me. "It's a day off work." Lorena was young, pleasant, and, as a surpassingly competent purchasing manager, the keeper of all receipts from Detroit. Each December 11, she told me, a priest comes to say Mass, and the statue comes down from the alcove and is carried around the plant. Above the entranceway but beneath the Blessed Mother were signs stating the Gestamp plant's "Filosofia," "Misión," "Valores," and "Visión" ("Ser proveedor nivel 1 de auto partes en Norte America"). Workers saw these signs as they exited the plant. They faced them on their way in, too, if they were among the many who turned to genuflect to the woman above before beginning their workday.

When Salvador and I walked onto the shop floor, I noted a smell similar to Budd, minus the smoke. "The oil, the lubrication, the motor," Salvador said. There were other similarities. Guys drove around in yellow Yale hi-los, as in Detroit, and went up on blue Genie extension lifts. The presses were the same presses I'd seen come down in Detroit over the course of many months, though it was difficult for me to connect the "Aguascalientes" that Salvador had spoken of the year before with the city, the plant, and the press line I was now seeing. The line had been cleaned up and painted blue and gray, the Gestamp company colors.

"You from Detroit?" one of the workers asked me.

"Yes."

He seemed concerned for my safety—a response I expected in the States, but was surprised to encounter south of the border.

Yet it wasn't uncalled for. In Mexico, there was no rain dripping in from the ceiling, no pigeons in the rafters, no pigeon shit in piles, no open pits to fall into. (One winter day, to demonstrate the Budd plant's myriad dangers, Eddie had thrown a heavy fire extinguisher through the layer of ice that had formed atop an open, water-filled pit. "Hypothermity in a matter of minutes," he said.) The Aguascalientes plant had working bathrooms and running water with which to wash one's hands. The plant floor gleamed. The designated walkways were indicated by gray paint with yellow borders. The intention was to keep pedestrians out of the way of hi-los, which carried parts around the plant at relatively high speeds, honking as they turned corners. Red "Alto" signs dotted the floor, for the benefit of pedestrians and hi-los both. All of the workers wore some combination of vest, T-shirt, shirt, and hat with the Gestamp company logo.

We climbed the steps to Salvador's office, on the second floor of a white brick building in the center of the plant floor. He opened his laptop, where he kept pictures he'd taken of 16-line and all its parts. He had pictures, too, of all the trucks, along with their license plates. "I take pictures of everything," he said. Salvador said it took eighty-five trucks total to move everything to Mexico. Lorena, who told me it had taken ninety trucks, said that Salvador took a picture of every truck leaving the Budd plant and "sent it to a girl here." That way, when the truck got to Aguascalientes, she could make sure that all the pieces had arrived properly. "When the first trucks arrived," Lorena said, "the cages were full of cigarettes and McDonald's wrappers."

I had Salvador pull up a Web site on which I'd posted pictures I'd taken of the Detroit plant. He seemed pleased to see the place and the people. When I got to a picture of Nedzad, Salvador, touched, told me to stop.

"I gave him my jacket—'Remember me,'" Salvador said. I thought he might cry. I thought I might. "Anything you need—me, Johan, Uli—you ask Nedzad."

Salvador and I walked down from his office to the shop floor and stood next to the plant's sole press line, which had been one of the Budd plant's many. The computers on presses 2, 3, 4, and 5 had been changed to Spanish, Salvador said, but 1 and 6 were still in English. For the moment, the line was down. Salvador helped three guys who were working on the electrical of press 1, the draw press. There was also a gearing problem with press 2. Salvador, seeking help, spoke on his cell to Johan, who was in Puebla. "Problems," he said when he'd hung up. "Problems, problems." He excused himself and went to work.

I was passed along to Hector Eduardo Padilla Michel—Eduardo, for short. The *ingeniero de calidad*, Eduardo took me to the *área de piezas master*, where an assembled body side for the Dodge Journey was displayed. The eleven different parts stamped at the Gestamp Aguascalientes plant were painted blue; the parts from Gestamp's Puebla plant were painted gray. The body side, Eduardo said, was assembled in Gestamp Toluca, the plant to which the Aguascalientes and Puebla plants shipped parts. From Gestamp Toluca, the assembled body side was shipped to the Chrysler assembly plant in Toluca, where the entire car was put together. Knowing all this didn't do for me what equivalent knowledge of parts and press lines had done for me in the Budd plant. I again felt as if I'd gained some insight into the planet's workings—something that I suspected but, in this case, would have preferred to block out.

That the line in Aguascalientes wasn't yet running on this morning, while not good, wasn't so bad either, Eduardo said, because there was a slowdown, or stoppage, at the Chrysler plant in Toluca due to the poor sales that were beginning to sink the global automotive market. The stoppage was to run from November 10 through November 24, Eduardo said. "Problems in the U.S.A.," he said. "Everybody has problems." He saw a bright side, however. "The Journey is a four-cylinder," he said. "Better on gas. Good car for U.S.A. right now!"

He said that the plant's original section was six years old, having been built in 2002. The new half of the plant, added to accommodate the press line from Budd Detroit, was just a year old. "Building it as presses arrived," he said. Since its arrival, employment in the plant had roughly doubled, to around 150 workers. The arrival of the press line from Detroit, he said, was "big news. We had some people, no work. Now, work. Good for me." He said that the plant stamped about fourteen thousand of each of the eleven parts each month. In normal times, he said, two trucks arrived per day. No trucks were arriving now, with the slowdown in Toluca. Before the stoppage, sixty-six hundred parts per day had been shipped.

Eduardo started at the Gestamp Aguascalientes plant in September 2007, "when this project began." Before Gestamp, he worked on wiring systems for a Japanese company, Sumitomo, that supplied the big Nissan plant. Eduardo lost his job at Sumitomo when the company moved its design and quality-control areas to the Philippines. His first job in Aguascalientes, he said, was for Siemens, where he worked in wiring systems, including the wiring system of the new-version Ford Thunderbird. I told him that the Budd plant in Detroit, where the press line came from, had done a lot of the Thunderbird body stampings—a coincidence of a kind.

"It's curious," Eduardo agreed.

I thanked Eduardo and found Salvador, who was now on the phone to Spain. By 11:30, the problem had been solved. They set up the line to bypass the second press, which had the gear problem, altogether. The robot simply passed the metal through without a stamp. The line started up, and I could feel the plant begin to shake. Salvador looked like a parent whose child, just as the expectant visitor had been promised, had at last begun to crawl. At the end of the line, half a dozen guys were inspecting and sorting the parts that came off the last press. They hung the parts on racks that were then taken by a hi-lo for storage in the plant's other half.

Salvador told me he had a meeting to go to. "Lot of problem," he said.

■

"Come," Salvador said after his meeting had ended. I had no idea where we were headed, but a young woman came out and opened the door to a two-story warehouse. On its second floor, Salvador motioned to what he wanted me to see: shelf after shelf, row upon row of spare parts for the presses from the Budd plant. This room, with junk all over the floor, was the only part of the Mexican plant that resembled the closed Budd plant: there was stuff everywhere. I'd seen wire baskets scattered about the Aguascalientes plant marked "Budd Co.," "Budd Detroit," "Budd Automotive," but the words didn't mean much, not at such a temporal and latitudinal remove. The sight of these press guts spilled all over the floor, however, was like the scent of an ex's perfume: it took me back.

"Come," Salvador said again. We walked to the plant's administrative offices, past a pretty secretary, and up to the second floor, where Salvador introduced me to his boss, Ignacio Pipió Domínguez, the plant's *gerente de operaciones*. I'd seen him once or twice in the Budd plant, but we had never been formally introduced in Detroit.

Ignacio knew of my arrival—or the arrival, at any rate, of a "writer." He seemed pleased by my interest but amused as to its source. He was a Spaniard who looked to be in his late thirties—a handsome, haggard, successful man of the world who smoked his cigarettes with panache. His urbanity suggested familiarity with the speed of customs clearance at the world's great airports. Despite the dismal world climate for auto sales, he exuded a sense of well-being. Salvador stood by silently as we talked.

Merely wishing to inform, Ignacio told me that "the project"—the moving of the Budd plant's 16-line from Detroit to central Mexico—had already been written about, in a piece in the *New York Times*. He took me into his office and pulled up the piece on his computer as proof. He smiled, leaning to the side so I could see.

"I wrote it," I said.

Aha! Now we were getting somewhere. Ignacio told me that it had taken one hundred trucks to move 16-line from Detroit to Mexico, that the installation of the Detroit presses in the Aguascalientes plant had taken from January through May, and that stamping had started in June. Yes, there was a slowdown now at the Chrysler plant in Toluca, and it was possible that the Christmas closure at Gestamp Aguascalientes might extend three weeks. There was nothing to be done. It was the world situation.

On my way out for the day I walked through the lobby, where several young men—job applicants, it seemed—were sitting. Like young men everywhere, they conveyed an uneasy combination of insecurity and swagger. I said so long to Salvador, who would be in Mexico City for training the next day. My guide would be Jorge Adalberto Guzmán Díaz, a maintenance manager.

"It is all arranged," Salvador said.

■

The Aguascalientes plant operated three shifts, Jorge told me the next day, but "in this moment, stamping is only morning, afternoon." With the slowdown in Toluca, three shifts of stamping were not needed. Prior to working at Gestamp, Jorge had worked in maintenance at Texas Instruments. He had also worked at the Nissan assembly plant I'd passed on the way from the airport. "It's a monster of a plant," he said. Aguascalientes, like Detroit in the previous century, had all kinds of plants, and people bounced around.

The pay wasn't much. Jorge said that line workers in the plant made about thirty-five hundred pesos a month. The technicians made about seven thousand pesos per month. Since the peso was worth about $^1/_{12}$ of the dollar, those monthly figures equaled the employees' yearly earnings in dollars. "Is difficult, is very difficult," Jorge said. "Workers leave often. Many rotations." He asked me what the minimum wage was in America, and seemed to find the figure I cited impressive enough. In the United States, he said, "workers win more money. For this reason, many Mexican peoples are looking for opportunities in America." He said that when he worked at Texas Instruments and told his Mexican friends in America what he made—well, he cupped his hand over his mouth in laughter, in imitation of their telephonic mockery.

Jorge began working at the Gestamp plant when it opened six years before. "Good job," he said, though he regretted the problems with press 2. "I have many doubts about stamping," he said. We went up to his cubicle, which sat outside Salvador's office, and he checked the numbers on his computer. Yesterday's afternoon shift, he said, stamped 1,712 parts. Fifteen of these were defective. His computer screen shook from the stamping half a football field away. "All the time," he said of the shakes. "All the time." This constant shaking and rattling caused the company IT guy headaches. "Is broken—three days old!" he quoted him as saying.

Still, he was happy to have the presses doing their stamping. "When all machines running," he said, "boss is happy. When not running, 'Maintenance! Maintenance! Where is maintenance?' One, two in the morning, asleep"—he made a

head-on-the-pillow motion—"get to plant—problem!" At
1:00 today, Jorge said, was a meeting with the big bosses—the
bosses from Spain. He was nervous. "Bosses want no problem!"

■

Jorge came out of his meeting looking stricken. "Many
problems," he said. "Boss wants to change parts." Stamping
different parts meant a die change.

It was a little after 3:00. Workers were starting to leave,
crossing themselves as they walked beneath the Virgin's statue
at the end of their shift. I went outside, to leave Jorge to his
troubles, and saw the second-shift workers arriving in a van.
The van picked them up along a designated route and
dropped them off just outside the gate. The workers whose
shift had just ended climbed into the van that the newly
arrived had gotten out of. Henry Ford's five-dollar day,
designed to allow line workers to purchase the cars they helped
make, hadn't yet dawned in Mexico.

I went back into the plant, up to the second-floor offices,
and spoke to Lorena, the purchasing manager. If you want
solid, useful information, ask a woman. If there'd been a
Lorena in the Budd plant, I'd have spent a whole lot less time
listening to delightful bellyaching about guys' bowels and balls
and more time learning the ins and outs of moving millions of
pounds of press line two thousand miles.

Lorena still had a list of contacts in Detroit, and she
flipped through the phone numbers she had amassed over the
months. "Phone calls to Detroit to find wood!" she said. "Sal-

vador would call—'I need wood of these measurements. Heated and treated.' " The wood was for the cribbing of the press pieces on the Fitzley trucks. So, in a binder, she'd kept a card for her wood contact in Detroit. Lorena had everything in this binder or that. She flipped through one and laughed: receipts from Salvador's and David's trips to McDonald's and 7-Eleven. "I could see where they were going, what they ate," she said, something of the disapproving mother in her tone. Dig to a sufficient depth when studying the movement of America's industrial capacity to other countries and this is what you'll find: records, preserved for posterity, of the Big Gulp purchases by Mexican engineers in a Macomb County 7-Eleven.

Starting next month, Lorena said, the plant would begin preparations for the stamping of a new job for Chrysler. The dies were being sent down from Detroit.

■

As I waited for my cab down in the lobby, I flipped through an English-language copy of *Automotive Industries* magazine. From the issue's introduction: "The result is that the industry can make more cars, components, and add-on bits than it has customers. There are two solutions. Most obvious is to close a couple thousand plants."

I put the magazine down and went outside. Ignacio, the plant manager, stood by the building, smoking by himself. I thanked him for allowing me to visit and said that it sounded as if things were going fine, what with the new Chrysler stamping job on its way. That Chrysler wasn't doing well

caused him only mild concern. "It's a crisis everywhere," Ignacio said, "but here in Mexico, we're okay. We'll grow." He
mentioned a bigger stamping job, for a 2010 GM model, that
was in the pipeline as well. "We plan, kind of," he said. "We're
a Spanish company. We don't plan like the Japanese. Americans, Spanish—we improvise. The Japanese, they plan."

My cab pulled up, but Ignacio and I kept talking. My
arrival from Detroit had brought back memories. He said that
they had found out about 16-line being up for sale on April 20,
2007. He remembered the date. His boss from Puebla, who
was now in Argentina, had received an e-mail about the line's
being on the block. Three days later a contract was signed,
and the day after that Ignacio flew to Detroit. For a time, he
flew between Detroit and Aguascalientes every three days. He
sounded exhausted saying it.

Two months before my visit to Mexico, the former Mexican president Vicente Fox had visited Detroit. "In the end,"
Fox said, "Michigan factories have to compete with factories
in Mexico and China. Companies like General Motors and
Ford and Maytag don't have an option. They either close the
doors and fire their workers, or they move where they can gain
economic competitiveness." Even in the economic depths of
November 2008, one could imagine America's manufacturers
one day returning to competitiveness and profit. Harder to
imagine, by a long shot, was the mass employment of middle-
class Americans in manufacturing making this profitability
possible. Manufacturers didn't need nearly the number of
employees they once did; those they did need—well, there

were billions around the globe who fit the bill, and Detroit hadn't submitted the low bid.

I told Ignacio that I needed to get my cab. He finished his cigarette and we shook hands. Despite his worldliness, he seemed as surprised by it as anyone—how thousands of tons of press line had come apart, piece by piece, and been put on truck after truck and hauled mile after mile across a border and then rebuilt, from the bottom up, based on pictures taken a year before and half a continent away. It hardly seemed possible, but the booms inside his plant's press shop were proof that it had succeeded.

"Next time Gestamp buys a line," I said, "they'll ask you to handle it."

"Maybe," he said.

Acknowledgments

Most of what is good in this book comes courtesy of other people. The mistakes are my own. Alert me to any errors at pc@paulclemens.com. I'll note corrections on my Web site and include them in any future editions, print or electronic, of the book.

The long list of those whom I have to thank is abbreviated by the fact that so many of these people appear in the book proper, where I hope my indebtedness and gratitude are plain. Among those who do not appear in the book but to whom I am indebted nonetheless are Paul Flancbaum, Thomas McDonald, Larry Wahl, Nanci Mellar, Willie Williams, Barry Edel, Jerry Roszka, Sherman Miles, Jerry Nowakowski, Bob Blaine, and Steve Merkley.

Thanks to Rob Franciosi for his readings of the manuscript and to Michael Scrivener, David Small, Adam Bellow, and Jeffrey Eugenides for their early support. Thanks to my agent at Russell & Volkening, Timothy Seldes, and to all at Doubleday, including Hannah Wood, who helped shepherd the book; Bill Thomas, who stuck by it; and, above all, Gerry Howard, who ruined a year of my life with rewrites.